DON'T INSIST YOU'RE RIGHT UNTIL YOU CHECK

MORE MISINFORMATION

- St. Bernard dogs of Switzerland never carried casks, of brandy or anything else.

- The "Franklin" stove—as designed by Ben Franklin—never worked.

- Sake is not wine, or spirits. It is a kind of strong beer.

- Dew does not fall.

- Lemmings make a nice metaphor, but they do not periodically commit suicide by marching *en masse* into the sea.

Also by Tom Burnam
Published by Ballantine Books:

THE DICTIONARY OF MISINFORMATION

More Misinformation

TOM BURNAM

BALLANTINE BOOKS • NEW YORK

Library of Congress Catalog Card Number: 80-11505

ISBN 0-345-29251-0

This edition published by arrangement with
Lippincott & Crowell, Publishers

Manufactured in the United States of America

First Ballantine Books Edition: July 1981

Once again, for Phyllis—and for all the others who have helped so much

One of the most striking differences between a cat and a lie is that a cat has only nine lives.

—Mark Twain

Introduction

What's exasperating about folk beliefs and fallacies is not that they are always entirely wrong. It's that they so often are half right, which is worse; for the half-truth is made to justify the error, and it is the error that persists. Washington really did cross the Delaware (but not the way the famous painting has it); Lindbergh flew the Atlantic nonstop, all right (but he wasn't the first); and Fulton actually built a steamboat (he wasn't the first either, nor did he call it the *Clermont*).

Cure frostbite by rubbing the affected part with snow, goes the folk belief. Yes, the part should be kept cold (see FROSTBITE, TREATMENT OF), but *only* until it can be properly warmed. Whiskey is good for snakebites. Yes, but only if it's externally applied as an antiseptic, assuming that there's nothing better available. If a child wants to run away, pack a lunch for the journey. Yes, it's best to keep a cool head, but the damage done by such an approach certainly outweighs the half-truth (in this case, less than half —much less).

So the search for truth, so often crushed to earth, goes on: the full truth, that is, unencumbered by the lie either big or little. It's not easy—or did you already suspect this? But it's rewarding, and it has to continue.

Not always, though, is the search successful.

Did the Japanese, as an old story current before and during World War II had it, really name one of their manufacturing centers "U.S.A." so that in the days before everybody drove a Datsun and took pictures with a Nikon, the Japanese could put "Made in U.S.A." on certain of their exports? I don't know, and can't find out.

Does it really take only three muscles to smile, and fifteen to frown? (The figures vary.) It seems to me that a smile is much the more complicated. All you do to frown is wrinkle your brow, and that can't take too many muscles, surely, whereas a smile spreads all over the face. My physician friends could not answer the question; apparently there are more important things to study in medical school. There is no literature on the subject, barring the constant repetition, sometimes in needlepoint, of the folk saying itself. Frowning, I gave up.

A tale repeated in advertising circles is that some anonymous genius, back in the days when canned goods were still under suspicion, managed to peddle a lot of slow-moving white salmon (as good as the red, but not so familiar to the public) by putting on the label the following bold—and quite accurate—statement: "This salmon is guaranteed not to turn red in the can." What genius indeed (shrewd merchandising variety)! What lack of documentation!

All my life I've heard the story, often from English teachers of the grimly purist variety (far less common, I might say, than is usually supposed, especially in colleges and universities), of the "fruit trees/fruit, trees" error said to have been made in a bill removing certain tariffs on imported agricultural products. Generations of cowed students have been warned of the consequences of that comma: the bill was supposed to exempt only fruit trees; but because somebody was *careless,* all fruit and all trees were exempted, with disastrous economic consequences. I wonder.

There is a horse known in the Pacific Northwest as the Appaloosa. The Nez Perce Indians apparently developed it. Its characteristics are spots of color on the rump, lack of hair on the tail, and pink on the nose. Among horsemen and -women it is believed that the name derives from "a Palouser," since it is associated with the Palouse (pronounced pa-LOOSE) country, an inland area that covers parts of Washington and Idaho and is notable for its Nez Perces, rolling hills, and fertile black soil.

Perhaps. Why doubt this explanation? Precisely because it is so logical, so reasonable, so—right. And that is what at once sets the hair on a linguist's neck upright in suspicion. Not because those interested in word origins are any more suspicious than anybody else; it's just that so many explanations of word origins are so logical, so reasonable—and so wrong.

Some still maintain that Mt. Everest rises to an even 29,000 feet, but that, when Sir George Everest (1790–

1866) calculated its height in the mid-nineteenth century, he added 2 feet. The reason? He didn't think anyone would believe such a nice round figure as 29,000, but 29,002 would have the aura of scientific responsibility. It does seem doubtful that such a tale is true, but I don't know how to prove (or disprove) it. The government of India says that Mt. Everest is 29,028 feet, give or take a few on account of snow.

The truth, the whole truth, and nothing but the truth: how simple a phrase, how complicated its implementation! But we must continue to search, for how else are we to rise above the unthinking brute that lurks within us all?

Acknowledgments

Forgive me if I say again what I've said before: There may be those who can do a book like this without help from others, but I'm not one of them. And the list keeps growing. So many at Portland State University have helped that I despair at a complete listing; perhaps, this time around, they will forgive a blanket, though heartfelt, "thank you," especially to my colleagues in the Department of English. But permit me to slip in a special word of gratitude to Ed Gnoza, Humanities Librarian, the Branford Price Millar Library at Portland State.

Following are some of those who have written with suggestions, comments, and corrections following the publication of *The Dictionary of Misinformation*. A fascinating bunch; indeed, one of my chief delights has been the intelligent and perceptive letters so many of you have sent.

Professor Thomas A. Bailey, Stanford University; Doug Baker, columnist, *Oregon Journal*, Portland; Steve Belko, Boise, Idaho, Commissioner, Big Sky Conference; Ralph Boas, Northwestern University, Evanston, Illinois; George A. Bowman, Pullman, Washington; Larry Brooks, Portland, Oregon; Capt. Peter T. Burke, Portland, Texas; Charles J. Cazeau, State University of New York, Buffalo; Howard J. Critchfield, Western Washington University, Bellingham; Kenneth D. Clapp, Vice-President, Humphrey-Browning-Macdougall, Boston; Samuel Y. Edgerton, Jr., Boston University; Edward A. Flinn, chief scientist, Earth and Ocean Programs, NASA, Washington, D.C.; Rabbi Yonah Geller, Portland, Oregon; Mrs. Paul Gerard, Brussels, Belgium; Bernard Grebanier, Speonk, New York; Marvin Grosswirth, public relations officer, "Mensa," New York; Walter Harding, secretary, The Thoreau Society, State University of New York, Geneseo; P. A. Hickline, Christchurch, New Zealand; A. S. Householder, Malibu, California; Kathy Humble, Portland, Oregon; Robert Huot, San Luis Obispo,

California; Warren J. Iliff, director, Washington Park Zoo, Portland, Oregon; Robert V. Keeley, Department of State, Washington, D.C.; Lysander Kemp, Austin, Texas; Alexander Kira, Ithaca, New York; John Lancaster, Special Collections Librarian, Amherst College Library, Amherst, Massachusetts; Mrs. Landes Lewiton, Amherst, Massachusetts; Dr. Frederick A. Lowenheim, Plainfield, New Jersey; Bill Lynn, Falls Church, Virginia; Bruce McCall, New York; David Maeth, M.D., Santa Cruz, California; V. J. A. Manton, curator, Zoological Society of London (England); Edward F. Mendelson, Yale University, New Haven, Connecticut; Thomas H. Middleton, Los Angeles; Arthur Mizener, Ithaca, New York; Professor Sylvère Monod, Paris, France; Professor Tauno Mustanoja, Kilo, Finland; James Nattinger, Ph.D., Portland, Oregon; Roscoe Nelson, attorney-at-law, Portland, Oregon; Dewey Newton, Woodburn, Oregon; Robert F. Niven, Los Angeles; Ted Odenath, Daytona Beach, Florida; Wayne Parrish, Pan American World Airways, Washington, D.C.; Mrs. Raymond Poindexter, Sumner, Washington; Dr. George Puterbaugh, Lake Oswego, Oregon; Dr. George B. Rabb, Director, Brookfield Zoo, Chicago; John Murray Reynolds, Princeton, New Jersey; Tom Rookard, Portland, Oregon; Norman P. Ross, New Canaan, Connecticut; Darrell Royal, Austin, Texas; Robert A. Scalise, San Luis Obispo, California; Frederick L. Schuman, Portland, Oregon; David R. Simmons, San Francisco; Robert W. Singer, M.D., Pittsburgh; James E. Sterner, Mexico, Missouri; J. N. Tarro, M.D., Lake Oswego, Oregon; John White, Cambridge, Massachusetts; Samuel Whitman, Long Beach, California; Wilford Willis, attorney-at-law, San Diego; and Franklin W. Young, Miami, Florida.

A special word of thanks should go to some special correspondents—Herbert Gross, South Orange, New Jersey; Norman Hickman, New York; George Johnson, Wausau, Wisconsin; Allen Walker Read, New York; John Rockwell, New York; Samuel Sherman, Moorestown, New Jersey; Tom Weatherly, Stockton, New Jersey; Digby Butler Whitman, Wausau, Wisconsin; Ben Woodhead, Marshall, Texas; and whoever lurks behind the mysterious signature "jones," of Seattle. And especially Gareth Penn, Napa, California, whose help has been very considerable indeed.

I have not been able to find out anything about George Stimpson, whose long-out-of-print books of oddities were useful. But at least I can spell his name correctly this time around, and I just did.

In addition to the well-known standard reference works constantly at my elbow, I should like to mention Rabbi R. Brasch's *How Did It Begin?*, first published in Australia in 1965. Though dealing primarily with the origins of customs and superstitions rather than misinformation, Rabbi Brasch's interesting book inspired further research that led to some usable items, including the one about Julius Caesar and the operation supposedly named after him.

I am sure that there are many present and former staffers at Lippincott & Crowell who have helped anonymously. Of those who have helped, but not anonymously, a very special word of thanks to the following: Robert L. Crowell, Hugh Rawson, Carol Cohen, Bernard Skydell, Patrick Barrett, and Paul Fargis.

Finally, two who helped greatly with the research—and, believe me, it was considerable—on this volume: Patricia Cooper and Gretchen B. Goekjian. Cynthia Wichmann did most of the final typing of the manuscript; not the least of her accomplishments was puzzling out my handwriting, and doing it so successfully.

So speaks the still small—well, I hope not *too* small— voice of gratitude, which, contrary to popular belief, is not a phrase entirely original with Thomas Gray (see I Kings 19:12).

TOM BURNAM

Lake Oswego, Oregon

A

abdication by a British monarch. Abdication is not, as many think, a unilateral process. When Edward VIII left his throne to marry the woman he loved in 1937, he did so by act of Parliament. British monarchs can't just call it quits; they must ask permission, following which Parliament draws up an article of abdication that sets forth specific requirements for both parties. Only after the act has been signed by the King (or Queen) and approved by Parliament is the abdication official. It does all seem very British.

Air Corps, Air Forces, Air Force. A World War II veteran who speaks of having served in the Army Air Force is mistaken. So is anyone who corrects his terminology by substituting "Air Corps." Or "Army Air Corps." Or simply "Air Force." The fact is that there was no Army Air Corps in World War II, nor was there an Air Force. On June 20, 1941, some six months before Pearl Harbor, the Army Air Forces (note the plural) were—was?—created. On July 26, 1947, the Air Force came into being.

There still are, as there have been in the past, many military airmen and women not in the Air Force, but a part of the other services. The Navy has its Naval Air Force, Pacific (or Atlantic) Fleet—less formally called simply Naval Aviation. The Marines have their Air Wing. The Army calls its air personnel simply army aviators, many of whom fly helicopters in what the Army calls "close combat support."

air pollution. It is no news that many U.S. cities suffer from air pollution problems. It may come as a surprise, however, to learn that cities that for years were proud of their clean air are now among the worst offenders: Denver, for example; and Albuquerque, New Mexico, whose air is worse than Boston's and much worse than Cincinnati's; and Fairbanks, Alaska, which ties with Washington, D.C.—all according to a National Wildlife Federation study done in 1975.

Neither the New York–New Jersey metropolitan area nor that old villain Pittsburgh is at the top of the list. (The New York area is slightly less polluted than Albuquerque, at least in terms of the atmosphere.)

The study lists the numbers of days in the year during which the air is unhealthful, very unhealthful, or hazardous. Among other interesting revelations are that Spokane has more than three times as many such days (126) as Omaha (40); that San Francisco with 127 is not so very far behind St. Louis with 140; and that Phoenix, with 118 "bad air" days a year, far outstrips Louisville, Kentucky (72), and Steubenville, Ohio (60).

Los Angeles is the worst, with 318; in the Mile High City of Denver, 177 days in 1975 were bad ones. Factory chimneys were once the principal culprits. Now it's the automobile—and topography. Cities close to mountains, such as Los Angeles and Denver, often find their atmospheres trapped in a stagnant pattern that encourages a temperature inversion, or a mass of warm air holding captive beneath it a colder mass that just sits there as the pollutants build up.

air pollution and fuel economy, automobiles past and present. Those who think that automobiles in the good old days were both more pollution-free and easier on gasoline should be aware that the Ford Motor Company has restored a 1930 Model A to its original condition and then put it through the EPA emissions and economy tests.

The results? The 1930 Model A emitted 3.6 times as much unburned hydrocarbons and 5.4 times as much carbon monoxide as are allowed by today's standards. In only one area was it acceptable: nitrous oxides emission. In gasoline engines, nitrous oxides increase with increases in compression ratio, which is why most automobiles have lowered this ratio in recent years. The Model A's compression ratio was only 4.2 to 1, about half of today's average for new gasoline-fueled cars.

As for fuel economy, the Model A, with just 40 horsepower, managed to achieve only 14.6 miles per gallon in city driving and 23.9 miles per gallon on the highway, figures exceeded by many automobiles now being manufactured with engines three times as powerful as the Model A's, or even more so.

In one area, the old Model A had an advantage: it could run on lead-free gasoline long before the term "lead-free" was invented.

airplanes, stalling of. An airplane does not stall because it loses power. If this were so, obviously sailplanes or gliders could not stay aloft. It stalls when the "angle of attack"—that is, the angle at which the wing meets the (apparently) onrushing air—becomes so great that the smooth flow of air over the wing, essential to lift, is destroyed by turbulence. Loss of power leads to (it does not "cause") a stall only if the pilot tries too hard to maintain altitude.

"A jug of wine, a loaf of bread" and—*who?* Most of us are aware that Edward FitzGerald (1809–83—and note the correct spelling with the capital "G") took considerable liberties with the original in his translations of Omar Khayyam's *Rubaiyat*. The fact that often enough the *Rubaiyat* is associated with FitzGerald rather than Khayyam is evidence of this.

In at least one case, however, the liberty taken is a fairly big one. Here is FitzGerald's version, known to almost everybody, of one of Khayyam's stanzas:

> A Book of Verses underneath the Bough,
> A Jug of Wine, a Loaf of Bread and thou
> Beside me singing in the Wilderness—
> Oh, Wilderness were Paradise enow.

The number of times this stanza has been inscribed in volumes presented, at a certain age, by callow youths to ripening maidens is impossible to determine statistically, but it must be considerable.

Here is a literal translation, done by A. J. Arberry, as quoted in F. L. Lucas, *The Greatest Problem and Other Essays* (1961, page 48):

> Let me have a loaf of fine wheaten flour,
> A flagon of wine, and a thigh of mutton,
> And beside me, amid the desolation, a comely youth—
> This is happiness no sultan's palace holds.

Strictly speaking, the "thou" of FitzGerald's stanza can, of course, refer to either sex. Perhaps it was the translator's Victorian audience that first made the assumption that here it must have referred to a female, an assumption that continues to this day.

Alaska as easternmost state. Contrary to popular belief, Alaska is not merely the northernmost state; it is, in fact, not only the most northern but also the most western—*and* eastern. This is not so absurd as it seems. That it is farthest west is easily confirmed by a look at the map—as is the fact that it is farthest "east." Some of the Aleutian Islands extend beyond the 180th meridian, which is the global dividing line between East and West.

Alaska and Hawaii, the southernmost state, thus between them hold all the locational records: farthest north, east, west, and south.

alibi. In the strict sense, "alibi" (the old locative case of the Latin *alius,* meaning "elsewhere") means only that kind of excuse which depends on one's presence at some other location. An accused person who can show that he or she was visiting an aged relative in a nursing home at the time the crime was committed has an alibi. (Unless, that is, the crime is the aged relative's murder in a nursing home.)

That an alibi is one form of excuse has, however, caused its meaning to be extended to include any kind of excuse. (See Ring Lardner's classic story, "Alibi Ike.") Most modern dictionaries list this second meaning as quite proper.

"All Americans are deaf, dumb, and blind." This remark, extraordinarily tactless and cruel in its presumed context, has been attributed to George Bernard Shaw. It is supposed to be what he said when Helen Keller was announced as a visitor and was described as deaf, dumb, and blind.

But the famous biographer Hesketh Pearson says the truth is quite different. What Shaw actually said to Helen Keller, when he saw how well she had overcome her handicaps, was "I wish all Americans were as blind as you."

altimeters (barometric). Not really "altitude meters" at all, in spite of the implications of the name. Altimeters of the kind still found in many small aircraft, and those sold for use in automobiles, are simply barometers. They measure atmospheric pressure, not altitude. Their dials may indicate altitude, but their mechanisms don't. That is why pilots must constantly check and reset their altimeters against some known reference—the atmospheric pressure at the airfield at the time of takeoff; and, in flight, a ground station in the vicinity. It should further be noted that barometric altimeters read in sea-level terms. They do not directly tell the pilot what he or she most needs to know: height above the ground.

Atmospheric pressure lessens with altitude. The rule of thumb is that every 1,000 feet of altitude is reflected in a 1-inch drop in the column of the mercury barometer against which aneroid barometers—that is, those dependent, like altimeters, on a clockwork-type mechanism rather than a column of mercury—are calibrated.

Atmospheric pressure, thus, does vary with altitude; hence the use of barometers calibrated to read in feet or meters. But other factors than altitude are involved. A storm front moving in may, in extreme cases, throw an altimeter off by as much as 2,000 feet—certainly, and commonly, by a few hundred. That is why many modern altimeters rely on electronic means to determine altitude (in this case, above the ground rather than above sea level—and more useful, in any case, to a pilot).

There are other instruments calibrated to read one function in terms of another. The conventional Pitot-tube airspeed indicator actually measures pressure, but the pressure is always directly proportional to airspeed no matter what the density of the atmosphere. The altimeter, however, is the only one in which the indications are so often more wrong than right that it needs constant correcting.

And, true enough, a magnetic compass must be corrected for deviation (built-in "mechanical" error) and variation (the difference between magnetic north and geographic north). But its readings do represent the direction of magnetic lines of force, which are relatively constant at ordinary latitudes. The altimeter, however, is so often a liar that it is potentially dangerous to pilots who are without recourse to other means of determining altitude.

"a man can die but once: we owe God a death . . . and let it go which way it will, he that dies this year is quit for the next." When Ernest Hemingway wrote "The Short Happy Life of Francis Macomber," he has the white hunter Wilson, who even by Hemingway standards is about as macho as one can get, admitting with some proper British embarrassment that he has always lived by these words of Shakespeare's.

And noble words they are, certainly. Who says them? One of Falstaff's roistering companions in the second part of *King Henry IV* (act 3, sc. 2, lines 250 ff.). He's a minor clown whose name indicates how we are expected to assess his character: Feeble, a "woman's tailor," who, says Falstaff, will be "as valiant as the wrathful dove or most magnanimous mouse."

Amazon jungles as flat. Recent surveys sponsored by the Brazilian government have given the lie to the old belief that the Amazon area is a flat rain forest. In fact, lowlands account for only about a fifth of the area, the rest being hilly with, often, mountain ranges.

Apparently, early explorers thought of this vast region as flat because they did not, or could not because of the impenetrable jungles, venture far from the rivers. The new surveys were done with airborne radar equipment.

Amazons and the Amazon River. The wholly fictional Amazons, said in Greek mythology to be a fearsome band of female warriors who cut off their right breasts to avoid interference with the bowstring, are usually credited with giving their name to the river. The reason is said to be that Francisco de Orellana, who first traversed the Amazon from the Andes to the sea in 1541, fought with a group of savages among whom were women warriors. However, this may not be the case; some believe that the name comes from the Indian word *amassona,* or "boat destroyer."

The Greeks apparently explained the word "Amazon" as deriving from two words that can mean "without," or "deprived of," and "breast." The *Oxford English Dictionary* is, however, a bit skeptical, suggesting that this may be ancient folk etymology, an attempt to account for a strange word from some foreign source.

There seems little need to demolish the belief that Amazons parted with their right breasts, any more than it should be necessary to prove that unicorns had no horns. Neither Amazons nor unicorns, to date, have been shown ever to have enjoyed an existence outside of fable and legend.

animals rejecting offspring handled by human beings. There are good reasons for not handling baby animals found in the wilds, but the belief that they will then be rejected by their parents is not one of them. Tagging or banding young animals is a common wildlife management tool. Hawks, eagles, waterfowl, deer, elk—even mice—have been so handled. It is extremely rare for a wildlife parent not to reclaim its young after such treatment.

Obviously a cub or a fawn that is taken from its parents and not returned for a long period of time may experience rejection. Or, as George B. Rabb, director of Chicago's famous Brookfield Zoo, points out, a baby animal taken from the mother before a proper bond has been established may be rejected.

In general, however, birds and animals do not regard handling by a human being as reason for rejecting offspring. Several years ago, according to Warren J. Iliff, director of Washington Park Zoo in Portland, Oregon, an orangutan baby was taken away from its mother and returned within a few days with total maternal acceptance.

There are two good reasons why persons hiking or camping in the wilds or along the ocean shore should not disturb young animals even if they appear to have been abandoned. The first reason is obvious enough: it can be dangerous if Mama Bear happens to show up. The second reason is suggested in the first: young animals appearing to be abandoned usually aren't. Female deer, according to Marlin Perkins of the popular TV program "Mutual of Omaha's Wild Kingdom," usually know where their fawns are and will come back to them. Baby seals are often thought to be abandoned when in fact their mothers are nearby; they should definitely be left alone.

"apple" that Eve ate. The Bible does not identify what it was that Eve took such a disastrous bite of. Genesis 3:6 (King James Version): "she took of the fruit thereof, and did eat. . . ." That the "fruit" was indeed an apple seems most questionable, unless the Garden of Eden was a chillier place than is usually assumed. Apples fit to eat require some 1,200 hours per year during which the temperature is below 45° F. (7° C.).

It has been suggested that the "fruit" may have been an apricot, which flourishes in the Holy Land, though it is not certain that apricots (native to China) were known in this region much before the beginnings of the Christian era.

Let us not be too hard on Eve for eating the forbidden fruit; her information about the tree of knowledge of good and evil was hearsay—and by way of a man, at that. For the tree was put into Eden before Eve was created; only Adam was told directly by God to stay away from it. Eve got her information from Adam, presumably; and later, of course, from the serpent.

Appomattox and Robert E. Lee's sword. The story that General Lee turned over his sword to General Grant after the surrender, and that Grant then returned the sword to Lee, is apparently without foundation. Grant denied it, anyway. In fact, Grant had specified that all rebel officers be allowed to retain their sidearms.

Arabic numbers. More properly "Hindu-Arabic." Arabian traders had a great deal to do with helping spread the form of numerals in almost universal use today. But most of them came from India, some being found in Hindu in manuscripts from as early as the third century B.C.

arbor and arbor. Somewhat surprisingly, "arbor" as a noun, meaning a pleasant vine-covered retreat, and "arbor" as in "Arbor Day" come from separate sources. The first sense derives from Middle English *erber*, meaning a plot of grass, in turn derived from the Old French for herb or grass, *herbe*. Arbor Day for tree planting is directly from the Latin for tree, *arbor*. ("Arbor" as a machinists' term for shaft or spindle also derives from the Latin word, which also meant "mast" or "shaft.")

ark. So firmly associated with the boat that Noah built is the word "ark" that many are puzzled by the "Ark of the Covenant," the chest or cupboard in which, in synagogues, the Torah is kept. But the word "ark" in Britain (compare Latin *arca*, "box"—from which, incidentally, "arcane" comes: that which is hidden or secret, as a box) has meant a chest or a box, once a ubiquitous household item in the days before built-in closets.

In the English Bible, "ark" is used to translate two quite different Hebrew words, one of which has the general meaning of "boat"—the baby Moses was found in an "ark of bulrushes" (Exodus 2:3)—and the other of the (sacred) chest taken with the Israelites on their journey to Palestine. In this sense it is used today, as said above, to define the place where the Sacred Scriptures are kept.

The common English surname Arkwright did not originally mean "boat builder," but "box maker."

artillery at the time of Waterloo. The cannon used at Waterloo ranged from six- to twelve-pounders, named for the weight of the iron ball they fired. (Some explosive shells were also used, governed by time fuses.) Since this was before the days of extremely powerful propellants, soldiers could often see the ball if it came straight toward them; and it was easily visible as it began to bounce.

Mark Twain's comment in "Fenimore Cooper's Literary Offenses" is interesting here: "For several years Cooper was daily in the society of artillery, and he ought to have noticed that when a cannon-ball strikes the ground it either buries itself or skips a hundred feet or so; skips again a hundred feet or so—and so on, till finally it gets tired and rolls. . . . [Yet] I wish I may never know peace again if [Natty Bumppo in *The Deerslayer*] doesn't strike out promptly and *follow the track* of that cannon-ball across the plain."

One wonders why men were so often killed by a cannon-ball they could see coming. David Howarth, author of *Waterloo: A Guide to the Battlefield* (1974), published for The Waterloo Committee by The Library of Imperial History, London, tells us why. And it is a fascinating commentary on what war once was, or was considered to be, and what it has become. Mr. Howarth says that even if one saw the ball coming, it was considered cowardly to duck it!

"As Time Goes By." A generation of Bogeymen (and women), addicted to the Late Show, has grown up thinking that the popular song "As Time Goes By" was introduced in the 1942 Warner movie *Casablanca,* starring Humphrey Bogart and Ingrid Bergman. It wasn't. Nor was it first sung by Rudy Vallee, although he did make an early recording of it for RCA.

"As Time Goes By" was written (words and music) by Herman Hupfeld. It was first featured in a musical called *Everybody's Welcome* in 1931. When Dooley Wilson's rendition of the song in *Casablanca* revived interest in it, RCA re-released the old Vallee recording.

Atlas holding up the world on his shoulders. It would be difficult to count the number of gazetteers that use as cover or endpaper a figure of the ancient Greek demigod Atlas bearing the world on his shoulders. Often the drawings are derived from a 1715 rendition of the famous 1696 map of the world done by the Italian cartographer Cassini.

But that was not Atlas's punishment. Although accounts vary somewhat depending on which classic source is consulted, the punishment of Atlas, who in some accounts is identified as participating in a rebellion against Zeus, was to carry not the world but the vault of heaven on his back.

In another version, Atlas, a king of enormous size, insults Perseus, who then tricks Atlas into gazing on the Gorgon's head, which turns Atlas into stone. Thereupon Atlas grows into a mountain, with heaven and all its stars resting on his shoulders. In any case, it's the sky, not the world, that Atlas was condemned to bear.

B

Babel and babble. One would suppose that "babble," for meaningless or repetitive prattle, springs from, or is at least related to, the Tower of Babel. But such is not the case; no direct connection between "Babel" and "babble" can be found, says the *Oxford English Dictionary*. "Babel" is the Hebrew for "Babylon"; as transliterated, *bābel*. "Babble," a much newer word, is imitative, or onomatopoeic, like the "Pow!" of comic strips or the snap, crackle, and pop claimed to be characteristic of a well-known breakfast food.

"Babble," like "prattle," is apparently an attempt at imitating a baby's first meaningless (except, perhaps, to the baby) sounds. "Ba" is one of the easiest syllables to pronounce and hence is likely to be among the first produced by infants. "Pa" and "ma" are equally easy, incidentally.

That is why "baby's first word" may well be, to the delight of its parents, "papa" or "mama."

"Baby Ruth" candy bar. Not named for Babe Ruth, though often thought to be in spite of the spelling. According to the National Confectioners Association, it was named "Baby Ruth" in honor of Grover Cleveland's daughter, Ruth, born in the White House.

However, a bit of chronology tends to throw certain doubts on this more or less "official" account. "Baby" Ruth Cleveland was born on October 3, 1891, and died of diphtheria on January 6, 1904. Cleveland himself died in 1908. The candy bar was not given its name until the early 1920s.

Another tale occasionally told is that the candy bar was named for an illegitimate child. Not so, True, as a bachelor Cleveland had had an illegitimate child, the result of a liaison in Buffalo. But Ruth was born to Mrs. Cleveland, a lovely creature of twenty-one at the time of their marriage; she was the daughter of Cleveland's late law partner and had been Cleveland's ward since she was eleven. Cleveland was fifty-four when they married.

For whom, then, was the candy bar named? According to the syndicated columnist L. M. Boyd, it was named by Mrs. George Williamson, whose husband was president of the Williamson Candy Company and who herself helped develop the formula for the candy bar, in honor of their granddaughter: information supplied, says Mr. Boyd, by a longtime family friend of the Williamsons.

bats entangled in hair. In spite of the old myth, which had even greater currency back in the days when coiffures tended to be high-piled and complicated, bats cannot possibly get entangled in hair. They have no hooks on their feet, or anywhere else.

Even though it's impossible for bats to be caught in anyone's hair, it should be noted that they can pose an extreme danger to human beings: rabies. Bats are mammals, and rabid bats are by no means unknown, posing a considerable potential (and often enough actual) danger in many parts of the country.

battery life—effects of quick charging on. Contrary to popular belief, high charging (or discharging) rates are not harmful to lead-acid storage batteries such as are used in automobiles. However, the efficiency of the fast charge is affected by its high current density. A quick charge does not completely rejuvenate a battery; what it does is to bring it up to the point where the automobile's own generator or alternator can take over and finish the job.

"The Battle of Waterloo was won on the playing fields of Eton." Did the first Duke of Wellington really say this? The present Duke doesn't think so, according to his friend and shooting companion Norman Hickman of New York. Nor does Elizabeth Longford, author of the definitive 1969 biography of the first Duke of Wellington, think so. As a matter of fact, Wellington did not really care much for Eton.

Not until three years after his death in 1852 was any such remark attributed to Wellington. The Count of Montalembert, a well-known journalist and parliamentarian, visited England in 1855 seeking material for a book. While not quoting the Duke directly, the Count remarks that one can understand how Wellington came to say when revisiting Eton, "C'est ici qu'a été gagnée la bataille de Waterloo" ("It is here that the Battle of Waterloo was won").

Then an English writer, Sir Edward Creasy, added his tuppence worth. In *Eminent Etonians,* Creasy has the Iron Duke passing the playing fields in his old age and saying, presumably about the players rather than the turf, "There grows the stuff that won Waterloo."

It all came together in 1889 with still a third writer, Sir William Fraser. In his *Words on Wellington* (this is the source quoted in Bartlett), Fraser repeats, in English, Montalembert's remark and for good measure throws in Creasy's—or Eton's—"playing fields."

The fact is that Wellington had no reason to love Eton. Nor, in fact, did Eton even *have* playing fields as the term is usually understood in the context of his reputed remark; there were no organized games when he was a student in the early 1780s. "Lonely and withdrawn," in Elizabeth Longford's phrase, young Arthur did not even finish his schooling there.

The boy who was to become the Iron Duke had no aptitude for the kind of learning Eton provided; he was removed so that all the family's resources could be applied to his younger brothers, Gerald and Henry, who were better students.

Not until thirty-four years later did Wellington choose to visit Eton. And in 1841, when included among his many other honors was a Chancellorship of Oxford University, he coldly refused to give so much as a shilling to a subscription drive for new buildings at Eton, saying that he had "determined that [he] would not subscribe to defray the Expense of addl. buildings at Eton College." Let the "publick" provide them, he added. So much for Eton—and its playing fields.

One is tempted to add one's own version, more consistent both with the Iron Duke's relationship with Eton and with his character: the Battle of Waterloo was won on the battlefield of Waterloo—part of which, by the way, is owned by the present Duke, who, fearful of its exploitation or subdivision by commercial interests, has resisted all offers of purchase.

"Because it is there." This famous response to a mildly impertinent question ("Why do you want to climb Mt. Everest?") was made not by Sir Edmund Hillary, to whom it is often attributed, but by George Leigh Mallory, who disappeared into the mists on his last attempt to scale Everest in 1924, never to be seen again.

"Beefeaters" (Yeomen of the Guard). The colorful Warders (to give them their proper name) who "guard" the Tower of London are not members of the Yeomen of the Guard, no matter how many tourists may think so. The Yeomen of the Guard are attached to the household of the sovereign; they were instituted in 1485, at the beginning of the reign of Henry VII.

The "Beefeaters" at the Tower came later, during the time of Edward VI (reigned 1547–53), son of the redoubtable Henry VIII and Jane Seymour. Though similarly costumed, they belong to the Yeomen Extraordinary of the Guard and are called Yeomen Warders of the Tower.

A further widespread misapprehension, shared by many British (it can be found printed on the place mats of an inn at Cambridge), is that "Beefeater" has nothing to do with eating beef but is rather a corruption of "Buffetier." According to this fanciful but quite false tale, William the Conqueror brought with him, in the eleventh century, yeomen-warders whose job it was to assist at his "buffet": "buffetiers," in other words. The name was corrupted to "beefeaters." Even those who market England's well-known Beefeater gin (see MARTINI, "BRUISING" IT BY SHAKING) were apparently taken in by the "buffetier" story; in 1978 they devoted part of a full-page newspaper advertisement to its perpetuation.

But it's all folk etymology, though of the purest kind. No such word as "buffetier" exists in English, or has ever existed; and (see above) in any case the Beefeaters came along many centuries after William the Conqueror. Nor was "beefeater" always, as it is today, associated with the glamour and color of those Warders. In the words of Sarah Barter Bailey, librarian at the Tower of London, "There have been several attempts to think up interesting etymologies for the term Beefeater as applied to the Yeomen of the Guard and the Yeoman Warders of the Tower. Most opinion nowadays favours the obvious derivation: 'beef-eater' was a seventeenth century slang description for a well-fed menial who stood around a great man's house. By a natural transfer, it came to be used of the royal guard . . . and finally came to be used only of the most conspicuously dressed royal guard as the custom of other great families having their own liveried household guards died out."

Whether or not an implicit contempt for authority was involved, "beefeater" as applied either to Yeomen of the Guard or Yeomen Extraordinary of the Guard was obviously a somewhat pejorative term in the beginning. (Compare the Anglo-Saxon word for domestic servant: *hlāf-aeta*, or "loaf-eater.") But as the centuries passed (and, perhaps, as the power of the monarch diminished), the term came to have its present more or less affectionate connotations—a process linguists sometimes call "elevation."

beggar. Once spelled "begger," this word is usually assumed to be derived from the verb "beg," by a process very common in English ("reader" from "read," "driver" from "drive," etc., etc.).

But the reverse seems to be the case. Although the *Oxford English Dictionary* shies away from a flat statement, it seems most likely that the noun "beggar" came first and the verb later, by a process linguists call "back formation."

An odd and interesting sidelight, especially to those who know Cole Porter's sultry and sexy "Begin the Beguine," is that "beg" may derive from the Beguines. And who were they? A thirteenth-century mendicant holy order whom it is very hard to imagine as doing the Beguine—though the phrase "to act the beguin(e)" (that is, to beg) is mentioned in the OED as perhaps relevant to the origin of "beg."

Back formation accounts for more words than many realize, from the somewhat disreputable "enthuse" to such standards as "edit" from "editor," which came first; "peddle" from "peddler," by much the older word; and "diagnose" from its ancestor "diagnosis." It is a common humorous device: "buttle" from "butler," "burgle" from "burglar" —the latter apparently created by W. S. Gilbert in a line from *The Pirates of Penzance* that goes "When the enterprising burglar's not a-burgling." ("Burgle" is sometimes used today in a nonhumorous context.)

As nature is said to abhor a vacuum—a somewhat dubious statement considering what outer space is largely composed of—so those who use a language will tend to fill in obvious gaps. "Notarize," once thought to be a barbarism—the *Oxford English Dictionary* did not even list it until 1976—is apparently derived from the noun "notary." The reason for its birth is obvious: just as "enthuse" says it more efficiently than "be enthusiastic about" and thus may someday achieve respectability, so "notarized" is the alternative to "witnessed by a notary."

Back formations often start under a linguistic cloud, for whatever reasons. "Donate" (for "give"), a back formation from "donation," was originally regarded by the British as a U.S. vulgarism. The common and inoffensive verbs "jell," from "jelly," and "resurrect," from "resurrection," were thought to be substandard not so long ago.

A different form of back formation involves the dropping of a final "s" that is erroneously supposed to be a plural ending. "Pease," as in "Pease porridge hot, pease porridge cold," is singular. But in relatively modern times it became mistaken for a plural; thus the creation of *pea* as a singular, and the modern spelling *peas* for the plural.

"Innings," incidentally, is used in Britain as a singular: in cricket, it's an innings. In American baseball it's an inning.

Beiderbecke, Bix, and his trumpet. Bix Beiderbecke (1903–31), the legendary Jazz Age musician, did not play the trumpet. His horn was the cornet. (Many overlook the fact that he was also an accomplished pianist.)

The trumpet, of ancient ancestry—the Greeks and Romans had them, though not with valves, which came many centuries later—differs from the cornet in bore and shape; a cornet looks a bit short and fat beside it.

Most people tend to assume that the cornet is the more "respectable" of the two, perhaps because the trumpet is so integral a part of the development of jazz. But the reverse is true; the cornet is regarded by some as inferior to the trumpet because the trumpet produces a more brilliant sound.

Bermuda Triangle "mystery." Millions of people have read of the mysterious disappearances said to have taken place within the so-called Bermuda, or "Devil's," Triangle. It all seems to have started with the loss of five Navy aircraft and their crews—the famous Flight 19. It was after this episode, apparently, that the term "Bermuda Triangle" made its way into popular usage—and many other instances of mysterious disappearances were alleged.

But although the exact place where the planes "disappeared" may never be known, the demise of Flight 19 was anything but inexplicable. That all five aircraft disappeared "simultaneously," a point often stressed by those who believe in the Triangle, is scarcely surprising; they were flying in formation, all with the same amount of fuel on board, all in the same kind of aircraft (Avenger torpedo bombers).

However, it would be arrogantly supererogatory to deal here with the presumed mysteries of the Bermuda Triangle. The seminal episode, Flight 19 and the search therefor, is the subject of a new book, *The Disappearance of Flight 19* (Harper & Row, 1980) by Larry Kusche, whose *The Bermuda Triangle Mystery—Solved* (Harper & Row, 1975) deals case by case with the examples most often cited and finds them quite explainable. Mr. Kusche, a conscientious researcher (and also a pilot), did what had to be done: rather than pretending to, he actually looked at the record, relying on original sources rather than hearsay or sensational journalism.

One book capitalizing on the Bermuda Triangle "mystery" became the nation's No. 1 best-seller. It is still taken seriously by those who have not bothered to read Mr. Kusche's account. To paraphrase Ben Jonson, truth hath an enemy called apathy.

Bernhardt, Sarah, and her wooden leg. Everybody knows two things about Greta Garbo: she has big feet (she doesn't), and she told people "I vant to be alone" (she didn't). Everybody knows one thing about "the divine Sarah" Bernhardt (1844–1923): during the last years of her career she wore, and performed with, an artificial leg.

Well, she didn't. True, her leg was amputated when she was seventy-two; years earlier, in 1890, she had fallen and had injured her knee on the deck of the ship bringing her to New York for her second appearance in the United States. It never healed properly; and finally, no longer able to bear the pain, she decided on amputation. Both her doctor and many of her well-wishers tried to persuade her to wear an artificial limb, but she refused. She was carried in a specially made chair, tailored to the dimensions of theater corridors and passageways, which could also be installed in her automobile. She went right on acting, but in roles that did not demand much if any movement; in Rostand's *La Gloire*, for example, she sat on a throne throughout the drama's five acts.

"Beware of the dog." This old warning—it goes back at least as far as the Roman Empire *("Cave canem")*—should be applied with caution. It does not, as often thought, relieve the dog owner of responsibility. It has been said that as a matter of law every dog is entitled to one bite, or "one bite free." What this means, as the late Bergen Evans reminded us in his *Dictionary of Quotations* (1968), is that an owner is presumed to be unaware of his dog's tendency to bite unless the dog has already bitten someone. (Apparently the potential victim is thus under obligation to inquire of the dog if this is, or will be, his first experience, bitewise.)

Obviously, a warning sign shows that the owner *is* aware of his dog's unfriendly tendencies; thus, the owner deprives himself of a possible defense in a possible lawsuit.

births and the blackout. It did not take long (nine months) to establish in folk mythology the increase in births said to have followed the great New York blackout of November 1965 after a series of massive and interconnected power failures.

This and similar beliefs (after the Chicago blizzard a couple of years later, a storm of "blizzard babies" was predicted) make for interesting psychological speculations. Is sex considered so shameful that one assumes it is more likely to be undertaken in the dark? Or is it taken so casually that it becomes merely an alternative to television?

One would suppose that shivering in the dark and worrying about the food in the freezer and looters on the loose are scarcely ideal conditions for lovemaking. In any case, the story is quite false, although even the *New York Times* helped to perpetuate it in a news item about the increased number of births at Mt. Sinai Hospital on August 8 of 1966.

But that was just one day at just one hospital, a random statistical variation. J. Richard Udry, director of the Carolina Population Center at the University of North Carolina, Chapel Hill, takes an interest in such matters. And he showed conclusively, in *Demography* for August 1970 (325 ff.), that there was no increase in births nine months after the blackout. (There was, in fact, a slight decrease.)

Basing his findings, as a good statistician—or a good reporter—should, on the number of births in the New York area between July 27 and August 14 of 1966, Professor Udry compared them with total numbers during this same period from 1960 to 1965.

His conclusion? Of babies born throughout the year, the percentage of those born between July 27 and August 14, 1960–65, varied between 13.9 and 14.1. For the comparable 1966 period, the percentage was 13.9. Though not statistically significant, this figure is actually a bit below the five-year average.

black children as result of tiny percentage of "Negro" blood. A myth now at last dying, but by no means dead, is that a small percentage of black blood, perhaps unknown to either partner, will show up when an apparently white couple has a coal-black child. It is, of course, nonsense.

Mark Twain knew better. In *Pudd'nhead Wilson,* the beautiful slave Roxana, one sixteenth black, bears a blue-eyed, flaxen-haired child by her white master. (The plot of *Pudd'nhead* revolves about this crucial fact, since Roxana, or "Roxy," exchanges the child in the cradle for the lookalike legitimate son of the white master, and no one except her knows the difference.)

A fascinating indication of how a stereotype can completely blind the observer to the truth is found in early editions of *Pudd'nhead*. Here is Twain's description of Roxana, or Roxy:

> From Roxy's manner of speech, a stranger would have expected her to be black, but she was not. Only one-sixteenth of her was black, and that sixteenth did not show. She was of majestic form and stature, her attitudes were imposing and statuesque, and her gestures and movements distinguished by a noble and stately grace. Her complexion was very fair, with the rosy glow of vigorous health in her cheeks, her face was full of character and expression, her eyes were brown[1] and liquid, and she had a heavy suit of fine soft hair which was also brown, but the fact was not apparent because her head was bound about with a checkered handkerchief. . . . Her face was shapely, intelligent, and comely—even beautiful.

But then an artist was engaged to do a frontispiece for the "Author's National Edition" of Twain's works, first published many years ago in twenty-five volumes and still, in its green binding, a familiar sight in libraries and used-book stores. The frontispiece is titled "Roxy Harvesting Among the Kitchens" (a reference to the custom of stealing, or "harvesting," small items by slaves who, in Twain's words, had themselves been robbed of "an inestimable treasure . . . liberty").

Roxy dominates the picture. And how is she portrayed? As a stout, buxom, coal-black woman with so-called negroid features: thick lips, broad nose, broad face!

Blackstone. Sir William Blackstone (1723–80), most famous of English jurists—indeed, the term "Blackstone" is almost a synonym for "law"—was not himself much of a lawyer. It has been said of him that he did not have any but the vaguest grasp of the elementary conceptions of law. Although apparently a good lecturer, he was shy and diffident; his own law practice was anything but successful.

What probably ensured his fame (greater, some have said, in America than in Britain) was the grace and lucidity of his style. Like Gibbon, Addison, Steele, Swift, and a

---

[1] Twain is on safe ground here also. Though brown is dominant over blue, it is quite possible for a brown-eyed parent to have a blue-eyed child.

host of others, he lived and wrote during the eighteenth century, that period of Anglo-Irish literary history often called the "Neoclassical" or "Augustan," during which the balanced sentence and the graceful phrase reigned supreme.

"blind as a bat." Bats are not blind; they can see, though not so well as other mammals. They use echolocation, which enables them to fly at night, when darkness protects them from other predators.

Echolocation is a kind of sonar; the bat emits high-pitched sound waves which are reflected back from any object they hit. The bat reads the echo and knows, instantaneously, the distance, size, and shape of the object. The sonar apparatus is quite sophisticated; bats use it to catch insects, and it has been shown in tests that blindfolded bats can fly easily through aerial mazes, even when the obstacles are thin threads strung across a room.

blue jays. The saucy, intelligent, and curious creature known to Westerners as the blue jay, or the California blue jay, is not a blue jay but either a Steller's jay or a scrub jay. There are no blue jays west of the Rockies.

body, average human. Those large charts, often in vivid color, that purport to show us what our organs look like have encouraged the belief that human beings resemble each other internally much more than is actually the case. There is no such thing as an "average" body—externally or internally. Most people, for example, have three arteries branching off from the aorta. But more than a third do not: there may be as few as one or as many as six. Stomachs vary in size, shape, and position so much that the textbook stomach of the charts is an idealization, not a fact.

These many differences, as Roger J. Williams, a member of the National Academy of Sciences and a past president of the American Chemical Society, points out, should remind us not only of our individual uniqueness but should also be taken into account in terms of the widely varying nutritional needs that exist among individual human beings.

boomerang. The word is Australian, but the boomerang is not exclusively an Australian device. Similar missiles were known in ancient Egypt and can be found in parts of Africa and India today. The Hopi Indians of Arizona know one form of the boomerang; apparently, Eskimos once used them—there is such a legend among some Eskimos.

Nor do all boomerangs return to their throwers. The notion that an Australian aborigine can kill a large animal (or an enemy aborigine) with a boomerang that returns obediently to its owner is quite false. The boomerang used for this purpose, sometimes called the war or hunting boomerang, is not designed to return to the thrower, nor is it thrown in the same fashion as the return, or "sporting," boomerang. When thrown with murderous intention by an expert, it is a murderous weapon. But its flight is straight, not curved; thus it doesn't come back but must be retrieved.

"Born with a gift of laughter and a sense that the world was mad." Years ago the late Alexander Woollcott told, with Woollcottian amusement, the story of this impressive-sounding quotation inscribed over a doorway of the Hall of Graduate Studies at Yale. It is not, as Woollcott gleefully pointed out, from the classics, or anything remotely resembling them. It's from the opening sentence of a romantic novel by Rafael Sabatini, *Scaramouche*. Vastly popular in its day (and still in print), it is not, true enough, the sort of thing that graduate students at Yale are likely to spend time analyzing, explicating, correlating, or dissecting.

Then how did so unlikely an inscription come to grace so likely a seat of learning as the Yale Graduate School? There seems to be more than one answer to this question —or, perhaps, there is one answer with a subanswer. The architect responsible, John Donald Tuttle, wrote to Woollcott following the appearance of Woollcott's comments in *The New Yorker* for November 17, 1934. Tuttle, then a young man working under Yale's favorite architect, James Gamble Rogers, said that it cut across his grain to use architecture of the sort mandated by Yale: architecture originally conceived so that archers could shoot arrows through slits and yeomen pour molten lead on the people below. So, "as a propitiatory gift to my gods," said Mr. Tuttle, he carved, or caused to be carved, the inscription over the door. He also suggested that there were other reasons for nervousness, on the part of the Yale Corporation, incorporated into the design.

However, Edgar S. Furniss, dean of the Graduate School at Yale when the Hall of Graduate Studies was built, has a different version. His account, in *The Graduate School of Yale* (New Haven, 1965), puts the blame on a Mr. Finnegan, "an Irishman of middle age with a battered face of mahogany hue, with snapping eyes of piercing blue given . . . to an incessant chatter of frivolity and whimsey," who was top boss of the construction workers and, as such, "not supposed to exercise any independent authority at all."

Supposed to or not, however, Mr. Finnegan did undertake some modifications; he believed, according to Dean Furniss, that graduate schools tended toward the pretentious; it would be "a wholesome experience for the university . . . to . . . exhibit in permanent form a declaration that its own graduate school would represent . . . the lighter and gayer concerns of mankind."

Mr. Finnegan implemented his belief, says Dean Furniss, through various means: decorative bricks sneaked into the structure with various devices—a cherub to symbolize President Angell; busts of the Yale comptroller and of the Yale chief architect, Rogers; miniature ovens, or "furnaces," to represent the new dean; and so on. (According to Furniss, the unauthorized busts were later modified to resemble Egyptian pharaohs.)

And it was Mr. Finnegan who was responsible for the Sabatini inscription. The reason for it? Mr. Finnegan, at first reticent, explained that he had meant it as a compliment to the new Dean Furniss, "but if it's going to cause you embarrassment, let's not give out any information about it."

Such is Dean Furniss's account. Since deans of graduate schools, especially those as distinguished as Yale's, surely do not lie, one must accept it. The remaining possibility, which reason strongly suggests, is that Mr. Finnegan was not working quite so independently as Dean Furniss believed but was actually in cahoots with the rebellious young subarchitect, Mr. Tuttle. In other words, Dean Furniss had the right information, but not all of it.

At least Mr. Tuttle or Mr. Finnegan, or either or both, saw to it that Yale, or the hall of its Graduate School anyway, did not join the vast legion of academic buildings that have had somewhere inscribed upon themselves the weary old quotation from Chaucer: "And gladly wolde he lerne, and gladly teche."

A final comment, for such irony as may be mined from it: the inscription as carved misquotes Sabatini. The inscription reads "a gift for laughter." Sabatini wrote "a gift of laughter."

boycott. As many are aware, this word derives from the name of Captain Charles Boycott, who in nineteenth-century Ireland, acting as agent for a wealthy English absentee landlord, dealt harshly with Irish tenant farmers. But "boycott" derives not from the fact that he did any boycotting himself but rather from the fact that he was the object of it. The tenants organized themselves and refused to have any further dealings with him.

Braille. Many think that Braille is merely conventional letters, figures, and symbols raised so that they can be perceived by the fingers. It isn't; it is quite unlike any conventional alphabet, consisting rather of raised dots bearing no physical resemblance to actual letters or figures. When "written" by hand, the dots are punched out on stiff paper with the help of a template and a small tool resembling an awl. Because it would be virtually impossible to punch the dots out from underneath, Braille is written backward so that for most European languages it can be "read" with the fingers in normal left-to-right order when the page is turned over.

Reading Braille is not, as some think, a one-finger exercise. A skilled reader uses both hands, to keep a word or two ahead, just as a skilled reader of regular type scans words and phrases, not just individual letters.

Brazil, language of. Brazilians do not speak Spanish unless they learn it as a foreign tongue. Their language is Portuguese. Once a Portuguese dependency, Brazil is, in fact, the only colony ever to assume rule over its mother country. When Napoleon threatened to invade Portugal in 1807, the prince regent, later Dom John VI, moved the seat of government to Rio de Janeiro, arriving there in March of 1808. Following Dom John's return to Lisbon in 1821, Brazil achieved its independence under John's rebellious son, Dom Pedro. In 1825 Portuguese recognition followed.

breast cancer. Many women—as many as 62 percent of more than 1,000 interviewed, according to the American Cancer Society—believe that a blow or an injury to the breast can cause cancer. Fortunately, this is not so. According to Philip Strax, M.D., author of "Breast Cancer Is Curable," a booklet obtainable from the American Cancer Society, "There has never been a proven case of breast cancer arising from an area of injury. There is no connection between the development of breast cancer and injuries to the breast or even frequent manipulation as sometimes happens in love-making."

"bug" in Great Britain. Tourists in London should be advised that asking for a "bug repellant" may invite a questioning stare. The British mean one thing, and one thing only, by "bug": bedbug. Say "insect" repellant if the mosquitoes find you palatable in Portsmouth.

bumblebees and the laws of aerodynamics. Often quoted is the statement that according to all the laws of aerodynamics, bumblebees cannot fly—but they do it anyway. There is obviously nothing whatever in the laws of aerodynamics that says bumblebees can't fly. If there were, they wouldn't —and they do.

Bunyan, Paul, as mythic folk hero. Whether or not, as some believe, there was a real logger of extraordinary strength and endurance who provided the original basis for "Paul Bunyan" stories, the fact is that the stories themselves were very largely the creation of two twentieth-century lumber-company public relations men: W. B. Laughead and James Stevens. Some have gone so far as to propose that Paul Bunyan was a hoax—that is, that no prototype for him ever did exist except in the fertile imaginations of advertising men and press agents.

Certainly it is true that, unlike the fictional Roaring Ralph Stackpole or the real Mike Fink and Davy Crockett, Paul Bunyan does not show up in print until 1914 (some say 1910). According to W. A. Botkin's *A Treasury of American Folklore* (1944), the Red River Lumber Company in 1914 issued a booklet of Bunyan tales written— and also illustrated—by Laughead. Poems and stories about Bunyan written by others followed, and in 1924 Esther Shephard gave the tales a Pacific Northwest orientation with her *Paul Bunyan,* aimed at a popular audience.

James Stevens wrote his *Paul Bunyan* in 1925, the year after the publication of the Shephard book. Stevens, who had worked in an Oregon logging camp, achieved his first national recognition with his Bunyan tales. He moved to Seattle in the mid-1930s to take a job with the West Coast Lumbermen's Association as public relations director, a post from which he retired in 1957

There may have been, as Stevens claimed, a French-Canadian logger during the 1830s (who spelled his last name "Bunyon" according to Stevens), a kind of logging-camp superman. If there was, it took him a mighty long time to be mentioned in print. Tall tales based on the escapades of Mike Fink and Davy Crockett—Fink died, or was killed, about 1823; Crockett fell during the siege of the Alamo in 1836—flourished during their lifetimes or only shortly thereafter. If Paul Bunyan was indeed modeled after a real-life figure who lived 150 years ago, it does seem odd—in fact, unprecedented—that nothing was printed about him until the twentieth century.

That mythical creatures may, for commercial reasons, be invented by advertising men is evident enough. Still, who knows but that sometime in the future an earnest folklorist will trace the Jolly Green Giant's origin back to a prodigious pea-picker with a pigmentation problem?

Butler, Nicholas Murray—and what happened to him in Poetry magazine. Without question Nicholas Murray Butler, or Nicholas Miraculous as he was sometimes called (though not to his face), was a remarkable person. A high school graduate at thirteen, a Ph.D. at twenty-two, he joined the faculty of Columbia University at the ripe old age of twenty-three. He organized, and was first president of, the famous Columbia University Teachers College; became president of Columbia itself in 1902, serving until 1945; ran with Taft for Vice-President on the Republican ticket in 1912 (they were soundly defeated by the Woodrow Wilson forces); was co-winner with Jane Addams of the Nobel Peace Prize in 1931; and died in 1947, loaded with honors, at the truly ripe old age of eighty-five.

But he was not universally beloved, possibly for reasons implicit in one sentence from a *Time* magazine review in 1939: "Dr. Butler's autobiography," said *Time,* "betrays no false modesty."

It was in June of that same year that the late Rolfe Humphries, himself notable as poet, classicist, and football coach at a boys' school, gave Dr. Butler his comeuppance —with the assistance, both unwitting and unwilling, of

Poetry magazine, then as now the most prestigious journal of its kind.

Humphries's accomplishment, all the more remarkable in that it met *Poetry*'s high standards, was at the same time one of the most famous, and yet least known, of literary practical jokes: famous among insiders, unknown to the general public.

Here, reproduced just as it first appeared in *Poetry* for June 1939, is Humphries's tour de force, perhaps sufficiently described as a rather cross acrostic:

DRAFT ODE FOR A PHI BETA KAPPA OCCASION

(Written in the tradition that there must be an average
of one classical allusion to the line, and that the
metre must be unrhymed iambic pentameter.)

Niobe's daughters yearn to the womb again,
Ionians bright and fair, to the chill stone;
Chaos in cry, Actaeon's angry pack,
Hounds of Molossus, shaggy wolvers driven

Over Ampsanctus' vale and Pentheus' glade,
Laelaps and Ladon, Dromas, Canace,—
As these in fury harry brake and hill,
So the great dogs of evil bay the world.

Memory, Mother of Muses, be resigned
Until King Saturn comes to rule again!
Remember now no more the golden day,
Remember now no more the fading gold,
Astraea fled, Proserpina in hell:
You searchers of the earth, be reconciled!

Because, through all the blight of human woe,
Under Robigo's rust, and Clotho's shears,
The mind of man still keeps its argosies,
Lacedaemonian Helen wakes her tower,

Echo replies, and lamentation loud
Reverberates from Thrace to Delos' isle;
Itylus grieves, for whom the nightingale
Sweetly as ever tunes her Daulian strain.

And over Tenedos the flagship burns.

How shall men loiter when the great moon shines
Opaque upon the sail, and Argive seas
Rear like blue dolphins their cerulean curves?
Samos is fallen, Lesbos streams with fire,
Etna in rage, Canopus cold in hate,
Summon the Orphic bard to stranger dreams.

And so for us who raise Athene's torch
Sufficient to her message in this hour:
Sons of Columbia, awake, arise!

Rolfe Humphries

And here, by the way, is what an indignant *Poetry* had
to say in August of 1939.

A STATEMENT

Not being accustomed to hold manuscripts up to the
mirror or to test them for cryptograms, the editors recently accepted and printed a poem containing a con-
cealed scurrilous phrase aimed at a well-known person.
This was not called to their attention until several weeks
after the issue had been published. The phrase in question is puerile and uninteresting, and would not be referred to except that it is necessary to disclaim editorial
responsibility. Apparently it is also necessary to state a
principle which one would have thought obvious; name-
ly, that any contributor who allows such matter to be
printed without the editors' knowledge is guilty of a
serious breach of confidence, and will automatically dis-
bar himself from the magazine.

Someone once asked Humphries if this "disbarment" was
for life. He grinned and said, "They forgave me finally."
Forty years have passed since the appearance of Mr. Humphries's "Ode." Perhaps the shade of Nicholas Miraculous
will also forgive him now.

butterfly, origin of word. How charming is the butterfly!
Symbol of the soul to the ancient Egyptians, of the gentle
west wind Psyche to the Greeks and Romans (but also, it
must be added, sometimes superstitiously associated with

death), lifelong study of the late Vladimir Nabokov, and the delight of tourists who watch the masses of monarchs in springtime on the Monterey peninsula in California, the butterfly has fascinated humankind for thousands of years. And it has also generated its share of misinformation.

It is often said, for example, that the word represents a transposition of sounds ("metathesis" to linguists): once it was the charming "flutter-by." Not so; it's been "butterfly" in English for as long as we have written records. Nor is it so named because its wings are often yellow.

Somewhat unromantically, to say the least, it seems that the butterfly very likely got its name from what its excrement looks like; both the renowned linguist Walter W. Skeat (1835–1912) and the renowned *Oxford English Dictionary* point to an Old Dutch word for butterfly: *boterschijte*, not difficult to translate even for those who know no Dutch.

buttery (noun). Not a room or a pantry where butter is stored, though it looks as if it ought to be. The word is related not to "butter" but rather to the Middle English *botery*, which stems in turn from the Old French word *boteillerie*, from *bouteille*, "bottle." A buttery, thus, is a place where liquor is kept, although sometimes in England it refers to a room in a college where provisions are held for sale to students.

The word *butler*, incidentally, has an analogous etymology (Old French *bouteillier*, "bottle bearer").

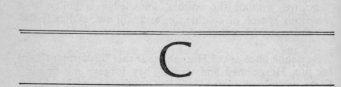

C

cabbage regulation myth. Poking fun at the language of government rules and regulations is one of America's favorite indoor sports. Now and then, however, the critics invoke mythology. A good example is the so-called Cabage Regulation, which has never existed. The history of the mythical cabbage rules is well told in the *New Republic* for April 23, 1977, pages 9–10. Here in large part, and with permission, is its account:

"Pipeline Pete," a rough-hewn, pipe-smoking fellow with a hard hat, is a creation of the propaganda arm of the Mobil Oil Corporation. His words of folk wisdom appear at the bottom of a column called "Observations," which Mobil puts in places like the Sunday *New York Times Magazine*. One recent Sunday (April 10, [1977]) P.P. was all riled up about meddlesome government regulations, one of his favorite topics. As reported by Mobil, here are Pete's thoughts:

Pipeline Pete says: "The Lord's Prayer has 56 words; at Gettysburg, Lincoln spoke only 268 long-remembered words; and we got a whole country goin' on the 1,322 words in the Declaration of Independence. So how come it took the federal government 26,911 words to issue a regulation on the sale of cabbages?"

These simple but honest reflections aroused our interest. . . . We called Mobil's public affairs office in New York, to find out which government agency had been leaving its heavy boot prints in the nation's private cabbage patches. . . . The people at Mobil said they didn't know. They had lifted the anecdote from an editorial in the Fall 1976 edition of *Progress*, the house organ of FMC Corporation, an agricultural concern in Chicago [which had] borrowed the story from the May 5, 1976, issue of *NAM Reports*, published by the National Association of Manufacturers here in Washington. The editor of that publication said she got it from an NAM director, whose name she could not remember, who had it printed on a card he carried around with him. . . .

There is no such regulation and there never was. . . . But the story of the phantom cabbage regulation, along with the comparison to documents of greater nobility but shorter length, has surfaced hundreds of times, usually in right-wing or business-oriented publications. (Both major publications of Dow Jones, Inc., *The Wall Street Journal* and *The National Observer*, have fallen for the hoax.) Max Hall, a research director at the Harvard Business School, has traced the story back as far as July 28, 1951, when it appeared in a farm journal called *New England Homestead*. At that time it included the Ten Commandments (297 words) instead of the Lord's

Prayer, and attached itself specifically to the regulations of the Korean War Office of Price Stabilization. Mr. Hall claims that as an oral tradition the story can be traced even further back, to World War II when it was applied to the Office of Price Administration. In recent years the story has detached itself from any specific agency and become an indictment of big government in general.

Mr. Hall has conducted a 26-year crusade against the cabbage lie. It began when he was public affairs director of OPS, trying to cope with the bad publicity. In 1954 he wrote a lengthy study of the phenomenon for the *Journal of Personality and Social Psychology.* Over the years various publications have exposed the hoax, including the *New York Times.* . . . But the cabbage myth never has lost its grip on the imaginations of the American business community. The number of words allegedly in the Declaration of Independence has varied from as low as 300, in the 1951 *New England Homestead* story, to a reported high of 3,000, in *NAM Reports* last May. There have been smaller variations in the count of the Gettysburg Address.[1] But the number of words in the cabbage regulations is always precisely the same: 26,911.

But it isn't true. Free enterprise survives in the cabbage industry.

It would be pleasant to think that the *New Republic* has finally laid to rest the Great Cabbage Regulation Myth. But history seems to reveal, alas, that if Truth, crushed to earth, indeed rises again, it may be only as prelude to another crusher. Members of the wagering fraternity would be well advised to place their bets now on a further appearance of that ubiquitous—and apparently eternal—cabbage regulation somewhere, some time in the future, and not the distant future either.

California sliding into the sea. Californians, because perforce they must, have long resigned themselves to living with the famous San Andreas Fault, which runs much of the length

---

[1] A hand count of these documents, not guaranteed, with hyphenated words counted as one, gives the following results: Declaration of Independence: 1,371; Gettysburg Address: 271; Lord's Prayer: 72, counting "Amen." Texts are those found in the *World Almanac* (Declaration, Gettysburg Address) and the September 1952 printing of the Book of Common Prayer of the Protestant Episcopal Church. —T. B.

of California. Perhaps because of publicity about it, a sizable number of people, not all of whom are cultists, fear that southern California may break off and slide into the Pacific. But not to worry; in the words of Edward A. Flinn, chief scientist of NASA's Earth and Ocean programs and also editor of the *Journal of Geophysical Research*:

[The prospect that California is in danger of sliding into the sea] is not at all ominous as far as immersion of the land is concerned, although the risk to life and property from large earthquakes is very real.

About ten years ago the evidence became overwhelming that the plate tectonic model of dynamic processes within the earth is correct, at least in its essential features. This model has the surface of the earth covered by about a dozen very large quasi-rigid plates (and a number of small ones), several hundred kilometers thick, and in motion with respect to one another, rather like paving stones. The plates move away from each other at the mid-ocean ridge system, where molten rock wells up from below, adding new material to the plates on each side as it freezes. The continents are carried along on the plates, which act like rafts.

The plates clash together at zones of convergence such as the Aleutian archipelago (and elsewhere where there are deep ocean trenches); one plate rides up over the other in these areas. In other parts of the world the plates are in relative horizontal rather than vertical motion—this is the situation in New Zealand, for example, and on the west coast of North America.

The boundary between the North American Plate and the Pacific Plate is the San Andreas fault system, and the two plates are moving past one another at about five centimeters per year, with Baja California and all of California southwest of the San Andreas going north. In ten or fifteen million years, Los Angeles and San Francisco will be suburbs of one another, and later still, Los Angeles will be located on a long thin island off the coast of Canada. There is absolutely no danger, though, that Los Angeles is going to sink beneath the Pacific.

It's possible that Angeleños might prefer sinking into the Pacific over the prospects cited by Mr. Flinn, no matter how far in future they may lie.

cancer induced in rats and other laboratory animals. A common—and potentially dangerous—misconception is illustrated in the widely circulated statement that for a human being to contract cancer from saccharin, it would be necessary to consume 800 bottles of saccharin-sweetened soft drinks daily. Similar rejection of laboratory findings is illustrated in such wisecracks as "Don't smoke cigarettes if you're a mouse" and so on.

Behind these popular cynicisms lies a misapprehension of how cancer-inducing agents are, and must be, assessed. Cancer incidence is directly related to dosage. Feeding what appear to be inordinate amounts of a suspected carcinogenic substance to a relatively small number of animals is the alternative to a procedure impossibly long and complicated: low or "normal" dosages to hundreds of thousands, perhaps even millions, of animals.

As Charles F. Wurster, a trustee of the Environmental Defense Fund, has pointed out, laboratory extrapolations from animal data are admittedly not precise, but they remain the best indicators available for estimating human response.

Often, another variation of *reductio ad absurdum* appears: *anything* taken to excess may kill. But there is a consideration that is vital, in the exact sense of that term: aspirin can be poisonous if taken to excess, but aspirin does not cause tumors, in rats or anything else. And that's the point Mr. Wurster is concerned with. The saccharin did cause tumors.

Incidentally, among the misconceptions about saccharin are that it causes weight loss or contains "negative calories." Saccharin is simply a flavoring agent, nothing more or less. It has been pointed out that it can conceivably increase a desire for sugar, rather than lessening it, since saccharin does not raise the blood-sugar level.

Capistrano, swallows of. Firmly fixed in legend—aided and abetted by a still often-heard popular song and those annual newspaper accounts—are the swallows that each year faithfully return to the mission of San Juan Capistrano on exactly the same date: St. Joseph's Day, March 19 (not, as is sometimes said, the first day of spring). But this annual "miracle," which yearly attracts bumper-to-bumper traffic, just doesn't happen.

Dr. Thomas R. Howell, professor of zoology at UCLA, joins with other experts in pointing out that the swallows are merely following, and not so exactly as the myth would have us believe, a typical pattern of bird migration. In fact, the swallows have been recorded as arriving in southern California, where the mission is located, as early as the last week in February and as late as the last week in March. Nor do they all arrive in a single flock. The species is actually very abundant and widespread over much of North America during the nesting season.

Further, says Dr. Howell, it is quite likely that many tourists and visitors confuse the Capistrano swallows, which do indeed winter in South America and migrate to California each spring, with the common white-throated swifts, which stay in California the year round.

As a matter of fact, not very many swallows call the mission home any more. In earlier days it was the most suitable building around. The Capistrano swallows (*Petro-chelidon pyrrhonota*) are natural cliff dwellers; their popular name is "cliff swallow." Today, there are many other stone or concrete structures in the area that are even more suitable as substitutes for the natural cliffs where they build their gourd-shaped mud nests.

For some reason, the departure of the swallows for South America never seems to attract much attention, which is odd in that the legend has them leaving on the October 23 anniversary of the death of San Juan (St. John of Capistrano), for whom the mission is named. They do leave in the fall, all right, but no more en masse or on the same day than is true of their arrival in the spring.

In any case, those who have been puzzled as to how the swallows made allowance for leap years may now rest their minds.

capital punishment. Contrary to widespread belief, the U.S. Supreme Court has never ruled that capital punishment, *per se,* is cruel and unusual punishment. That is why there have been executions since the Supreme Court ruling of 1972. What the Court did say, in effect (*Furman* v. *Georgia*), is that when the decision to impose capital punishment is left to the discretion of a jury so that discrimination as to race, religion, wealth, social position, or class can play a part in its imposition, *then* capital punishment is cruel and unusual and thus forbidden by the Eighth Amendment. ("Excessive bail shall not be required, nor excessive fines imposed, nor cruel and unusual punishments inflicted.")

Note that although the question of race has been uppermost in the minds of many concerned with capital punishment, the Supreme Court did not confine itself to this issue.

carrots and vision. That eating lots of carrots will improve one's night vision is not so. True, the vitamin A that the body converts from the carotene in carrots is thought to be related to visual acuity. But many other foods contain carotene. And in any case, the liver stores plenty of vitamin A. One reason this myth persists is that during World War II experiments designed to sharpen night vision among soldiers and pilots involved extra doses of vitamin A. No observable improvement resulted.

"Casey at the Bat"—and its baseball strategy. "Casey at the Bat," certainly one of the best-known of American popular poems, is often regarded as anonymous. It is not. It is often thought to have been written by a rustic rhymester with no pretensions to education or "culture." It was not.

"Casey" was created by Ernest Lawrence Thayer and first appeared in the *San Francisco Examiner* on June 3, 1888. And who was Ernest Lawrence Thayer? Heir to the American Woolen Mills, says *The People's Almanac* (1975), a student of philosophy under William James at Harvard, and editor of the famous *Harvard Lampoon* at a time when the young William Randolph Hearst was its business manager. When Hearst took over his father's *Examiner,* Thayer was invited to write a humor column. "Casey at the Bat" was one result—which became famous when DeWolf Hopper, the actor, made it his own, reciting it countless times in countless theaters. Hopper, born in 1858, lived on until the mid-1930s.

Perhaps because few associated "Casey at the Bat" with so sophisticated, or at least educated, an author as Thayer, the text has been regarded as fair game by many who have not hesitated to modify it to suit local tastes. At least one version, printed in 1936 in *The Best Loved Poems of the American People*, callously shifts the locale from Mudville to, of all places, Boston.

But how well did Ernest Lawrence Thayer know his
baseball? Not very well, says Ed Renfrew, vice-president
for Research and Development of American Color and
Chemical Corporation of Lock Haven, Pennsylvania, who
calls himself "a critic of unimportant things." As described
in a version of the poem published without attribution in
Taylor's Popular Recitations (1903), a fascinating hodge-
podge of pieces "delivered" by now-forgotten actors and
actresses during the days when audiences flocked to hear
such gems as "My Sweetheart of Long Ago," "The Dying
Actor," and "A Yaller Dog's Love for a Nigger," here is
the situation:

The outlook wasn't brilliant for the Mudville nine that
  day;
The score stood four to two, with but one inning more
  to play;
And so when Cooney died at first and Burroughs did
  the same,
A sickly fear came o'er the patrons of the game.

If only the mighty Casey could get a whack at the ball!
Unfortunately there are two hitters ahead of him—Flynn
and Blake—and "the former was a hoodoo, the latter was
a cake."

But Flynn let drive a single, to the wonderment of all,
And Blake, the much despised, tore the cover off the ball.
And when the dust had risen and they saw what had
  occurred,
There was Blake safe on second and Jimmy hugging third.

So Casey the indomitable will have his chance after all.
Scornfully he lets two strikes whistle past him as he stands
motionless in "haughty grandeur." Thayer, a Harvard man,
was well aware that humbled pride is the commonest of
themes in classic literature. And, sure enough:

The sneer is gone from Casey's lip, his teeth are clenched
  in hate,
He pounds with cruel violence his bat upon the plate;
And now the pitcher holds the ball, and now he lets it go,
And now the air is shattered by the force of Casey's blow.

Thayer also knew that, in classic tragedy, resolution follows crisis at once, without further ado; the next and final stanza is:

Oh, somewhere in this favored land the sun is shining bright,
The band is playing somewhere, and somewhere hearts are light,
And somewhere men are laughing, and somewhere children shout,
But there is no joy in Mudville—mighty Casey has struck out.

To all this Dr. Renfrew (he holds a Ph.D. in chemistry) responds:

"Casey at the Bat" may deserve its firm position in American folklore, but if so, it has to be for reasons other than good baseball. The strategy is dreadful. Consider the lineup: "But Flynn preceded Casey and so did Jimmy Blake;/The former was a hoodoo, the latter was a cake." Why in the world would a competent manager put two very weak hitters just ahead of his best slugger?

But with two out, bottom of the ninth, Flynn got a single and the much-despised Blake tore the cover off the ball. "And when the dust had risen and they saw what had occurred,/There was Blake safe on second and Jimmy hugging third."

In such a situation, the runner on first has to start with the crack of the bat and run all out. There is no way he should have held at third on such a long double, despite the purist argument that no chances should be taken when a team is two runs behind. And despite the old saw that the potential winning run should not intentionally be put on base, I feel that it was a grave strategic error to pitch to Casey, the most feared hitter in the league, with first base open. The next hitter, whoever he was, was not as good as Casey and should have been pitched to, with a play at every base.

An old saying, coined by this writer on the golf course, goes as follows: When you have a choice between luck and skill, choose luck every time. Perhaps the winning pitcher—or the manager—followed this principle.

castrato (plural, castrati). It seems hard to believe that as recently as the nineteenth century—the man believed to be the last castrato, Giovanni Battista Velluti, died in 1861—what the *Britannica* calls "the abominable practice" of castrating boys so that their voices would not change existed. But it did. Mozart, among others, wrote operatic roles for castrati. They were quite common in the seventeenth and eighteenth centuries.

However, it is hard to determine whether the practice, as is often assumed, was always ruthlessly inflicted on unwilling boys (sometimes, it is said, so they could remain church choristers). Particularly in the eighteenth century, castrati were often well paid and frequently idolized. It seems likely that some were willing participants—although obviously the deeper moral issue, whether (like Adam and Eve) a true choice is possible when it is impossible to assess its results, remains. (Adam and Eve could not know what sin meant until it was too late.)

According to Grove's *Dictionary of Music and Musicians,* a common story (told, in the instance cited, about Baldassare Ferri, 1610–80) was that the singer had had an accident in his boyhood resulting in his remaining a soprano. However, this appears to have been said so often about so many castrati that it was apparently a convention accepted but not necessarily believed. That the story was told at all indicates some reservations, on the part of seventeenth-century music lovers, about depriving a male child of his sexual future so that operagoers could continue to enjoy his voice.

catacombs of ancient Rome as hiding places. According to the *New Catholic Encyclopedia,* there is no evidence that the famous catacombs of Rome were used as refuges during periods of persecution. They were used, at least during the fourth century, for burial and memorial services.

Celsius (centigrade) thermometers and the metric system. It is widely assumed that the Celsius temperature scale, also called "centigrade," is an integral part of the metric system. It isn't, really; in a sense, the two coexist. In 1742, long before the International Bureau of Weights and Measures was established in 1875 for the purpose of "international unification and adoption of the metric system," a Swedish astronomer, Anders Celsius (1701–44), proposed the scale long called "centigrade."

Not until 1927 was the centigrade scale internationally adopted; not until 1948 did the International Committee on Weights and Measures and the U.S. National Bureau of Standards recommend that "centigrade" be replaced by "Celsius" in honor of the inventor. ("Centigrade" is merely a descriptive term deriving from the Latin for "hundred" and "gradation.")

Since the Celsius scale, in which zero represents the freezing point and 100 the boiling point of water, is a decimal measurement—that is, based on units of ten—it obviously fits neatly into the decimal-based metric system of measurements. But it is a marriage of happy convenience between compatible cousins rather than an offspring of the same ancestry.

It might be added that the marriage did take a bit of arranging in terms of compatibility. Interestingly enough, Celsius himself identified zero as the boiling point, 100 as freezing! Old dictionaries so identify the extremes of the scale. In honoring the inventor of the centigrade scale, the scientific community perforce reversed it, to bring it into a more apparently consistent relationship with the metric system.

Although Americans are now becoming accustomed, as Europeans long have been, to temperatures given in Celsius, it should be pointed out that "illogical" though the Fahrenheit system may be (it was invented by a German instrument maker, Gabriel Fahrenheit [1686–1736] early in the eighteenth century), in practice it provides a somewhat more accurate rendition of temperatures. The reason is that the Fahrenheit scale has 180 divisions between freezing and boiling rather than only 100. Only if the Celsius temperature readings are carried out to a couple of decimal places, as they rarely are in general use, are they capable of exceeding Fahrenheit readings in terms of reflecting small temperature changes. For example, in a two-digit temperature indication of the kind common on display thermometers, both 69° F. and 70° F. would be rendered as 21° C. (20.56° C. for 69° F., 21.11° C. for 70° F.).

ceremony, to stand on. Standing on ceremony is today taken to mean insistence on formalities; "Let's not stand on ceremony" means dispensing with whatever interferes with the business at hand. But this is far from its original significance. The expression comes from Shakespeare's *Julius Caesar* (act 2, sc. 2, lines 13–14) in which Calpurina, Caesar's wife, says to her husband, "Caesar, I never stood on ceremonies,/Yet now they fright me."

The "ceremonies" Calpurnia had in mind, however, are the rites and procedures of augury as practiced by seers in attempting to foretell the future. Later in this scene a servant answers Caesar's question, "What say the augurers?" by replying that they "would not have you to stir forth today./Plucking the entrails of an offering forth,/They could not find a heart within the beast"—a bad omen.

Calpurnia is saying that she never believed in signs or portents before, but that she does now. Her remark has nothing to do with "ceremony" as the word is commonly used today.

Our word *auspicious* derives, in interesting fashion, from the "ceremonies" of the Auspex, an "augurer" who studied the flight of birds. That which is auspicious, figuratively speaking, is that which is upward-looking—like the attitude of an Auspex while on the job. King Claudius, in *Hamlet,* remarks that he has married his brother's widow, Gertrude, with "an auspicious and a dropping eye," a sophisticated little figure of speech which nicely contrasts "upward looking" with "dropping" or "downcast" (with perhaps a secondary implication of weeping, or dropping, tears).

cesarean operation, or "section." It is almost universally believed that the operation by means of which the baby is delivered through an incision in the abdomen is named after Julius Caesar, because he was born in this fashion. But he could not have been born in this fashion, for reasons shortly to be made apparent.

Those few who are aware that "cesarean" derives not from "Caesar" but from the Latin verb *caedere,* "to cut" (past participle *caesus*), may nevertheless assume, as Pliny (A.D. 23–79) did, that Caesar was so named *"a caeso matris utero,"* in Pliny's words: that is, after his mother's cut womb. Not at all; Julius was not the first of the *gens* Julia to be called "Caesar" and thus could not have been named after the operation. At least two earlier members of his family, famous enough to be remembered, had been named "Caesar." One of them, Lucius Julius Caesar, was consul in 90 B.C., at which time the one who was to become the most famous of all the Caesars was not yet into his teens. And there were others.

In other words, practically everything that practically everybody believes about the operation itself, or the name for it, is false; and this includes standard reference works of generally impeccable reputation and authority.

It is, perhaps, not too surprising that Pliny was the one from whom stem all the mistaken beliefs about Caesar and cesareans. As Gareth Penn, California scholar and classicist, reminds us, Pliny is particularly suspect in matters obstetrical; it was his considered—or unconsidered—belief that weasels conceive in the ear and give birth through the mouth. (An analogous belief about opossums still crops up occasionally to this day.) Pliny also tells us, among other fascinating if inaccurate fantasies, that diamonds first soaked in the blood of a billy goat can be cut with a butter knife.

The cesarean operation itself had been known and practiced for many centuries before Julius Caesar's birth. From as early as the eighth century B.C. (Julius was born about 102 B.C., assassinated in 44 B.C.) it had been routine for this means of delivery to be employed on Roman women who died in an advanced stage of pregnancy or while in labor. However—and a very big "however" it is in speaking of the cesarean with a capital "C"—it was invariably performed *only on the mother's dead body*. Julius's mother lived on for many years after his birth.

How, then, did Caesar get his name? According to two Roman writers (Sextus Pompeius Festus, fl. c. A.D. 150, and Nonius Marcellus, c. A.D. 280), from the Latin for hair, *caesaries*. One story has it that he was born with a full head of hair, though there is a more likely reason for the name. (If the story is true, it might be interpolated, Caesar had difficulty hanging onto it; there are those who maintain that he combed his hair forward in a holding action against his creeping baldness.)

Another suggestion is that "Caesar" may derive from the Latin for eyes of bluish gray, *caesius,* as if Caesar may have been born, if not bright-eyed and bushy-tailed, then perhaps blue-eyed and bushy-haired.

The fact is that all Roman citizens had three names (remember that Caesar was actually Caius Julius Caesar). First there was the *gens,* or "gentile," or clan name, which came second and proved that its bearer was a citizen.

Caesar, as said, was a member of the *gens* Julia. The third name was the *cognomen,* or aftername; most likely, some ancestor (perhaps Lucius Julius Caesar himself), who may well have been either bushy-haired or blue-eyed or maybe even both, had first been called "Caesar." By the time of Julius's birth, however, most cognomens had lost their significance, just as today few stop to think about the origins of such common family names as Smith or Miller.

The *praenomen,* or as we would say "first" name, served the purpose it serves today: primarily to distinguish siblings from each other. Only men, however—and this is an interesting sidelight on one aspect of Roman culture—had distinctive forenames. Women used the clan name. Caesar had only one daughter, known as Julia after his *gens.* Other subsequent Julias were known by number—the tenth, for example, would have been Julia Decima. As Alfred Duggan remarks (*Julius Caesar,* 1955, page 28), it must sometimes have been confusing in the nursery.

Since Julius Caesar was an only son, probably few if any persons ever called him "Caius"; there was no need, obviously, to distinguish him from other male siblings. "Caesar" was sufficient. The combination by which he came to be known to posterity, "Julius Caesar," was probably not used in his lifetime and may, as Duggan suggests, have arisen to distinguish him from his successor, Augustus, who took to calling himself Caesar Augustus.

Caius Julius Caesar had such an enormous impact on Western history that Kaiser and Czar are variants on his name. It is this impact, no doubt, that gave impetus to the mistaken notions about the operation called "cesarean" and the origin of the term.

The modern German word for the operation, incidentally, is *Kaiserschnitt,* or "imperial cut," which, as the indomitable Mr. Penn further remarks, sounds a bit like something one might ask for in a high-class *restauration.*

chain stores as modern invention. As early as the seventeenth century, the house of Mitsui in Japan, which started humbly enough as a brewer of sake in Ise and then opened a pawnshop and began also dealing in rice, opened branches in several cities. According to W. Scott Morton's *Japan: Its History and Culture* (Crowell, 1970), this was the beginning of one of the great companies of modern Japan. And, it would also seem, of the chain-store concept.

chaise "lounge." A corruption of the French *chaise longue*, or "long chair"—which, of course, is what a chaise longue is. But since it is also a sort of couch, or "lounge" as Americans often use the term, the confusion is understandable. As so often happens (the loss of the accent mark over the last letter of "coupe," for example, and the subsequent shift in pronunciation from "coopay" to "coop"), the French *chaise longue* will very likely become entirely Americanized into "chaise lounge." Nor will this represent a linguistic catastrophe or a triumph of barbarism over Culture; it's a perfectly normal linguistic phenomenon. "Bus" (for "omnibus") was once regarded as an ignorant vulgarism. On the other hand, "et" for "ate" was quite the proper form, not so long ago, in high-class English circles.

chastity belts. Like the "right of the first night" *(jus primae noctis, droit du seigneur)*, the supposed medieval law that entitled the lord of the manor to spend the wedding night with the bride of any of his vassals but that almost certainly never existed, the chastity belt is equally suspect. It is most unlikely that the chastity belt, a lockable device said to have been fastened around the strategic zones of the wives of medieval crusaders and other peripatetic knights, ever existed—except as a joke or a hoax.

True, there are examples in museums, notably in the Cluny Museum in Paris. In 1950, however, the Cluny Museum stopped displaying all but one of its collection of chastity belts (the one exception was allowed to remain on public view as a curiosity). The reason? Like fakes, hoaxes have no place in a museum—and a French scholar, Edouard Haraucourt, had come to the conclusion, some years before, that this is just what the "chastity belt" is: a hoax.

Common sense would indicate that a true chastity belt of the type supposedly worn by wives of knights who might be away for many months is a practical impossibility, given the necessary functions of the human, and especially female, body, unless it could be periodically removed—in which case it could scarcely serve its presumed purpose.

Christian Brothers Winery, ownership of. An oft-told tale—told so oft, in fact, that the winery is tired of hearing it—is that the Christian Brothers Winery in California was sold some time ago to a secular corporate conglomerate.

The only Christian Brother still connected with the Christian Brothers Winery, so the tale goes, is Brother Timothy, the cellarmaster often featured in national advertisements; he is said to have been kept on so that he could mislead the public by continuing to be so featured.

There's not a word of truth in all this. The Christian Brothers continue to own and operate the winery. The president is Brother Frederick; the well-known Brother Timothy is vice-president; Brother Cassian is assistant to the president; and Brothers Kenneth, Alvan, and James, among others, also hold important positions.

It may be that confusion between manufacture and distribution accounts for the mistaken belief that the winery is no longer connected with the Catholic Church. Fromm and Sichel, Inc., of San Francisco, an affiliate of Joseph E. Seagram & Sons, Inc., has exclusive and world-wide rights to distribute the Christian Brothers wines. But the order (as Mt. La Salle Vineyard) operates as a profit-making—and taxpaying—corporation; the winery supports, or helps support, a variety of Christian Brothers endeavors, especially schools in California, Oregon, and elsewhere.

The order itself is an old one, having been founded in the late seventeenth century at Reims, France, by St. Jean Baptiste de la Salle. Christian Brothers take the three vows (poverty, chastity, obedience) and devote themselves to teaching youth.

Churchill as class dunce. That Winston Churchill (1874–1965) was always at the bottom of his class in school, as is often said, is by no means true. Or so, at least, says a man who ought to know: John Bartlett, headmaster of Stoke Brunswick School in Sussex, which Churchill attended before entering the famous Harrow.

According to Headmaster Bartlett, contemporary records show that during his last year at Stoke Brunswick, Churchill was at the top of his class in every subject except geography —and in this he was second.

Somewhat ironically, it is Churchill's own words that helped foster the myth of his incompetence as a student. In *My Early Life* Churchill remarks that he was considered unfit to learn anything but English, and he tells the story of his failure to answer a single question of the Latin test he took as part of his entrance examination for Harrow. What happened, apparently, is that Churchill simply suffered a bad attack of examination nerves; old reports and class lists unearthed by Bartlett prove that Churchill was able to translate both Vergil and Caesar and was indeed a prize student.

True, Churchill did have some scholasitc problems later, if the accounts of some of his biographers—and of Churchill himself—are taken at face value. But it is equally obvious from his elementary school record that such difficulties as he had were no reflection on his intelligence or ability.

cirrhosis. Usually followed by the phrase "of the liver," cirrhosis in fact may affect other organs. It is a form of tissue degeneration resulting in fibrosis, with nodule and scar formation. However, it does most commonly affect the liver. In spite of popular belief, it is not a disease confined to alcoholics, although alcoholics frequently suffer from it. Nor does it directly result from excessive drinking; the kind of liver cirrhosis associated with alcoholism is actually a result of protein deficiency, a type of malnutrition often found in alcoholics.

civilian. The common—sometimes, seemingly, even somewhat contemptuous—use of "civilian" by the police with reference to members of the public blurs a crucial distinction. In a democracy police are themselves civilians, subject to the same laws they enforce. Only members of the military, operating under their own code of military justice, give up their civilian status—and most of their civilian, or "civil," rights.

Colorado as a mountain state. Only a little more than half of Colorado is mountainous. The rest is prairie. Nor are Colorado's mountains, beautiful as they certainly are, really very high except in absolute terms: that is, elevation above sea level. The vast central plains of the United States rise slowly as they extend westward; by the time one reaches the foothills of the Rockies in Colorado, the plain is about 5,000 feet high (Greeley, Colorado, 50 miles from the mountains, is at about 4,500 feet; Denver, as everyone knows, is about 5,200 feet high. Both are built on flat ground.) Thus, a 14,000-foot mountain in Colorado, and there are many, is in effect some 9,000 feet above the observer's point of view at best. By contrast, Mt. Rainier in Washington State, itself a 14,000-foot mountain, rises from near sea level. Thus, visitors from Washington State who see Colorado's mountains for the first time often express some disappointment; they just don't seem very high.

Brochures about Denver that are produced in Denver frequently refer to it, or her, as "Queen City of the Plains."

Colosseum. There is considerable confusion surrounding the Colosseum, the remains of which are one of Rome's best-known tourist attractions. It is often confused, for example, with the Circus Maximus, said to have been constructed several centuries before Christ and over the centuries modified and enlarged by various people, including Julius Caesar. The Colosseum came along much later; it was begun by Vespasian about A.D. 75 and completed by his son Titus in A.D. 80. After Flavius, the *gens* (patrilinear clan name) of the emperors, it is also known as the Flavian amphitheater. It came to be called the Colosseum not because of its size (which in any case was nothing compared to the Circus Maximus) but because a colossal statue of Nero was put up nearby.

No modern stadium comes close to the capacity of the Circus Maximus, which was said (depending on the authority) to accommodate from 250,000 to 350,000 spectators. The Colosseum compares with a medium-sized college stadium today in terms of capacity: it held some 40,000 to 50,000. (It may also have been the precursor of the modern domed stadium; it is said that a great canvas "roof" could be spread over it to protect the spectators from the weather.)

And in spite of popular belief, it is highly unlikely that any Christians were ever thrown to lions in the Colosseum, or martyred there in any other fashion, though gladiatorial combats and other sufficiently bloody spectacles were presented.

It was not until the eighteenth century, under Pope Benedict XIV (reigned 1740–58), that the Colosseum was consecrated to the passion of Christ, commemorating the blood of martyrs said to have been shed there. (Pope Benedict's edict had a practical effect: for centuries the Colosseum had been used as a quarry for other buildings, a practice that stopped with the edict.)

However, ancient Christian sources, according to the *New Catholic Encyclopedia,* make no mention of Christian martyrdoms at the Colosseum. There may have been persecution of Christians at the Circus Maximus, however; Tacitus, at least, tells us that Nero participated in such persecution both there and at his gardens.

It would seem, incidentally, that Christian persecutions in ancient Rome were at least as much political as religious; in the words of Michael Grant (*Nero,* American Heritage Press, 1970, page 160), "[Christians] kept themselves to themselves in an even more suspicious fashion than the Jews, indeed to a degree which, in an extrovert, nationally minded community, must inevitably lead to hostile rumours." Their unwillingness to participate in veneration of the emperor-god made them suspect politically, and they often enough suffered the fate of minorities everywhere, especially "different" minorities.

Colossi of Memnon. These twin statues in Egypt, recently believed to be in danger because of seepage from the Aswan high dam, have been called by the wrong name since the times of ancient Rome. They are actually representations of Amenhotep III, himself a great one for temples and statues, who reigned about 1,400 years before the birth of Christ. It was the Romans who named, or apparently renamed, the statues.

A poem by Charles Darwin mentions the "sacred Sun in Memnon's fane" and refers to the reason the statues were such a popular tourist attraction in Roman times:

> Spontaneous concords choired the matin strain;
> Touched by his [the sun's] orient beam responsive rings
> The living lyre and vibrates all its strings;
> According aisles the tender tones prolong,
> And holy echoes swell the adoring song.

It is good that Darwin's reputation does not depend on his poetry. His reference is to the fact that after one of the statues was damaged in an earthquake in 27 B.C., it gave forth a mysterious musical note at sunrise. One theory is that the sound resulted from passage of air through cracks in the stone, a result of temperature changes at dawn.

The Romans believed, or liked to pretend to believe, that the sound was the voice of Memnon greeting his mother Eos, goddess of the dawn. Anyway, the emperor Septimius Severus spoiled the fun in A.D. 170 by having the statue repaired, upon which the mysterious music ceased. (The *Britannica* says, however, that some modern travelers claim to have heard the sound.)

"Come with me to the Casbah." The late Charles Boyer, one of the silver screen's greatest lovers, was given an even more intriguing image by being attached to this sultry statement. He is alleged to have extended the invitation to Hedy Lamarr in *Algiers* (1938), but according to Boyer himself, he never uttered it in any play or motion picture. He said it was devised by a press agent.

"coon." Not originally a racist term for blacks, "coon" was first applied to whites, as early as 1839: specifically, to members of the old Whig party, which at one time had a raccoon as its emblem. By the end of the nineteenth century, however, it had come to be used as another word for "Negro"—or, more accurately, for "nigger."

Ironically, "coon" for blacks was popularized in 1896 by a song written by Ernest Hogan, who was himself black. Called "All Coons Look Alike to Me," the song surely was intended as irony, for Hogan was surprised and bitterly disappointed by the resentment it aroused among blacks. H. L. Mencken tells the story in Supplement One to his classic work *The American Language* (New York, 1945, pages 632–33). According to Edward B. Marks, author of *They All Sang* (New York, 1935), as cited by Mencken, Hogan's song had an immediate impact of a sort evidently not foreseen by its composer. It was whistled by whites as an insult; the refrain became a fighting phrase. Hogan apparently died haunted by what he felt to be the crime he had unwittingly committed against his own people.

But Hogan should not bear the whole blame. Two other songs, both written by whites at the turn of the century ("Every Race Has a Flag but the *Coon*" and "Coon, Coon, Coon"), further established the term in the American vocabulary. And not, it might be added, in the vulgate vocabulary only. As anyone who recalls the 1930s can certify, "coon" was often used by persons who would have regarded themselves as quite "genteel."

Like "coon," "a coon's age" did not originally have any racial implications, though it undoubtedly picked them up later. "A coon's age" goes back at least as far as the first half of the nineteenth century; Eric Partridge and Mencken agree that its first reference was to the raccoon, which was believed to live an unusually long time—a belief, incidentally, not based on fact. (A raccoon's normal life span is about ten years, a figure which is surely not the stuff of legend.) Nor did the old expression "a gone [rac]coon" originally have any racial (or racist) significance.

Cooper, Dan, and the statute of limitations. Those who tend secretly to admire Dan—often improperly referred to as "D.B."—Cooper for his boldness in highjacking a Boeing 727 in 1971 and getting away with $200,000, and who have since counted the years following Cooper's escape, should be aware that there is no statue of limitations for capital crimes, among which air piracy is included. This was true when Cooper took over, and parachuted from, that 727. So even if he is alive and well in Rio, he is not, nor will he be during his lifetime, beyond the law.

Copenhagen, pronunciation of. American tourists. sophisticated enough to know that the letter "a" in almost all European languages is sounded like "ah" sometimes try to impress their Danish friends by saying "Copenhahgen." They shouldn't. The Danes much prefer that Americans who cannot pronounce the name of their favorite city in the Danish way should simply say "Copenhaygen." The broad "a" pronunciation, at least among older Danes, is too uncomfortably reminiscent of the way the occupying Germans said the word during World War II.

Those who would like to essay a close approximation of the Danish might try "KER bn HOWN," with the "r" in the first syllable suppressed so that the sound is like the *oe* in "Goethe." Since the attempt, however, might inspire a response in Danish, it is no doubt best to stick to the American pronunciation—without the broad "a."

corned beef. Not so called because corn, the cereal, has anything to do with its creation. "Corn"—as in "peppercorn"—originally meant a grain or a seed, usually coarse. The preparation of corned beef at one time involved the use of coarse grains, or "corns," of salt. Hence the name.

corsair and pirate as synonyms. A corsair was a warship especially fitted out for privateers, not to be confused with pirates; nor should "corsair," obviously, be taken as a synonym for "pirate." Privateers put to sea with the authority of their governments. Pirates were, and in some areas of the world still are, brigands out for profit, sanctioned by no one but themselves.

cottage cheese as diet food. Those who are condemned, or who condemn themselves, to lunches called "waistliner specials" or those found in the "calorie counter" section of the menu are resigned to cottage cheese, along with the overdone ground-beef patty and anemic slices of tomato. But they might as well enjoy a baked or boiled potato. As potato growers often point out, sometimes with exasperation, just half a cup of cottage cheese contains more calories than a medium-sized potato: 100 as opposed to 90.

Or perhaps a few potato chips to break the monotony: eight or ten large ones add up only to 100 calories. Even french fries can be enjoyed in moderation: half a dozen contain fewer calories (about 90) than half a cup of cottage cheese.

A square of butter ¼ inch thick is 50 calories; even adding this means that a baked potato will come to only about 140 calories. Mashed potatoes? With milk and butter added, a full cup comes to 230 calories. The difference between half a cup of mashed potatoes done with milk and butter, and half a cup of cottage cheese, is, thus, just 15 calories.

cougars as dangerous. Fearsome tales of cougars ("pumas," "panthers," "mountain lions," sometimes "catamounts") stalking adults for miles and then pouncing for the kill are fiction, not fact. Like any wild animal, a cougar wounded, sick, or cornered can be dangerous, especially a mother with kittens. Even so, given a choice, some authorities say that cougars will attempt diversion rather than attack.

Cougars are, in fact, rather shy and prefer to avoid human encounter. Like wolves, they have been given a reputation as killers which is quite undeserved. It is unfortunate that bears have been treated so sentimentally ("Goldilocks," Gentle Ben, Smokey), whereas cougars are so often regarded with fear. For bears really are dangerous, as Yellowstone Park rangers know very well even if tourists do not; people in tents or sleeping bags have been killed by bears and many others have been maimed. But not by cougars.

covered wagons. "Get those wagons in a circle!"—the cry familiar to those who watch old Westerns on television or comedians who imitate John Wayne—was not heard only in case of an imminent attack by Indians. Nor, as a defensive device, is putting wagons in a circle anything new.

In fact, putting the wagons in a circle most likely happened every night, whether or not hostiles were in the vicinity. A circle, aside from its obvious psychological significance in maintaining a sense of community, helped prevent the escape of horses, oxen, or other animals which might break free from their hobbles or tethers. Further, a circle is the most efficient boundary in that it can contain the most area—not to mention that putting the wagons in a square is fairly absurd on the face of it; leaving them stretched out in a long line even more so.

Helmut Nickel reminds us, in his *Warriors and Worthies: Arms and Armor Through the Ages,* published in 1969, that the Hussites[1] of the fifteenth and sixteenth centuries used, as the backbone of their defense, the *Wagenburg.* And what was the *Wagenburg?* A ring of wagons—and covered wagons at that—from which the halberdiers would sally out.

coy mistresses and "quaint" honor. Published three years after the author's death in 1678, Andrew Marvell's "To His Coy Mistress" is widely admired, anthologized, and quoted as one of England's greatest poems. (Surely it is also one of the most persuasive invitations to seduction ever written. What answer had a seventeenth-century maiden, or indeed has a twentieth-century one, to "The grave's a fine and private place,/But none, I think, do there embrace"?)

The title of what many think to be Robert Penn Warren's finest novel comes from Marvell's opening lines ("Had we but *world enough, and time* [italics added],/This coyness, lady, were no crime."). And few are not impressed with that sad sense of the passing years expressed in "at my back I always hear/Time's wingèd chariot hurrying near."

But not so many are aware, though most scholars are, of the ribald, not to say vulgar, pun Marvell sneaks into one of the lines that follow:

1 Hussites were followers of the Reformation preacher John Huss (1369?–1415), a strong opponent of clerical abuses. They engaged in many battles with supporters of the established church.

". . . yonder all before us lie
Deserts of vast eternity.
Thy beauty shall no more be found,
Nor, in thy marble vault, shall sound
My echoing song: then worms shall try
That long preserved virginity,
And your quaint honor turn to dust,
And into ashes all my lust."

The pun lies in that word "quaint." The plain fact is that "quaint" or "queynte" is an old euphemism for a four-letter word even today not very often seen in print: "cunt," for the female genitalia.

(The mighty *Oxford English Dictionary,* somewhat amusingly, asks the reader to discover for himself the meaning of the obsolete noun *quaint:* "[See quot. 1598]." "Quot. 1598" turns out to be from John Florio, an English lexicographer who died in 1625: "a woman's quaint or priuities," which is to say "privities" or "private parts." He said it, protests the OED in effect; we didn't.)

Those who know Chaucer's delightfully bawdy adventure, "The Miller's Tale," will recall that Nicholas, a young "clerk," or scholar, seizes opportunity by the forelock, in a manner of speaking, when the carpenter in whose house the clerk lives is away from home. The carpenter has a young and beautiful wife, and—but here are Chaucer's words:

[it so happened]
That on a day this . . . Nicholas . . .
Whil that hir housbonde was at Oseneye [a nearby town]
. . . prively he caughte hire [her] by the queynte . . .
And heeld hire harde by the haunche-bones.

There's no pun involved in Chaucer's straightforward account. It took the sly and gifted Marvell to accomplish that.

cretins and Christians. "Cretin," thought by many to have some kind of medical meaning, perhaps because it looks as if it might belong in a medical dictionary, is derived, in fact, from "Christian." The term was first applied to deformed and mentally deficient dwarfs found in some Alpine valleys; since a nineteenth-century observer comments that they have enormous goiters, their condition may well have to do with a nutritional deficiency.

"Cretin" comes from a French word that was originally a dialectal variant of *chrétien*, "Christian." The *Oxford English Dictionary* suggests that, as is true in some Romance languages and in some English dialectal usage, "Christian" was used as a general synonym for "human being," the implication being that, brutish as cretins appear to be, they are actually human. Whether or not this explanation is true, there is no question that "cretin" did, in fact, start out as "Christian." Today the term is broadly applied to anyone with apparent extreme mental deficiency.

Crichton, the Admirable. Except for *Peter Pan, The Admirable Crichton* is James Barrie's best-known drama. It is the story of an English butler, Crichton, who believes firmly in knowing one's place and keeping it. However, when he is shipwrecked on an island in the Pacific with his master, Lord Loam, and various other aristocratic types, he becomes the one on whom the rest depend; his qualities of leadership and character far outshine theirs. (When they are rescued and return home, however, he reverts to his old self in an ending often criticized as a dilution of Barrie's apparent theme throughout most of the play.)

Barrie, a Scotsman, must have known that he cribbed his title, though not many others do. For there really was a person known as the Admirable Crichton, although—an irony intended, no doubt, by Barrie—he was anything but a butler. He was, in fact, the son of Robert Crichton, Lord Advocate of Scotland during the time of Mary Stuart and her son, James VI, and of Elizabeth, daughter of Sir James Stewart of Beath—through whom, incidentally, he claimed royal descent.

The real Crichton was born about 1560, four years before Shakespeare. He was a child prodigy; when only ten years old he entered St. Salvator's College in St. Andrews, where he got his B.A. at fourteen and his M.A. a year later. He went on to a distinguished career as scholar, linguist, and debater. He died (according to some disputed accounts, in a street quarrel with a prince of Mantua) sometime between 1582 and 1585.

And he became known to history as the Admirable Crichton, an epithet first applied to him in 1603 with the publication, by John Johnston, of a book about Scottish heroes.

croissant, origin of. Fanciful stories have been spun about the origin of the *croissant,* the delectably flaky roll that nobody but the French and the Austrians seems able to do quite so well. Oldest of the tales related to the *croissant* starts with Hesychius of Miletus, somewhere around A.D. 500. Hesychius almost certainly never saw a *croissant;* but he did spawn the story that when Philip of Macedon (382– 336 B.C.) laid nocturnal siege against Byzantium (later "Constantinople," still later "Istanbul"), the rising moon revealed him and his forces. Thus Byzantium adopted the crescent moon as its emblem. Or so says Hesychius, writing some 800 years after Philip's reign.

Many centuries later, in 1453, when the Turks captured the oft-besieged Byzantium (at this time, "Constantinople") and made it capital of the Ottoman Empire, its crescent was taken over as the symbol of the Ottomans, or Turks. Some two centuries after their conquest of Constantinople, the indomitable Turks in 1683 laid siege to Vienna under the sign of the crescent.

A Viennese baker, so the tale goes, heard the Turks tunneling under the walls. He sounded the alarm; the Turks were repulsed. And so the Viennese bakers' guild got a patent from the city fathers to make a crescent-shaped roll commemorating the defeat of the Turks. When Marie-Antoinette left her native Austria for Paris, she brought with her the *croissant;* and thus, as my scholarly correspondent Gareth Penn points out, when a Parisian has a *croissant* for breakfast, some 2,300 years of history are consumed.

But Mr. Penn also points out that the whole thing is a mishmash of misinformation. Hesychius's fanciful account to the contrary, the crescent emblem derives not from the moon but from a pair of stylized ram's horns. It could not have been taken over from the Byzantines in 1453; the Turks had displayed the crescent at least a hundred years earlier. As for that Viennese baker in 1683, he couldn't have heard any tunneling, because there wasn't any within the city, where the bakers were. The Turkish mines were directed against the outer fortifications.

Even stranger tales are told about the origin of the *croissant,* some of them self-evidently false. Half a dozen works on gastronomy, including the father of them all, *Larousse Gastronomique,* have a variation: the invention of the *croissant* dates from the Turkish siege of Budapest in 1686. The only problem is that Budapest was already Turkish in 1686—and had been for almost 150 years! So obviously it wasn't the Turks that did the besieging of Budapest in 1686. It was actually, of all people, the Austrians. It does not seem likely that the Austrians waved *croissants* as they attacked, although this tale seems as persuasive as the others.

The true origin of *croissant* is interesting enough in itself. The Latin word from which it comes, *crescens,* meant simply "growing, waxing." The Romans did not use *crescens* with any thought of shape, moonwise or otherwise; this was a medieval development. When the Romans wanted to describe something shaped like a crescent, they had a quite different word that obviously springs from *luna,* or "moon," all right—but not necessarily the new moon any more than the old one: *lunatus.*

Croissant in modern French (Old French *creissant*) means, as an adjective, "crescent-shaped." As a noun, its application to pastry shaped like a crescent is obvious.

cuckold (see CUCKOO**).** Anyone who knows Shakespeare is aware that in his works there are many references to cuckolds and cuckoldry, as also to the "horns" cuckolds are said to wear. (To be cuckolded is to be duped by an unfaithful spouse or sweetheart.) "Cuckold" derives from "cuckoo" and has reference to the European cuckoo's habit of taking over the nests of other birds. The horns of the cuckold, however, have nothing to do with cuckoos, who may or not be horny but who do not wear horns.

The horns sardonically (and figuratively) placed upon the cuckold's brow derive either from the legend of the amorous Jove, who in the form of a bull raped Europa, or from what the *Oxford English Dictionary* says was once the practice of implanting a castrated cock's spurs on the root of the cut-off comb, where they are said to grow into horns. (There does seem to be a German term for cuckold that is cognate with "capon.")

Further complicating the whole issue is that in Shakespeare's plays "horn," as Eric Partridge pointed out in *Shakespeare's Bawdy* (1948), sometimes means, for fairly obvious reasons, the penis, especially the erect penis. (It is from this metaphor that the slang term "horny" apparently derives.)

cuckoo. Those who know only the American cuckoo may be puzzled by a term deriving from it, CUCKOLD (which see). Only European cuckoos take over the nests of other birds; American varieties build their own.

The roadrunner of the American Southwest, immortalized with his ubiquitous "beep-beep!" in countless animated cartoons, belongs, by the way, to the cuckoo family.

Curtiss Ascender of World War II. An unusual aircraft design came off the Curtiss drawing boards during World War II. Its stabilizing surfaces were in front, so that it would appear to be flying backward. Some anonymous wit proposed the perfect name for it: the Curtiss Ascender. Unfortunately, neither name nor plane ever really got off the ground.

"custom more honored in the breach than the observance." Few famous remarks are more universally misapprehended than Hamlet's reply to Horatio (*Hamlet,* act 1, sc. 4, lines 13 ff.). When Horatio hears noises within the castle at Elsinore and asks Hamlet what it's all about, Hamlet explains that King Claudius is up late carousing. Each time the King "drains his draughts" of wine, the kettledrum and trumpet "bray out."

Horatio asks if this is a custom. Hamlet replies:

> Ay, marry, is' t [it is]:
> But to my mind, though I am native here
> And to the manner born, it is a custom
> More honour'd in the breach than the observance.
> [Other nations] . . . clepe [call] us drunkards. . . .

Hamlet's meaning, clearly, is that celebrating the King's drunken revelries in this fashion is a custom that would be better "honour'd" if it were not followed at all: "in the breach [rather] than the observance." Change Shakespeare's "more" to "better" and you have his meaning—which is far removed from the common interpretation: that whatever custom is under question has fallen into sad neglect. Quite the opposite!

D

death, exact time of determined by autopsy. Many a scene from detective stories or mystery movies comes to mind. "I will prove beyond the shadow of a doubt," says the defense attorney, "that the victim could not have been murdered at midnight, but in fact was alive and well until eleven o'clock the following morning, at which time my client was in another city." Following which, the forensic pathologist gives his testimony.

Unfortunately, it's not that easy. It is impossible to tell the exact time of death from the examination of a corpse. In the words of William J. Brady, M.D., chief state medical examiner for Oregon, "The most important fact to be stressed in any discussion of determining the post-mortem interval is that *no specific time of death can be given by the pathologist.* Unless the death is observed, physicians can only *give a range* of a probable post-mortem interval" (italics are Dr. Brady's).

One chemical test of value involves the rise in the potassium in the eyes' vitreous humor following death. However, after the first day of death, even this test can give only a plus or minus twelve-hour variation.

Death, proof of after disappearance. There is no universal fixed interval of time after which a person who has disappeared is "legally dead." It is often believed that anyone who fails to show up, or to be found, after seven years is automatically assumed to have died. But it must be shown that a search has been made, or there must be corroborative proof, before any such assumption will hold up in court. Time alone is not enough.

debate. Readers of the Bible and Shakespeare may be puzzled by the use of "debate," which to us connotes a reasoned discussion. However, it once meant "fight," or "strife." Its

New Testament Greek counterpart was *eris,* and Eris, goddess of strife, threw the golden apple that provoked the jealousy of Hera, Athene, and Aphrodite—and there was plenty of strife out of that! In Isaiah 58:4, "ye fast for strife and debate" means "you fast in order to squabble and fight." In *King Henry IV,* Part II (act 4, sc. 4, line 2), "this debate that bleedeth at our doors" does not refer to just an argument; it means an insurrection.

Deseret. Not always a misprint for "desert," as Mormons or those who have lived in Mormon country know. "Deseret" is a word occurring in the Book of Mormon, where it is said to mean "honeybee." A beehive, Utah's state emblem, appears on the state seal, and Utah's nickname is "Beehive State." In fact, the name under which Mormons, who still comprise almost three fourths of the population of Utah, wanted the state admitted to the Union was "Deseret." But their efforts failed, and "Utah," after a Shoshone Indian tribe, was chosen—or, as some Mormons think, inflicted upon them.

Salt Lake City's leading evening newspaper, published under the same auspices as the leading morning paper, the *Salt Lake Tribune,* is called the *Deseret News.*

deserts. Perhaps because the dunes of the Sahara figure so largely in history and folklore, many people forget that a desert, technically, is any area—hot, cold, or in between—whose vegetation is insufficient to support a human population. It may have no visible sand whatever; both polar regions are properly referred to as deserts.

"Deutschland, Deutschland über alles" as a Hitler song. Many people, although not the dwindling number who recall World War I, associate "Deutschland, Deutschland über alles" with Hitler and the Nazis, supposing it to be (like the Horst Wessel song, indubitably Nazi) a hymn for that Third Reich which fell so far short of its thousand-year promise. It is, and was, not, as Dr. Franz Langhammer of Portland State reminds us.

"Deutschland, Deutschland über alles" (Germany, Germany above all) was actually written as "Das Lied der Deutschen" ("The Song of the Germans") by August Heinrich Hoffmann von Fallersleben (1798–1874), to

Haydn's melody for the Austrian national hymn of 1797. The text appeared for the first time on August 26, 1841.

dew. "Who hath begotten the drops of dew?" asks the Voice from the Whirlwind (Job 38:28, King James Version). John Greenleaf Whittier (1807–92) has one answer: Robin Redbreast ("He brings cool dew in his little bill,/And lets it fall").

With due allowance, so to speak, for poetic license, it must be said that dew does not fall, no matter what Whittier and other poets seem to think. It is created, or begotten, when air is cooled to the point at which it can no longer hold water vapor in suspension. Not surprisingly, this condition is the "dew point."

As a blade of grass, or a leaf, cools down at night, a thin layer of air next to these objects also cools down; and when the temperature of that air reaches the dew point, its excess vapor condenses on the plant surface as dew.

However, what most people see as the characteristic "dew" formation—the early morning droplets on leaves and petals so often evoked in poetry—is not likely to be dew at all. The droplets are mostly exuded from the plant itself, as part of the normal process by which leaves are supplied with water from the soil. They are usually seen only in the morning because, during the daytime's heat, the exuded water evaporates as it is formed.

"Diamonds are forever." They're durable, all right. But while most of us don't think of diamonds as inflammable, in fact they are. It takes a mighty high temperature to do it, but diamonds will burn. After all, they are pure carbon, which is what coal largely consists of.

Dietrich, Marlene, as the Blue Angel. One of Marlene Dietrich's most famous roles was in the Josef von Sternberg film *The Blue Angel*. But it was not Marlene who was the "blue angel," in spite of popular belief. Much of the action of the film takes place in a cabaret; it is the cabaret that is called "The Blue Angel." Marlene played a character named Lola-Lola.

dinosaurs, those dumb. The lumbering dinosaur, long a symbol of stupidity, actually had a normal-sized reptilian brain, given its weight and dimensions. And, as Stephen J.

Gould says in *Natural History* for May 1978, after all, the dinosaurs survived for a hundred million years. Not bad for a stupid critter—and better so far than *Homo sapiens,* whose origins go back only some 50,000 years, and whose continued presence on this globe does sometimes seem in question.

discomfit. Has nothing to do with discomfort, as many suppose. It's an old military word that means by derivation "disrupt the preparations"; hence, "throw into confusion."

"Don't give up the ship, boys!" That's the way it seems to have come down to us. But it's a fairly far cry from what Captain James Lawrence (1781–1813) actually said to the men of the U.S. frigate *Chesapeake* as he was carried below, mortally wounded. According to Bartlett, his words were "Tell the men to fire faster and not give up the ship; fight her till she sinks."

And by the way, his words did not accomplish their objective. The *Chesapeake* was captured by the British.

"dord"—and other "ghost words." A persistent story that crops up in academic circles, and sometimes in newspaper columns, is that "dord," defined as a term in physics and chemistry for "density," was a made-up word deliberately inserted in Merriam-Webster unabridged dictionaries in order to catch plagiarizers. (See the entry on Who's Who in America.)

And sure enough, it does appear in early printings of the famous 1934 (second) edition of the Merriam-Webster unabridged. But it isn't there to catch the copycat. It was all a mistake—most unusual, for the Merriam-Webster people. Allen Walker Read, the renowned linguist, tracked down the story. What happened is that a preliminary entry reading "D or d," for the upper-case and lower-case *abbreviations* for "density," got misread as one word: "dord."

A staff member discovered the error in 1940, and the "word" was ordered deleted. For whatever reason, however, the deletion did not actually occur until 1947, giving the incorrect story all the more time to become established.

The expression "ghost word," as used by Professor Read, who points out that the philologist W. W. Skeat used it in 1886, identifies words that, like "dord," for various reasons (often, a mere misprint) pop up and then disappear. In a paper read before a seminar on lexicography at the Modern Language Association meeting in New York in 1976, Read gave several other examples. Among them are "leonic;" a misspelling by Thomas Wolfe for "leonine," and the changing by a printer of Robert Louis Stevenson's *howf* (Scottish for "shelter") to "howl"—which was then carefully explained as a Scottish spelling for "hovel"!

Obviously a ghost word ceases to be such when it comes into widespread use. Before it does, however—if it does, and few do—it poses a constant problem for dictionary makers: to include or not to include?

Dracula and vampire bats. Count Dracula, a fictional character invented by Bram Stoker (1847–1912), was not called a vampire because he sucked the blood of living beings, like the vampire bats of Central and South America. In fact, the vampire bats, which do indeed suck the blood of cattle and other domestic animals, were named after the vampires (Slavic *vampir*) of Transylvanian legend: corpses that arise from the grave at night and suck the blood of sleeping victims.

Though they subsist entirely on blood, vampire bats would pose little danger of anemia unless they attacked en masse: they live on about a teaspoon of blood a day. They are far more hazardous as carriers of disease, including rabies.

There was, incidentally, a real Transylvanian Dracula, but Stoker borrowed his name rather than his exploits. He was Vlad IV, a fifteenth-century prince of Walachia (a region south of the Transylvanian Alps). Vlad's father was Vlad Dracul—Vlad the Devil—hence "Dracula" for the devil's son.

The protagonist of the 1897 novel was "finally" killed when a pointed stake was driven through his heart. The real Dracula also has an association with pointed stakes; he mounted his captive enemies on them. So, besides "Dracula," he has become known as Vlad the Impaler.

driver education and driving records. A funny thing happened on the way from Driver Education class; the new graduate had an accident. Or not so funny; the accident was fatal. Quite contrary to the opinions of those thousands of schools, teachers, and state driver-licensing bureaus who favor courses in driver education, the Insurance Institute for Highway Safety claims that some 2,000 fatal crashes occur yearly that would not occur if various states did not license sixteen- and seventeen-year-olds who complete a driver education course.

If the institute is correct in its figures, driver education is less important than age as a criterion for issuing drivers' licenses. It cannot be said, obviously, that driver education is wasted on all sixteen- and seventeen-year-olds, since there is no way of knowing how many fatal accidents would have occurred if those states that license at eighteen or later had simply lowered the age to sixteen or seventeen without regard to completion of a driver training course.

Nevertheless, the fact apparently remains that highway fatalities are higher in states where sixteen- and seventeen-year-olds take driver education training as a prelude to issuance of driving licenses they would not otherwise be qualified for on the basis of age.

"Dry Sack." Selling sherry in a miniature gunnysack seems a straightforward enough merchandising device, but it involves a veritable jungle of linguistic and vinicultural confusion and misinformation, some of it going back hundreds of years.

First, in one sense "dry sack" is probably tautological. "Sack" as the name for a white wine common in Shakespeare's day (Falstaff and his drinking companions—which includes just about all his companions—were forever calling for it) is apparently cognate with French *sec,* or "dry."

In the sixteenth century in England, the pronunciation "seck" for "sack" (the container, that is) was common in provincial areas, thus associated with illiterate or uneducated usage, as in saying "git" for "get" today. Those who could afford to drink imported wine instead of homemade beer avoided the pronunciation "seck," lest they be misunderstood and thought tainted by rusticity.

A further confusion arises—are you ready?—with the fact that sack (the wine, that is) was not, however, always dry in Shakespeare's England. Most likely, "sack" or "sec" (from Old—and Modern—French *vin sec,* or "dry wine") was originally a dry wine, but the term was extended to any white wine imported from Spain or the Canaries, "dry" or not, just as today "whiskey" in America covers a variety of beverages made from various materials—rye, corn, barley, wheat—whereas in Britain whiskey (Br. "whisky") is made from barley.

But how does sherry get into the act? The "Dry Sack" that people buy today is sherry, not just any white wine that comes from Spain or the Canaries. "Sherry" comes from "Xeres" (now Jerez), the town in Spain near which it was—and is—made. "Sherry" is a corruption—or an English attempt at pronunciation—of Xeres or Jerez. A line from Ben Jonson written in 1614 seems to indicate that in Shakespeare's day sherry and sack were distinguished from each other, sherry being considered superior. ("Sack? You said but e'en now it should be Sherry.")

It is the confusion between "sack" meaning "bag" and "sack" as a high-class pronunciation of "sec" during Shakespeare's time that accounts for the burlap in which expensive sherry is often dispensed today.

E

eagles carrying off babies. According to any number of experts, there seems to be no provable instance of an eagle's carrying away a human baby, although this is an enduring myth. In Marlin Perkins's words, "No documented cases exist in which eagles have carried off human babies. On one of the Mutual of Omaha's 'Wild Kingdom' programs, we tested the ability of eagles to lift objects and found they could not lift an eight-pound weight attached to the leg."

Among others who agree that eagles are not baby-snatchers are George R. Rabb, director of Chicago's Brookfield Zoo; Robert R. Maben of the Oregon Department of Fish and Wildlife, who adds that it seems illogical that a bird weighing only ten to fifteen pounds could pick up a human baby and fly away with it; and V. J. A. Manton, curator, the Zoological Society of London.

Eden, Garden of—expulsion from. It is commonly believed that Adam and Eve were expelled from the Garden of Eden

for eating the fruit of the tree of knowledge of good and
evil. They were not. From Genesis 3:22–23, King James
Version:

> And the Lord God said, Behold, the man is become as
> one of us, to know good and evil: and now, lest he put
> forth his hand, and take also of the tree of life, and eat,
> and live for ever:
> Therefore the Lord God sent him forth from the
> Garden of Eden, to till the ground from whence he was
> taken.
> So he drove out the man; and he placed at the east of
> the garden of Eden Cherubims, and a flaming sword
> which turned every way, to keep [guard, watch over] the
> way of the tree of life.

Note that there are two trees involved—not one. Of the
two, it's the second, obviously—the "tree of life"—that
most concerns the Lord. The fruit of the first tree has given
Adam knowledge of good and evil. But it's not until the
Lord realizes that Adam can achieve immortality if he
tastes the fruit of the second tree that expulsion from the
garden occurs.

Note also that Eve is not mentioned as being expelled—
only Adam. However, the next chapter has them raising
Cain together, so obviously she must have accompanied
him.

eel, electric. There is no such thing; what is commonly
called an "electric eel" belongs to the carp family. There
are no eels capable of giving shocks like the South American fish of the order Ostariophysi (eels belong to Apodes),
which is often wrongly referred to as the "electric eel."

An analogous misconception is that the lampreys that
were such a scourge in the Great Lakes (at one point seem-
ing on the verge of eating all the other fish) are a form of
eel. They are not; they may look like eels, but they too belong to a different order, the Cyclostomata.

Eels are, incidentally, fish; they are not snakes, aquatic
or otherwise. Like other fish, they have gills, although they
also breathe partially through their skins; they can thus
survive for a time out of water. Freshwater eels can make
long journeys through wet grass; there are even records of
eels crawling out on land to forage.

Eiffel Tower mounted on hydraulic jacks. Many French men and women, and no small number of tourists, believe that the Eiffel Tower is mounted on great hydraulic jacks, presumably so that it can be brought back to level in case of earthquake or other disaster.

There's no truth in it, although in this instance there is some historical foundation, so to speak, for the belief. When the tower was built, sixteen 800-ton hydraulic jacks were used to position its base. Once it was in place, however, the jacks were removed as the solid masonry foundation was established.

Einstein's theories, public understanding of. It is often said that when Einsteinian relativity first became a matter of interest to the public, only twelve men in all the world could understand it. An absurd statement when first made, it has not improved with age. For there is clearly no way of arriving at any such figure; it had to be simply plucked out of the air. A species of word magic, or perhaps more accurately number magic, it became at once a matter of fixed popular belief.

elephants drinking through their trunks. An elephant no more drinks through its trunk than a human being drinks through the nose. What an elephant does is to suck water into the trunk and then squirt it into its mouth. Young elephants suckle not with their trunks but with their mouths.

energy, saving it by turning off the TV picture tube. Many older television sets incorporate into their circuits an "instant-on" feature. A small trickle of current keeps some components warm so that the relatively long wait before the screen comes to life is avoided. Earnest conservationists often point out that if this part of the circuit is disabled, energy will be saved.

True enough, in a narrow sense, although the energy saved will not be very much; the "instant-on" circuit draws only five or ten watts. But beyond this meager saving should be considered the energy it costs to build a new picture tube—a quite considerable amount, one would suppose. Keeping such electronic parts as picture tubes warm avoids overloading them, and shortening their lives accordingly, when the current first reaches them. The reason is that resistance to electrical current increases with temperature in the materials commonly used as conductors. The more resistance, the less current is used.

Whether constantly turning light bulbs on and off (as President Lyndon Johnson was said to do when he was in the White House) actually saves energy is also at least open to question. The first rush of current to a cold filament means that light bulbs last longer if left burning constantly—not to mention wear on the switches, which it also takes energy to manufacture. Obviously, the saving would depend on the wattage of the bulb; a large one should no doubt be turned off when not in use. But it's not so simple a question as some think; it's really a matter of balancing one kind of energy saving (current consumption) against another (manufacturing new tubes, bulbs, and switches).

"England expects that every man will do his duty." Lord Nelson's famous message to the fleet just before the battle of Trafalgar appears to have been the result of a somewhat hasty huddle on the quarterdeck.

As told in A. T. Mahan's *The Life of Nelson* (1897; reprinted 1968), Nelson originally said to one of his captains, Sir Henry Blackwood, "I will now amuse the fleet with a signal," or a message "telegraphed"—which is to say, sent by coded flags—to the fleet. The first suggestion was "Nelson confides that every man will do his duty." But someone suggested "England" instead of "Nelson." Nelson agreed and asked his signal officer to display the message.

The signal officer, however, a Lieutenant Pasco, pointed out that "expects" would be a better choice of words than "confides." The reason had nothing to do with felicitous phrasing. In naval terminology "expects" was "in the vocabulary" and "confides" was not. Certain common words—those in the vocabulary—could be expressed by a single number; others had to be spelled out letter by letter, an obviously time-consuming process. Again, Nelson agreed; and so the words later to be learned by many an English schoolboy were sent, or displayed. They owe the form in which they have come down in history, however, to the strictures of the naval flag code of the time.

English horn *(cor anglais)*. Neither English nor a horn—it's a woodwind from Vienna. How the name got attached to it is something of a mystery. A common explanation is that the French name for the instrument was *cor anglé*, or "angled horn." *Anglé* sounds like the French *anglais* ("English"); hence the misnomer. Actually an oboe with a difference, the English horn does have a bent, or "angled," mouthpiece. (It differs from the oboe also in having a bulbous bell.)

True, the French for "horn" is *cor* (Latin *cornu*, from which obviously comes "cornet"). But there is no French verb with a past participle of *anglé*. French *angle*—no accent—means "angle," right enough. But it's a noun, of course, as is the French *angler*, meaning—well, "angler," or one who fishes.

There is a French adjective *anglé*, but it means "angular," not "angled." And the English horn was anything but angular when it appeared in Vienna during the latter half of the eighteenth century; it was then, in fact, curved. (It finally straightened itself out.)

So the *cor anglé* explanation is almost certainly folk etymology, coined by someone somewhere suffering from that little learning Alexander Pope so properly warns us against ("A little learning is a dangerous thing").

When the French speak of *le cor*, they are referring to what, in English-speaking countries, is called FRENCH HORN.

English sparrow. For starters, neither English nor a sparrow, as Eugene Kinkead points out in *The New Yorker* for May 22, 1978 (pages 40 ff.). And, like the starling, it was deliberately introduced into the United States, although for a different reason. (The starling was brought in from England in 1890, along with such other birds as the skylark, by a misguided Shakespearean who thought Americans should know the birds mentioned in the Shakespeare canon.)

The "English sparrow" was imported in the hope that it would control certain noxious worms and insects; attempts to import it go back to the 1840s, although it was not until the 1860s that it established itself on the North American continent. It became such a pest that its importation was forbidden in 1900, at a time when wholesale attempts at extermination were everywhere being considered or attempted.

The term "English" was applied because the first birds to be brought to the United States came from England.

Actually, they are—and were—found all over Europe; as early as 1874 the terms "European" or "house" sparrow were used but did not stick in the public mind.

That it is not a sparrow was established in 1927 by an M.I.T. professor, Peter P. Sushkin; it is, rather, a weaver finch.

It was the automobile—interestingly, or perhaps even ironically, enough (one form of pollution defeating another) —that began to effect the reduction in the hordes of sparrows during the first quarter of the twentieth century. Sparrows loved the oats and other grain that horses scattered, by one means or another; as the horse disappeared, the number of sparrows lessened. When it was further discovered, as Mr. Kinkead points out, that, unlike most birds, sparrows will eat Japanese beetles—and aphids, cutworms, and other pests—the prejudice against them diminished to the point where, in 1960, the law against importation was repealed.

An odd and little-known fact is that English sparrows, or weaver finches, that are raised in captivity (especially in conjunction with canaries and other songbirds) can learn to sing quite melodiously.

It is not true that all the English sparrows in America are descended from exactly eight pairs. The species was reintroduced over and over until it finally took hold.

"Eros," statue of, in Piccadilly Circus. If there is any remembered sight that inspires nostalgia in the tourist or symbolizes London in the movies as the pigeons of St. Mark's symbolize Venice, it is the statute of "Eros" around which Piccadilly Circus revolves.

But it is not a statue of Eros, the god of love, at all. The boy with the bow and arrow actually represents, quite in contrast to the popular belief, the Angel of Christian Charity. The whole structure of which "Eros" is a part was placed there as a memorial to the seventh Earl of Shaftesbury, who died in 1885. The memorial was unveiled in 1893.

eyes, old wives' tales about. Coexistent in the American tradition are the story of Abraham Lincoln's studying by the light of the fireplace coals and the frequent admonition by parents to their children not to read in dim light or they will "ruin their eyes." But reading in dim light does no permanent damage, according to Merritt L. Linn, M.D., an ophthalmologist who practices in Portland, Oregon. Better light may reduce eyestrain, true; but strain does no lasting harm.

Among other old wives' tales cited by Dr. Linn are the following: Excessive reading does not harm the eyes, nor does reading in bed. And the mother who tries to discourage her children from too much TV by citing possible eye damage finds no support from Dr. Linn, who says that any excessive use of the eyes may cause fatigue and strain, but no permanent damage.

No proof exists that contact lenses can cure nearsightedness—that is, permanently alter its course. Nor are dimestore glasses necessarily harmful; they may be just as useful as much more expensive ones. There is no fixed interval for changing eyeglass prescriptions; glasses are often adequate for many years. (However, Dr. Linn emphasizes, eyes should be examined at regular intervals for the detection of possible disease.)

Holding reading material too close—or for that matter, too far—is not harmful. And those inexpensive sunglasses so often the subject of warnings, especially on the part of those who manufacture or sell expensive sunglasses, will do no harm. Nor is there any basis for the belief that wearing glasses too soon in life invariably weakens the eyes; in virtually all cases there is no proof that the structure of the eyes is affected in any way by the presence of absence of lenses.

Finally—insofar as adults are concerned—there is no danger of dependency on glasses. They make one see more clearly or reduce strain, but no permanent ill effects result whether an adult wears glasses or not. Children and babies are another story, however. They can develop loss of vision (amblyopia) if they do not have the proper glasses.

eyes, transplanting of. A fairly widespread impression is that eyes, like kidneys, can be removed from a donor or an eye bank and "transplanted." This is not true. *Parts* of eyes can be transplanted, but not whole eyeballs. In the words of Merritt L. Linn, M.D., an ophthalmologist of Portland, Oregon:

There are approximately one million little nerve fibers that lead from the eyeball to the brain. When the donor

eye is removed these fine nerve fibers are cut. There is no
way of reattaching them to a new "host." However, parts
of the eye can be transplanted, such as the clear window
of the eye (the cornea) or the outer coating of the eye.
The outer coating can be transplanted to patch a dis-
eased portion or injured portion of another individual's
eye.

Many medical and surgical techniques once thought impossible are now common, if not commonplace. It may be
that some day the reattaching of a million nerve fibers will
be accomplished. But it lies in the future.

eyes as indicators of injury or death. In spite of the common scene in movie or television melodramas in which
someone from the Emergency Squad or the coroner's office
lifts the eyelid of an accident or shooting victim, peers
closely, and says, "No need to hurry with that ambulance,"
the fact is that there is no surefire way to determine
whether the victim is merely unconscious or is dead simply
by examining his or her eyes. The eyes of an injured person
may be "looking" in any direction or no direction (whites
only showing), yet the victim may recover fully and completely.

F

falling asleep and freezing to death. Many years ago, the
famous Arctic explorer Vilhjalmur Stefansson (1879–1962)
warned against a dangerous myth: that persons in danger
of freezing should press on, not stopping to rest. If they did
stop, they might fall asleep; if so, they would never wake
up.

The myth persists. ("Resist the urge to doze off, even for
a minute," a recent Sunday newspaper article says in part.
"You may never wake up.") And it continues to be a most
dangerous myth. For, as Stefansson pointed out, it encour-

ages those who are lost in the cold to flounder along until they are completely exhausted; at which point, true, it is possible to go to sleep forever.

Body temperature does drop during sleep. But, as Stefansson also pointed out, there is no danger that one *who is not exhausted* will die of cold during a nap. Cold is a reliable alarm clock, as anyone whose bedcovers slip to the floor on a winter night can certify. The answer, according to Dr. Cameron Bangs, the Oregon physician nationally known for his treatment of cold-weather casualties, is to keep active, yes—but not to the point of exhaustion. The best course is fifteen- to thirty-minute rests, followed by periods of activity to increase body-heat production.

Few people who die of exposure, it might be added, actually "freeze to death." They die of hypothermia, or subnormal body temperature. And it can happen at temperatures well above freezing, especially if one is wet. Many have "frozen to death" in a 40° rainstorm, or rainstorm and windstorm, especially if they have driven themselves until they (quite literally) drop.

Dr. Bangs further emphasizes the necessity of preparing some kind of adequate shelter *before* one reaches the point of exhaustion.

"falsehood." Folk etymology continues its strange and wonderful ways. Readers of Ripley's "Believe It or Not!" were informed recently that the word "falsehood" derives from the wearing of a doctor's hood by medieval rogues who wished to pass themselves off as physicians.

Well, it's a falsehood. The suffix *-hood* (as in "brotherhood," for example) comes from Middle English by way of the Old English *-hād,* in turn cognate with German *-heit,* meaning "state" or "condition."

The noun "hood" is from an entirely different source: a Middle English word meaning—what else?—a covering for the head.

The research involved in this project was a two-minute trip to the dictionary. (Any dictionary will do.)

fingerprinting, originator of. Alphonse Bertillon (1853–1914), the French inventor of the complicated system of measurements then used for identification of criminals, is often also credited with the invention of fingerprinting. Not so. Sir Francis Galton, the English physiologist, anthropologist, and psychologist, invented—or discovered—modern fingerprinting techniques about 1880. Bertillon, as a matter of fact, did not think much of fingerprinting as a positive means of identification; after Galton's discovery, he adopted it only reluctantly, and even limited it to certain classes of individuals, notably women and children.

Fitzgerald, Hemingway, and the very rich. An often repeated literary anecdote has F. Scott Fitzgerald saying to Ernest Hemingway, "The very rich are different from you and me." Hemingway is said to have replied, "Yes, they have more money." But that's not at all the way it was.

The statement about the very rich was certainly made by Fitzgerald, but not in conversation with Hemingway. The remark is found in one of Fitzgerald's best-known—and best—short stories, "The Rich Boy," the third paragraph of which opens as follows:

> Let me tell you about the very rich. They are different from you and me. They possess and enjoy early, and it does something to them, makes them soft where we are hard, and cynical where we are trustful, in a way that, unless you were born rich, it is very difficult to understand.

When Hemingway wrote one of *his* best-known (and best) short stories, "The Snows of Kilimanjaro," which appeared in the August 1936 *Esquire* magazine—ten years after "The Rich Boy" was first published in *Redbook* in 1926—he takes a rather cheap shot by having the narrator, a dying writer named Harry, remember "poor Scott Fitzgerald" and his "romantic awe" of the rich, following which "Harry" remembers that "someone" had said, "Yes, they have more money."

The episode is, thus, entirely fictional. Hemingway had the advantage of hindsight in contriving "someone's" answer. Moreover, only in the earliest appearances of the Hemingway story—the 1936 *Esquire* first printing, and in an anthology published by *Esquire* shortly thereafter—is Fitzgerald identified as Fitzgerald. When Fitzgerald read the story he wrote a somewhat angry, somewhat sad, somewhat plaintive letter to Hemingway asking that Hemingway please lay off him in print and, in effect, stop treating him as if he were dead.

Following Fitzgerald's letter, "Scott Fitzgerald" became "Julian" in "The Snows of Kilimanjaro," and "Julian" it has remained in the many subsequent reprintings.

A. Scott Berg, in a recent biography of the famous editor who worked with both Fitzgerald and Hemingway (*Max Perkins: Editor of Genius,* 1978), claims that the put-down remark was not even original with Hemingway; that, much to the author's chagrin, the comeback was made—by a woman—as a topper to Hemingway's own observation about the rich.

fleur-de-lis (or -lys). Not a lily, as commonly thought, but an iris. The conventionalized heraldic symbol associated with the old French monarchy may not, in fact, represent any kind of flower. Some argue that it is, rather, a stylized representation of the head of a lance or spear. A somewhat fanciful explanation is that early French kings, often named Louis, carried a scepter adorned with a flower—the *"fleur de Louis."* But this *"fleur"* smells a bit like folk etymology.

flies, how they cling to ceilings and walls. Many think that the common housefly has miniature suction cups on its feet, thus enabling it to walk on the ceiling. Not so; most flies, the housefly among them, have claws to help them cling to the comparatively rough surfaces of walls and ceilings, and the housefly has an additional apparatus that serves nicely on even the slickest glass or metal: pads *(pulvilli)* with hairs that are coated with a sticky goo—better arrangements, really, since suction cups would inhibit the instant takeoffs for which flies are notable.

foils, "buttons" on. That fencers customarily use sharp weapons that are rendered safe by placing some kind of protective button on the end is quite counter to actual practice. Since the sixteenth century, standard procedure has been to fence with weapons that have simply been "bated," or blunted; modern foils and other fencing weapons all have the blade drawn and shaped to a blunt end that is integral with the blade and cannot come off.

When Hamlet and Laertes engage in their fencing match —or what Hamlet at first supposes to be merely a fencing match, at any rate—Laertes uses a foil both unbated and "envenom'd," or with poison tip. Only too often, a director

ignorant of Elizabethan—or, for that matter, contemporary
—practice will have Hamlet pick up a weapon with a button on the end, while Laertes takes one with a sharp point;
and many a spectator has asked himself how in the world
Hamlet could be so imperceptive as to fail to note the
difference between his and Laertes's weapon.

But that was not the way it was. As Shakespeare's audience knew, weapons used for fencing were blunted, not
"buttoned," in Shakespeare's day, just as at present. Since a
sharp rapier amid a group of "bated" weapons would be
indistinguishable except on close examination, Hamlet is
easy prey to Laertes's murderous trick.

The whole scene, in fact, is carefully prepared by Shakespeare. King Claudius, who knows Hamlet very well, and
whose original idea the unbated weapon was—Laertes is
the one who thinks of adding the poison—remarks when
he is persuading Laertes to do his dirty work for him,

> [Hamlet being] Most generous and free from all
>   contriving,
> Will not peruse the foils; so that with ease
> Or with a little shuffling, you may choose
> A sword unbated. . . .

Claudius was right. Just before the contest, Hamlet does
ask if "these foils have all a length"—that is, if they are all
the same length. An "unbated" foil would be somewhat
longer; bating, or blunting, a foil was commonly done by
filing. But Hamlet is too much the gentleman, too "gener-
ous and free from all contriving," to pursue the matter
further; he is satisfied when Osric, who acts as referee, as-
sures him that they are.

folk myths and fantasies. Among the figments and fantasies
that surface periodically, none are more durable than these
following. Most editors, reporters, and columnists, though
by no means all, know them well. Some start from the
merest germ of truth; others seem to generate themselves,
as once it was thought that crocodiles are fathered by the
sun and borne by the Nile's muddy banks. (Today, they
are sometimes believed to grow to enormous size in Manhattan's sewers, flushed there when small by children getting rid of their pets.)

All the tales that follow share certain characteristics.

They are often repeated, but never documented; they are believed without proof. They are always attributed to someone else; never can be found anyone who is personally, directly involved. Many—perhaps most, perhaps all—of these tales illuminate certain subliminal areas of the human psyche, some darker, some lighter: a wish to see the high and mighty cut down to size; an instinct for revenge; a delight in the discomfiture of others because, perhaps, it seems to make our own discomfitures easier to bear; a deep distrust of those who have chosen ways unlike our own. ("See, I told you so!")

The Snake in the Coat. This one recently swept the Pacific Coast, showing up in press reports and columns from Seattle to San Diego. A woman in a large department store tries on an expensive fur coat imported from an exotic, usually tropical, area. She decides not to buy it, and it is returned to the rack.

Shortly thereafter the woman becomes very ill. She is rushed to her doctor, who—some diagnostician!—decides that only the bite of a certain rare but deadly snake, unknown in the area, can account for her symptoms. Sure enough, on her arm are two tiny marks of the sort classically described as "telltale." She is treated and recovers (or, sometimes, dies).

But how could she have been bitten by such a snake? Someone remembers the coat; so it is back to the department store, where, following a frantic search, the coat she tried on is found and the sleeve seam ripped out. (In some versions, the husband or friend who goes back to the store must buy the coat before being allowed to mutilate it.) Sure enough, out falls a coral snake or a Gaboon viper, which is promptly killed on the spot. Sometimes, it is said, all the coats in the expensive shipment will be ripped open and other snakes found. Attempts to document the story invariably fail. It always happened to someone else's friend, who in turn says it was told to him or her by still someone else, and the trail vanishes.

The Dead Grandma in the Station Wagon. A family is vacationing in the wilds, far from home. They have taken aged Grandma with them. They stop for a picnic, leaving Grandma to rest in the rear seat. When the picnic is over, the children try to rouse Grandma, who has apparently fallen asleep. But she is not asleep; she has died.

What is now to be done? There is no one within miles.

So they tuck Grandma into a sleeping bag, zip it up, and place her, with due tenderness and respect, on the floor of the station wagon. If they are driving a car or a pickup camper, as in some versions, they may tie her to the luggage rack on the roof. Driving to the nearest town, they stop first at the police station to report the death. When they come back out to take Grandma's body to the mortuary, they find that the station wagon or the car or the camper is missing; it has apparently been taken by someone bold enough to steal a car in front of the police station. Here the story ends, the rest being left to the reader's or listener's imagination.

So often is this tale repeated that it is the subject of at least one scholarly attempt to trace its genesis. Robert H. Woodward, writing in *Northwest Folklore* for Summer 1965 (vol. I, no. 1, page 20) points out the similarity between this story and the fictional experience of the Joads, in Steinbeck's 1939 novel *The Grapes of Wrath,* who do carry the body of Grandma Joad with them for a while after she dies.

The Cement in the Basement. Like all such tales, this one may vary in detail. A common version has the driver of a large cement truck, ordered to deliver a small amount through a basement window so that the floor can be patched, unable to shut off the flow. A variation adds both deliberation and motive. The driver's cheating ex-wife has just finished building the downstairs recreation room the driver had always wanted—in the house his wife unfairly got away from him during the divorce proceedings, and in which she now lives with her lover. Sometimes a swimming pool, rather than a basement, is involved. The essential is always wet cement (or fuel oil or coal), a lot of it, in the wrong place.

A Denver newspaper, some years ago, printed (without, as usual, names or places) a somewhat analogous tale. Young and arrogant (the arrogance gives the story its punch), the passengers in a new, expensive convertible playfully—and dangerously—tailgate a state highway truck of the kind used to spread road oil. But they overdo it; the convertible gets too close, its hood touches the release valve, and hot oil drenches the car and its occupants.

The Bartender and the Waitress. This one showed up in a San Francisco newspaper. It may well crop up again. No names were mentioned; no specific location was given.

A cocktail waitress, so the story goes, became involved with the bartender. At first they spent their passion in a nearby motel. But then it occurred to the bartender that he could save money if he drove the family pickup camper to work.

The bartender's wife, already suspicious but without proof, stakes out the camper. Sure enough, shortly after the midnight closing, she sees the waitress and her husband enter the door in back. She waits for what she estimates to be about the right time; then, using her own duplicate set of keys, she quietly locks the back door, gets into the driver's seat, and takes off—fast. Driving at such reckless speed that the occupants cannot risk jumping out even if they could open the door, she takes them for a wild ride over the roughest and most winding roads she can find.

As will be abundantly obvious later, the husband and his inamorata become violently ill in back. Still driving fast, the wife roars to their hillside home, slams the camper into reverse, and backs it against the concrete retaining wall on one side of the driveway, completely blocking any possible exit. The wife then goes comfortably to bed, after a phone call or two. When morning comes, she moves the camper away from the wall; trembling and ashen, the two lovers totter out—to be greeted by the wife's lawyer *and* the waitress's husky husband.

The Recipe from the Ritz. It may not be the Ritz, but it must be ritzy. While living it up on vacation, a tourist (almost always it is a woman) particularly enjoys a special dessert at a very expensive restaurant. She asks the waiter if she might just possibly be given the recipe; it would so impress her friends back home.

But of course, madam. The chef appears in person, apparently pleased at this tribute, and reveals the recipe to the woman. Back home at last, she finds in the mail a bill for $500 from the ever-so-friendly chef. Often as this tale is told, it contains such built-in absurdities that one wonders why it keeps turning up. Why would the woman suppose the chef wants her home address? How would he hope to collect? And recipes are kept secret, when they are, for the very reason that invalidates this fable: there is no way to protect them short of a patent—and this would require revealing the recipe!

The Violinist and the Snob. This lovely little story—it's been told about various violinists and other musicians—

involves the famous fiddler who is invited by a well-to-do hostess to play for the guests at a party. She asks about his fee. One thousand dollars, she is told. "You understand," says the hostess, "that you will be expected not to mingle with the guests." "In that case," says the violinist, "my fee will be one hundred dollars."

The Repentant Car Thief. Most recently heard on a national TV news show, this one is quite durable. And international; it has been reported out of Grenoble, France, among other places. A couple discover that their automobile has been stolen. Scarcely have they had time to report its loss to the police, however, when they discover it once more parked in its accustomed place. On the front seat is an envelope. In the envelope is a note expressing embarrassment and shame and adding a plausible enough reason for the "borrowing" of the car: some emergency or other. Also in the envelope are two prime-seat tickets to a sold-out event (opera, ballet, rock concert, whatever) which, the repentant thief hopes, will partly atone for his misdeed. The grateful couple use the tickets—why not?—and on their return home discover that their house has been ransacked.

The State Trooper Decoy. This grim little story involves a stretch of road in California (in some versions, Texas) that seemed to invite speeding and thus had a bad accident record. State police headquarters decided to try a man-power-saving experiment: a full-size wooden cutout of a highway patrol car, complete wtih driver, painted in the proper colors and set up so that it looked like the real thing.

And for a while it helped. Seeing what they thought was a police car waiting to nab the unwary, motorists slowed down. But soon the deception was discovered by those who traveled the road regularly; and it became a popular sport to take potshots at the decoy. (Western drivers are notorious for this kind of thing, as many a bullet-ridden road sign testifies.)

The rest of the story tells itself. The highway patrol decided that the decoy, pretty well punctured by now, was not doing much good any more. So they put a real car and a real driver in its place. So guess what happened, one day, to the (real) highway patrolman.

The Truck Driver and the Motorcycle Gang. Like the Dead Grandma, this one represents the biter-bitten theme,

one of the most durable in literature, folk or otherwise.
The driver of a large truck-trailer combination stops at a
roadside café. He finds it temporarily taken over by a particularly brutal motorcycle gang. The gang decides—for
some reason or none—to pick on the truck driver, and they
rough him up considerably.

Shaken and bruised, the driver finally manages to escape.
Back in the cab, he sees the gang's motorcycles neatly
parked along the roadside. Aiming accurately, he mows
down the whole row and pulls out onto the highway, leaving behind a mangled mess of Yamahas, Harley Davidsons,
and Triumphs.

Grandfather's Gold Watch. A somewhat ironic twist to
the biter-bitten theme has been around for decades; a variation cropped up in *Parade* magazine in September of
1972, reported as truth. A salesman who prizes the expensive gold watch his grandfather left him picks up a hitchhiker, who, when he climbs into the car, bumps rather
clumsily against the driver. The driver thinks little of it
until he reaches for his watch, to find it gone.

The salesman slams on the brakes, grabs the hitchhiker
by the throat (or in some Western versions, pulls a gun on
him), and says, "All right; let's have that watch." The
hitchhiker hands over the watch. The driver stuffs it back
into his pocket, none too gently shoves the hitchhiker out,
and roars away. When the salesman gets to his motel, he is
told to call his wife. "Did you know," she asks, "that you
left Grandfather's watch on the bureau this morning?"

In the *Parade* version, updated as such stories often are,
the object is a wallet and the locale a subway. It was the
same basic story, however. And with the usual vagueness
as to specifics.

Those who watched *The Prisoner of Second Avenue,* the
mid-1970s film adapted by Neil Simon from his play, saw
the tale of the wallet/watch exploited in a crucial scene.
The protagonist, "Mel Edison," played by Jack Lemmon,
chases down and subdues a mugger only to discover, when
he returns home in triumph, that the wallet he "recovers"
is not his; he's left that one at home. Whether or not this is
Art imitating Life, or the reverse, only Mr. Simon and perhaps the editors of *Parade* know. Certain it is, however,
that the tale of the hitchhiker and the watch long antedates
both the *Parade* and the Simon variations.

The Gentleman and the Horn Blower. Another biter-bitten theme shows up now and then. An elderly driver gets stalled in busy traffic. He cannot restart his car. From behind comes a continuing horn blast, although the old gentleman is obviously doing the best he can to get going. Finally the bedeviled driver gets out, walks back to the horn blaster, reaches swiftly inside, pulls out the ignition key, and throws it as far as he can.

The Everlasting Rolls-Royce. It is widely believed, though not by Rolls-Royce owners, that any time a Rolls-Royce part fails regardless of age, all the owner need do, no matter whether in central London or central Africa, is call or cable the factory. Posthaste a replacement part will be sent, by air if quicker, no charge of course. Such legends as this are, or at least ought to be, self-defeating. If it were true, as Bruce McCall of *Car and Driver* magazine reminds us, every Rolls-Royce ever built would be in mint condition as owners summoned their free replacement parts over the years. (Old-timers may remember the $100,000 purportedly to be paid to anyone who could hold down the throttle of a Stanley Steamer for one minute.)

The Black Widow Spider in the Hairdo. Now that "hippies" are no longer the objects of quite so much fear and revulsion as once they were, this one may fade out. It had some currency during the sixties. A "hippie" lets her, or his, hair grow into a dirty, tangled mess. A black widow spider builds a nest there and, it goes without saying, finally bites her host or hostess, who expires in properly deserved agony. (Black widow spiders are, in fact, shy and reclusive creatures; it is impossible to imagine one seeking out a coiffure.)

The Playful Retriever. Truman Capote told this tale (with himself as the culprit) for some years before finally admitting it was a bit of creative imagination. A summertime visitor to a friend's (or date's) apartment, somewhere above the tenth floor (altitudes vary with the teller), amuses himself, while friend or date is dressing, by throwing a ball that friend's or date's dog retrieves. But the visitor miscalculates, the ball bounces out an open window, and the dog bounces right out after it. Not daring to tell what happened, the visitor slinks away into the night.

The Captain's Wife and the Fish Dish. As used-car salesmen are wont to say, an oldie but a goodie. On a fine summer night, an army captain's wife is having a big dinner party for the general and other assorted brass. Her husband is up for promotion, and she hopes to impress her guests with the *pièce de résistance,* a fish mousse. She goes to the kitchen to fetch it only to discover her beloved pet cat nibbling at one end. What-the-helling it, she puts the cat out, cuts off and reshapes the end of the mousse, and serves it.

The last guests make their farewells. As the captain and his wife start back into the house, they find their pet cat lying dead beside the outside stairs. Good Lord, thinks the captain's wife: the mousse. I've poisoned the lot of them. Frantically she calls the departed (soon to be, she fears, the late) guests; the dinner party ends up at the base hospital having stomachs pumped. The next morning, as the wife glumly ponders the catastrophe over a cup of coffee, a neighbor knocks at the door. So sorry about your cat; we saw it get hit by a car last night, but we just couldn't bear to ruin your party with the sad news, so we put it outside by the stairs.

The Naked Lady and the Meter Reader. This one has many, many variations. Although it may have started as a joke, it is often heard as fact. Essentially, it involves a lady who, for whatever reason (just out of the bathtub, e.g.), is in the nude. In one version she strolls toward the kitchen, hears the screen door open, realizes it must be the delivery boy with the groceries. She takes refuge in a closet, hears footsteps, gets nervous, makes a noise. The door is opened; it's the meter reader. "Oh," says the lady. "I thought you were the delivery boy."

A version in which the lady herself is not naked has her worried about her little boy, who is. He gets away while being bathed; his mother hears a noise in the basement and calls out, "Are you down there running around stark naked?"

"No, ma'am," comes the answer. "Just reading the meter."

There is even a naked-man version. He sleeps in the buff, goes downstairs for a drink of water, and gets goosed by the cold, wet nose of his only too friendly dog. With a yelp and a jerk, the man bangs his head on the cupboard overhanging the sink and falls, unconscious. His wife hears the noise, comes down, and calls an ambulance. The man comes to as they are taking him down the front stairs on a stretcher; when he blurts out the story of his mishap, the bearers laugh so hard they drop him and he ends up with multiple leg fractures.

The Volkswagen and the Pachyderm. Lady comes to the city to shop—New York, let us say, though the story has popped up everywhere, or at least everywhere a circus might conceivably visit. She first picks up a case of liquor and puts it into the trunk, or front, of her red VW "bug." She has other errands, so she parks near Madison Square Garden. It's circus time; elephants parade by and one of them, whose trick involves a red platform, parks his bottom on the luggage compartment, caving it in and smashing some of the bottles.

The trainer is nice about it, though; he leaves a note explaining what happened and says that the circus, through its insurance, will pay for the damage. Pleased to find the note, and to discover that the car is still drivable, the lady starts for home only to be stopped by the police: a red VW has been involved in a hit-run accident nearby. With the odor of booze in the air, the lady tries to explain how the front end of her car came to be damaged. "I see," says the cop, sniffing the bourbon-scented atmosphere. "An elephant sat on it." She's finally saved either by the trainer's note, or a call to the circus, or both. (A common variation has the woman attempting to explain what happened to *her* insurance company.)

The Seventy-five-dollar Porsche. This one swept through a Western city not long ago and will no doubt show up elsewhere, for it has all the essential ingredients—including a singular lack of documentation; the tale turned out to be impossible to trace. A man sees a classified advertisement offering a late-model low-mileage Porsche for seventy-five dollars. Assuming that it must be a misprint, he nevertheless calls the telephone number listed in the ad.

No, it's not a misprint, explains the woman who answers, although she seems quite aware of the car's actual value. The man tells her to hold everything; he'll be right over. Sure enough, the car is as represented: low mileage, beautiful condition. The man whips out his checkbook and buys the car on the spot. Curious, he asks why the woman is willing to sell a twenty-thousand-dollar automobile at such a figure. "My husband," she explains, "ran off to San Francisco with his secretary and wants a divorce. He called long-distance and asked me if I'd please sell his car and send him the money." The inherent implausibilities in this story did not prevent its appearance, as a news item, on at least two television newscasts.

The Exploding Candy. Not long ago a new taste sensation appeared on the kiddy market: a candy releasing small amounts of carbon dioxide, a harmless gas that gives soft drinks (and for that matter champagne) their bubbles. In the mouth, the candy teases—or assaults—the palate with tiny explosions. Hardly had the stuff hit the junk-food market when it was reported (in one instance, out of Spokane, Washington) that a greedy child had gulped down several packets at once. They exploded in her stomach, with fatal—and quite impossible—consequences. The moral is as old as Aesop. The story is quite false.

The Parakeet and the Vacuum Cleaner, the Cat and the Microwave Oven. Analogous tales, though one is much the grimmer. A woman accidentally sucks up her pet parakeet, which has escaped its cage, while Hoovering the carpet. In most versions, the parakeet survives, though with both feathers and dignity considerably ruffled. Another woman —or perhaps the same one?—gives her long-haired cat a bath. It occurs to her that there must be a quicker alternative to toweling it dry. She has a new microwave oven, and—but this is a tale for ailurophobes, who can finish it for themselves; the writer is an ailurophile.

The Fish in the Trunk. There are many variations of this one: for example, the dead cat in a shoe box being carried to the veterinarian's for disposal which gets stolen along the way. (New Yorkers like to tell the tale of the young lady and her dog, a boxer; minor-league thugs who prey on people struggling with their luggage are not mythical in Manhattan, although the story almost certainly is. The dog dies on a Friday; the ASPCA says it can't send around a truck until Monday but will accept the corpse if she can lug it in. So she stuffs the dead dog into a large suitcase. As she's huffing and puffing up a subway stairway, a young man gallantly offers to help, takes the suitcase, and bounds away with his prize.)

Man goes fishing in August. Gets his limit, puts it into his car trunk, properly iced. As he pulls into his garage back home, he hears the phone ringing inside the house. An emergency requires his immediate departure to another city for a stay of some duration. Preferring a taxi to long-term airport parking, he calls one, packs hastily, and leaves. Two weeks later he is back home again. What happens when he gets around to opening the trunk of his car can be only too vividly imagined.

A variation is the unsalable Buick. It's almost new, in fine shape, offered at a very low price. Only problem is that a gangster-type murder victim was left in the trunk of the car, which was found abandoned some weeks after the crime.

The Vanishing Hotel Room. Or "the vanishing lady," which is how Alexander Woollcott identified this famous old chestnut when he retold it years ago in his *While Rome Burns* (1934). A woman and her daughter check into a first-class Paris hotel; they are just in from India. Though the city is crowded—Woollcott's version places the time as that of the Paris Exposition of 1900—they are lucky enough to be given an elegant room, unforgettable in its details: old-rose wallpaper, plum-colored draperies, an oval satinwood table, a mantel with an ormolu clock.

The mother is exhausted from the long trip; indeed, she looks and feels so bad that her daughter calls the house doctor. The daughter knows no French, but that does not matter; the doctor speaks English. And he tells the daughter that her mother is, indeed, ill, but that if the daughter will go to the doctor's house, on the other side of the city, the doctor's wife will provide the necessary medication. The doctor scribbles a note, in French, to be given to his wife.

In the crowded city, traffic is fierce; the daughter's trip takes hours. Finally she reaches the doctor's house; the wife reads the note, leaves the girl waiting for what seems like an interminable time, finally comes back with a small package which she says is the needed medicine.

Another agonizing slow trip across the width of Paris brings the girl back to the hotel. But when she asks for the room key, the clerk stares uncomprehendingly. It's the same clerk, but he professes never to have seen her. Nor is her name, or her mother's, on the register. When she insists, the clerk, shrugging, takes her to the room. In effect, it does not exist; it resembles in no particular—wallpaper, draperies, furnishings—the room she recalls so well. And, like the room, her mother has ceased to exist; the house doctor (a quite different person) has, like the clerk, never heard of her. Their manner implies that the sick mother is the creation of a sick mind.

So some versions of the tale end, if the simple inducing of paranoia is its presumed purpose. If the tale is continued, it is finally discovered (by the persistence of the girl herself, or a skeptical stranger who befriends her) that the mother was desperately ill with the plague. She dies shortly after the daughter has been sent for the "medicine," is spirited away, and a crew of hastily recruited workmen in great secrecy redo the room. The alternative, obviously, is panic that will empty the city and cost millions upon millions of francs.

It is not hard to see why this tale, in one version or another, is retold so often; it strikes at our darkest fear, the loss of self, of identity. Woollcott, who was not taken in by it—he calls it "a fair specimen of folklore in the making"—found its story the basis of a 1913 novel, *The End of Her Honeymoon*, by Mrs. Belloc Lowndes, and of another later novel by Lawrence Rising called *She Who Was Helena Cass*. In more recent times, it has been the basis of the plot in several movies and television dramas, including *So Long at the Fair*, a Jean Simmons vehicle of the early 1950s. Woollcott says that the story appeared in a column by Karl Harriman in a Detroit newspaper in 1889. It may, of course, be even older.

The tale is no longer told on shipboard by, in Woollcott's words, "those rootless widows who wear buttoned shoes with cloth tops" and whose families persuade them to go traveling. But that's only because the shoes and the ships are gone; it may well be repeated, even as you read this, in the Stratolounge of a Boeing 747, with details altered to fit the telling and the teller.

The Dangerous Drink. A Prohibition tale. In a speakeasy, someone takes a swallow of his first drink, then asks why the lights have suddenly gone out. A hand is passed before his face; he's blind. What he got was wood alcohol. A highly moral tale, obviously; why the others in the room have not gone blind is not revealed.

Spanish Fly and the Gearshift Lever. Another grim one, also highly moral—and completely absurd, though once fearfully told (and believed) by any number of young males. A youth contrives to sneak a large amount of Spanish fly, widely—and quite falsely—thought to be an extremely powerful aphrodisiac, into his date's drink. The story predates the Pill; as the lustful youth starts their drive out into the country, he remembers that he lacks proper precautions. He stops at a nearby drugstore to buy condoms. When he gets back to the car, he finds that his girl friend has impaled herself on the gearshift lever.

The Baby-sitter and the Toilet Seat. The seat must have been freshly repainted, preferably with something based on epoxy, or other ingredient equally mucilaginous. Enough said.

Atrocity Tales. No one could possibly collect all the atrocity stories bred by riot and war, and rumor and myth multiply so fast in troubled times that documentation is impossible. Since war is itself an atrocity, no doubt some of the stories are true. And, as at My Lai, some are without question true.

Now and then, however, a story may reveal itself as inherently suspect, like the World War II tale (a variation of a World War I tale) about the American prisoner in a Japanese camp. The prisoner is allowed to write to a friend or relative. He speaks well, in his letter, of his captors: the Japanese are not the monsters they are made out to be. He goes on to comment that the stamp on the letter ought to be of particular interest to the recipient, who has for so long been an ardent philatelist; why not steam it off and add it to the collection?

Never having been interested in stamp collecting, the recipient, puzzled, nevertheless follows instructions. When the stamp is off, underneath, in cramped miniature handwriting, are the words "They have cut out my tongue." How the prisoner contrived to lick the stamp is not explained.

The One-liners. In addition to the tales just discussed, there are what might be called one-liners, not narratives but suppositions that spread like wildfire. One of them is a recurring nuisance, though a nuisance with tragic overtones, to such organizations as the foundations that help provide guide dogs for the blind. Periodically—how, why, when, no one knows or can foresee—there sweeps through a region or even the nation a belief that if one sends the cellophane tear strips from a cigarette package to some place or other, for every thousand strips a free dog will be provided a needy blind person.

Not uncommonly, a service club or some similar group will place itself, in entire good faith, in charge of such a collection only to learn what is invariably the case: the strips are worthless. No one is going to get a "free" dog, or a free anything else. The objects to be saved and those to be gained vary: beer-can tabs for a kidney machine; candy-bar wrappers for artificial limbs.

A nonphilanthropic variation has been around for years. It was especially common during the Great Depression of the 1930s. If a cigarette package contained somewhere the symbol V8, sending the package to the manufacturer would result in the sender's receiving a free automobile. As usual, there were variations, but the essential factor was always the "secret" symbol and a payoff of great value. Certainly there are legitimate offers: for every label, we'll give a dime to the Olympic Games fund. The distinguishing feature of the phony "prize," however, is always its absolute anonymity; never is there any public announcement. Yet many continue to swallow it all whole.

Only rarely is a folk myth traceable to its source. But sometimes it can be done. It is impossible to know how many people continue to believe the tale of the six Pennsylvania students who, high on LSD, stared directly at the sun and blinded themselves. The story, carried on national news service wires some years ago, was soon revealed as a hoax. The man responsible, himself blind, confessed. His motive, as expressed, was the obvious one: a warning to the young to stay away from dangerous drugs. Unfortunately, the revelation that it was all a lie made the "warning" worse than none at all. But expressed motives are seldom true motives. No doubt the teller of the tale wanted a place in the sun for himself. One must surely pity him.

footballs, baseballs, and bats. Ah, the crack of the willow against the horsehide, the "thunk" of the punter's foot against the pigskin! So embedded in the American consciousness are these more or less immortal phrases that it seems almost a shame to point out that baseball bats are not made out of willow, baseballs are not horsehide, and footballs haven't been pigskin for lo, these many years.

Actually, footballs never were made out of pigskin. A pig's *bladder* is said to have been employed long ago, when the game was in its infancy. Baseball bats are hickory or ash. And baseballs have a cowhide cover, as do footballs.

Baseballs *were* covered with horsehide until the 1973 season, when, according to the A. G. Spalding Company, whose plant at Chicopee, Massachusetts, supplies baseballs for both major leagues, high-quality horsehide became in short supply. In 1969, Spalding engineers had begun the search for a suitable replacement. After many experiments with tanning processes, cowhide was finally rendered functionally equivalent to horsehide as a baseball cover.

Ford, Model A. Everybody knows that the Model A Ford, which ended the reign of the famous Model T, was introduced in the 1920s. Not so. The first Ford Model A came out in 1903. It was followed by an alphabetical succession of models before the "T" came along after the Ford Model S of 1908. The name of the "new" Model A was a return to a much earlier designation.

forgery and uttering. Forging a signature is to simulate it with intent to defraud. Uttering is putting the forgery into circulation.

It is quite possible to be convicted of forgery for signing one's own name: as, for example, if John Smith mistakenly receives through the mail a check not meant for him. If he knows that he is not the John Smith for whom the check is intended, it's just as much forgery for him to endorse it "John Smith" as if he had actually altered the name of the payee.

French and their livers. Some fifteen years ago, the actress Olivia de Havilland wrote *Every Frenchman Has One,* a title that rivals *Once Upon a Mattress* as a combination of come-on and put-on. *Once Upon a Mattress* took its inspiration from the old fable of the princess and the pea. What every Frenchman has, in the de Havilland book, turns out to be a liver.

Indeed, both to Frenchmen and Frenchwomen, the liver ranks very high, perhaps even taking second place, as the organ most likely to be blamed when things go wrong. But it's all a myth, according to the French Association for the Study of the Liver. As reported in the *New York Times* (June 13, 1976), Dr. Jean-Pierre Benhamou, director of the association, says that the belief both in France and elsewhere that the French have very bad livers simply isn't so.

This does not mean that the French do not constantly talk about "liver complaints": quite the contrary. Whether or not this obsession derives from a submerged guilt complex because of the way geese are force-fed to enhance the creation of *pâté de foie gras,* the fact is that in France everything tends to be blamed on the liver, including skin eruptions, headaches, and stomachaches.

No medical texts, says Dr. Benhamou, mention anything like the "liver crisis" so often invoked in France. Though millions of francs are spent annually for nostrums believed to alleviate liver problems, many such "crises," he thinks, are psychosomatic or possibly the result of drug abuse.

Whatever the reasons, it appears that fifty million Frenchmen—and women—can indeed be wrong. Their livers are as good (or as bad) as anybody else's, no matter what they may think.

The United States is not without—or has not been without—a lesser but similar phenomenon. Those who follow such matters closely will recall that Carter's Little Liver Pills, known to generations of our forebears, are now, as a result of FDA action, simply Carter's Pills.

However, the most likely American counterpart of the French liver would seem to be the bowels. Judging from advertising messages, one would suppose that there is scarcely a soul in the United States not suffering from constipation or "irregularity."

French Foreign Legion as haven for criminals. There is a widespread misconception, fostered by many a romantic movie, that if anyone is sought after by the police, he can find refuge in the Foreign Legion, no questions asked. The fact is that the Legion does not admit criminals to its ranks.

forward pass, Notre Dame University, and Knute Rockne. Regardless of the opinions of loyal alumni or those dedicated souls who rewatch the reruns of Pat O'Brien as Knute Rockne, the forward pass did not originate with Rockne or at Notre Dame, nor was it first used in Notre Dame's game against Army at West Point in 1913.

True, Notre Dame did use the forward pass with devastating effect against Army in 1913. It was a victory all the sweeter because Army had scheduled Notre Dame merely because it had an open weekend and thought that this obscure Midwestern team might provide a breather. But the Gus Dorais–Knute Rockne passing combination turned the game into a 35–13 rout. (What might be taken as evidence that the military mind is not so inflexible as sometimes assumed is the fact that Army learned its lesson; in its final game—with Navy, of course—it won an upset victory, 22–9, using as its principal weapon the previously scorned forward pass.)

But the forward pass had been legal since 1906, used by many teams in spite of conservative objections to it. The famous Amos Alonzo Stagg claimed, in fact, that in 1906 he had dozens of pass plays in his repertoire. The forward pass was first proposed to the rules committee by Walter Camp, though it was adopted under restrictions that today seem unthinkable; for example, failure to complete a pass resulted in a 15-yard penalty from the spot where the ball was put into play, *and* loss of a down!

"Foursome, threesome" (in golf). Contrary to almost universal American belief, neither foursomes nor threesomes are recognized in the rules of golf, if by these terms is meant three or four players each playing a separate ball. A "threesome," according to the rules, is a match in which one plays against the other two, each side playing only one ball. That is, two of the players must play the same ball, so that in a "proper" threesome there are only two balls in play. In a foursome as defined in the rules, there are two sides, each consisting of two players, each side again playing the same ball for the same total number of balls, two. There is no provision in the rules for the common American "foursome," which the British do not ordinarily, as a matter of fact, allow on their golf courses.

The maximum number of golfers playing together as a group, each competing against the others with his own ball, is three—again according to the rules. And this group is not called a "threesome"; it is called a three-ball match.

Franklin and the "Franklin" stove. We all know—don't we?—that Benjamin Franklin played no part whatever in founding *The Saturday Evening Post*.

It may seem like a low blow further directed at one of Colonial America's greatest men to reveal that he had little or nothing to do with the "Franklin" stove. But it's true. What he invented did not—indeed, could not—work. Only after others had extensively modified his original proposal was it a success.

Franklin had no understanding of the laws of thermodynamics. In fairness, it must be said that nobody else had either, during his lifetime. It was not until the nineteenth century that the scientific principles underlying combustion and heat were discovered. To Franklin and his contemporaries, heat was a fluid behaving like water except that it flowed up instead of down. When anything combustible burned, it was thought to release this "fluid."

The story of Franklin's efforts to improve on the inefficient fireplaces of his day is told in "The Myth of the Franklin Stove," by Samuel Y. Edgerton, Jr., in *Early American Life,* a publication of the Early American Society (June 1976, pages 38 ff.).

It was Franklin's notion, based on his misunderstanding of the way hot gases behave, that he could make a stove more efficient by drawing the smoke out of the bottom instead of the top. This, in Mr. Edgerton's words, "became an obsession—and a fatal flaw—in all his thinking about heating."

It seems clear enough that Franklin's original design was neither a technological nor a commercial success. His brother, the merchant Peter Franklin, ordered eleven of the "stoves" (they were actually designed to operate, in rather complicated fashion, in conjunction with an existing fireplace). In twenty years, he sold only two.

The reason, apparently, is that they simply did not work. They could not work because, although heat itself does behave something like a fluid—it "flows" from an area of high temperature to an area of low temperature no matter what the direction, up, down, or sidewise—heated *air* does not; it rises. Thus any attempt to "siphon" smoke out of the bottom of the "Pennsylvanian Fire-place" was bound to fail.

Others, notably a man named Rittenhouse who may or may not have been David Rittenhouse, Franklin's colleague in the American Philosophical Society, finally modified Franklin's original design and made it workable. When the iron stove whose descendants are now found in almost every hardware store appeared in the last decade of the eighteenth century, it was in fact called not the Franklin but the Rittenhouse stove.

Interestingly enough, the one device that might properly be called the "Franklin" stove is a curiosity, so far as known never manufactured, that Franklin designed some forty years after his "Pennsylvanian Fire-place." In 1785 he proposed what seems, to a modern taste, a most unusual device: a coal-burning stove in the shape of a Grecian urn atop a pedestal whose smoke (as in Franklin's earlier design) was supposed to be drawn downward before being exhausted—that same "fatal flaw" again.

Though Franklin's own design for this rather funereal device was never implemented, apparently Charles Willson Peale, the noted American portrait painter (1741–1827), did actually construct a similar stove—but, in place of the urn, with a bust of George Washington on top of the pedestal!

Ironically, considering the appeal to energy-conscious conservationists today of the so-called "Franklin" stove, Franklin's original 1744 design would have consumed inordinately wasteful amounts of fuel.

The true "father of housewarming" in Colonial times, Mr. Edgerton says, is really not Franklin but another Benjamin: Benjamin Thompson, who fled to England from Massachusetts in 1776, came to be known as "Count Rumford," and in 1795 wrote a pamphlet about chimney fireplaces that truly did revolutionize household heating in Europe and America. And Mr. Edgerton quotes an amusing "epitaph" proposed for Franklin's grave by some anonymous wit who had come across Franklin's 1785 design for that mortuarian urn-and-pedestal heating device:

> Let fortune inscribe on this urn:
>   "Here lies the renown'd inventor
> Whose fame to the skies ought to burn,
>   But inverted, descends to the center."

"freeze plugs" in automobile engine blocks. A widely held but quite erroneous belief is that the circular plugs found in most automobile engines are there to prevent damage in case of freezing. Indeed, these plugs are usually called "freeze plugs." It is believed that if the block freezes, the plugs will pop out and prevent major harm. At least one large independent supplier of automobile parts lists "freeze plugs" as among items replaced in their remanufactured engines.

But the plugs are not there for any such purpose; they are, rather, simply a result of the manufacturing process. Once, in fact, called "Walsh plugs," perhaps after their inventor, they are explained as follows by Dante J. Lanzetta, Jr., of the General Motors public relations staff:

There is nothing which General Motors calls a "freeze plug." . . . There are holes in the block, for the purpose of shaking out sand from the casting molds. Since these may connect to the water jacket or oil gallery, they obviously must be sealed in the manufacture of the engine. We do this either with concave expansion plugs or with cup plugs, press-fitted into an interference counter-bore. . . . These plugs must be engineered so that they will *not* pop out under normal engine water (or oil) pressures, but they will usually pop out if water in the area of the water jacket near the plug freezes. [However] a localized freeze-up in an engine area remote from the plugged shake-out hole can still crack the block, so don't neglect your anti-freeze in the hope that some "freeze plug" exists. . . . It is . . . a popular misconception.

Perhaps the "freeze plug" myth started with a more or less accidental popping out of one such "plug" under freezing conditions. But, as pointed out, it was never designed for such a purpose and certainly cannot be relied on to prevent engine damage.

It may be that the "freeze plug" myth arose, or is at least kept alive, by the fact that air-cooled engines (the now defunct General Motors Corvair, Volkswagen "Beetles," and all Porsches until recently) do not have so-called "freeze plugs." Air-cooled engines cannot, obviously, freeze; hence the "confirmation" of the myth.

The real reason air-cooled engines do not have plugs, however, is that they are not cast with the double walls required by liquid-cooled engines. There is thus no casting sand to be shaken out. And no need for shake-out, or "freeze," plugs.

"French" horn. Known to musicians simply as "the horn," this sophisticated descendant of the hunting horn, with its soberly beautiful range of tonal colorations and its notorious tendency to betray even the skilled player (perhaps it resents the indignity of a fist up its fistula) is known as the French horn only in English-speaking countries. (To the French, as to musicians, it is simply *le cor,* or "the horn.") How the term "French" got applied to it no one knows. According to Winthrop Sargeant, writing in *The New Yorker* for March 14, 1977 (page 50), the International Horn Society is doing its best to get what Sargeant calls "the absurd adjective 'French'" removed from its name.

Incidentally, ENGLISH HORN (which see) is often mistakenly assumed to derive from a French expression!

"Frisco." Few words enrage a native more than this term for Baghdad-on-the-bay; some hate it with a purple passion. Say "San Francisco" unless you don't mind being classed as a vulgar barbarian.

"From each according to his abilities, to each according to his needs." Not from the *Communist Manifesto*. And not a concept original with Karl Marx (or his coauthor Friedrich Engels). In fact, there is some doubt as to whether the words are Marx's at all. According to Bartlett, the statement is in quotation marks; Bartlett takes this as an indication that Marx may have been quoting or paraphrasing. However, since the statement follows the words "[Let] society inscribe on its banners," the quotation marks are not very firm evidence.

In any case, Marx did not say this until 1875 (the *Manifesto* was first published in 1848), in an essay: "From each according to his ability, to each according to his needs." Much earlier, however, a French radical reformer, Claude Henri, Count of Saint-Simon (1760–1825; he renounced the title at the time of the French Revolution) had said, "The task of each be according to his capacity, the wealth of each be according to his works." Not quite the same sentiment, but close.

As a matter of fact, a major part of the concept can be traced back as far as the King James Bible. From Acts 4:34–35:

> Neither was there any among them that lacked: for as many as were possessors of lands or houses sold them, and brought the prices of the things that were sold,
> And laid them down at the apostles' feet: and distribution was made unto every man according as he had need.

frostbite, treatment of. Perhaps related to whatever perverse impulse leads many to believe that a bucket drawn from the hot-water tap will freeze faster than a cold one (it won't) is the common notion that the way to treat frostbite is to rub snow on the affected area.

This is a fallacy, and a potentially dangerous one. In the words of Cameron C. Bangs, M.D. (see FALLING ASLEEP AND FREEZING TO DEATH),

> once a limb is frozen it should be kept frozen without increasing the amount of freezing, if possible, until it can be properly thawed. Proper thawing is in large vessels of hot water, between 105° and 110°, which I would call hot and not warm. Once the extremity has been thawed it should not be used for walking, feeding, etc., and it should *never* be refrozen as the most severe damage occurs when extremities are thawed and then refrozen. This is the reason that it is rare that we recommend the extremity be thawed in the field or on the mountain, because of the danger of refreezing.

Dr. Bangs adds that advocating the use of such devices as portable hand warmers (or warm rocks, etc.) for thawing frostbite "is incorrect as it would provide very slow thawing which would be more harmful than keeping it frozen and then thawing it rapidly."

G

"Gee, our old La Salle ran great."[1] This line from "Those Were the Days," the song that introduces the popular television show "All in the Family," is not really consistent with the general theme either of the song or the show. Nobody in the Bunkers' economic circumstances would have owned a La Salle, old or new. Though intended as a somewhat less expensive alternative to the Cadillac (as the Bentley was to the Rolls-Royce), the La Salle, built by Cadillac, was nevertheless aimed at an upper-crust, high-income segment of the population.

[1] Lyric by Lee Adams. Used by Permission of owner. © 1971. New Tandem Music Company. All Rights Reserved.

Produced from 1927 to 1940, a La Salle cost some $2,500 at a time when Chevrolets were going for about $500—more than twice the price differential between Cadillac and Chevrolet today. (The cost of a Cadillac these days is about double that of a fully equipped, full-size Chevrolet, not five times as much.)

One La Salle model was a luxurious five-passenger convertible sedan with a V-8 engine—hardly Archie Bunker's kind of car. (The name La Salle was revived briefly in the mid-1950s for an experimental, and fancy, two-seater sports roadster with a V-6 150-horsepower fuel-injected engine. It's even harder to picture the Bunkers in this one.)

The La Salle was discontinued, interestingly—and relevantly—enough when, in 1940, it cost so little less than a Cadillac that its market vanished.

"General" Custer at the Little Big Horn. George Armstrong Custer was not a general when he and more than 200 of his men were killed at the Little Big Horn battlefield in what is now Montana in 1876—hadn't been one for years, as a matter of fact. During the Civil War, or War Between the States, Custer, an 1861 West Point graduate, had become the nation's youngest major general. After the war, he reverted to his regular rank of captain, later advancing to lieutenant colonel. It was in this rank that he served until his death.

The term *massacre,* often applied to the death of Custer and his men, is quite inaccurate. They died in battle.

Gerber baby, origin of. A persistent myth, aided in its propagation by "Ripley's Believe It or Not!" and at least one recent national TV quiz show, is that Humphrey Bogart was the model for the picture—a trademark—used by Gerber Products Company in connection with its extensive line of baby foods.

He wasn't. As sometimes happens, however, there does appear to be a tenuous basis for the belief. John B. Whitlock, director of public relations for Gerber, tells the tale as follows:

It appears that the Humphrey Bogart story arose from the fact that his mother was an accomplished artist and frequently sold drawings and illustrations for commercial purposes. It is entirely possible and, in fact, probable that an early drawing of Humphrey Bogart was used for some baby food advertisement or some baby need illustration early in the 1900's. Gerber baby foods, however, were not introduced until 1928, at which time Humphrey Bogart would have been approximately 29 years old. We are sure, therefore, that the Bogart illustration has never been used for a Gerber baby food ad.

In 1928, when company officials sought an illustration for a proposed national ad to introduce Gerber prepared baby foods, leading artists of the day were invited to submit their work for consideration. Artist Dorothy Hope Smith, then living in the Boston area, sent in a small charcoal sketch of her neighbor's baby asking if this were about the age and size illustration desired. That charcoal sketch became the now famous Gerber baby which is literally known around the world.

For many years, at the request of the family, the identity of the original model has not been general public information. However, in recent years the model herself, Mrs. Ann Turner Cook of Tampa, Florida, has granted several local newspaper interviews in which she is identified as the "Gerber Baby."

gifts for golfers. Those who do not play golf are often unaware that many gadgets advertised (sometimes even in golfing magazines) as ideal gifts for golfers are disallowed by the rules. Two prime examples are pocket range finders, or devices that measure the distance to the flagstick, and clubs whose heads can be adjusted during play.

Other devices that tempt the unknowing at Christmas or birthday time are not illegal but are a waste of money, since no golfer wants them. They are the various gadgets, often designed to be worn on the wrist, that keep track of the score: push a small button and the stroke is registered. The problem is that they don't record the score hole by hole, but only the cumulative total. Thus they deprive the golfer of the pleasure of recalling, over a round of postgame drinks, how beautifully Hole No. 6 was played. They also deprive his or her opponent of the pleasure of pointing out the disaster that occurred on No. 10.

Better make it a Gift Certificate.

gin, cotton. It is probably not true that Eli Whitney once said, "Keep your cotton-picking hands away from my gin."

If he did, however, he was using a word that bears no relation to the essential ingredient in a Martini. "Gin," with reference to the various devices used to separate cotton from its seeds (Whitney's was not the first, merely the most successful), is a contraction of "engine." "Gin" as the name of the beverage comes from *geneva*—not the city, but a corruption of the French *genièvre*, "juniper," source of gin's characteristic flavor.

"Engine" derives from the Latin *ingenium*, from which we also get "ingenuity." In its short form it formerly meant the kind of "engine" used to trap birds or animals, as in Shakespeare's *Henry VI*, Part III, when an enemy of the Duke of York's remarks, as the Duke is struggling with his captors, "Ay, ay, so strives the woodcock with the gin" (act 1, sc. 4, line 61).

glaciers, composition of. Glaciers are composed primarily of ice, all right; but they are not "ice" in the same sense as ice cubes or the substance hockey players skate on. Glacial ice is actually compressed snow; in any region where snowfall exceeds melting, the weight of the snow as it piles up compacts the snow beneath until it becomes ice. In other words, it's primarily the compaction, not the "freezing," that makes a glacier.

gladiators and Nero. With all the bad that can be said of Nero—and there is much, a good deal of which is true—it is also true that he disliked the spectacle of violent death. When he built a wooden amphitheater, a forerunner of the Colosseum, in A.D. 57, he ruled that no gladiators, not even condemned criminals, were to be killed in the various games presented. In effect, the gladiators were to engage in fencing matches.

He could not, apparently, make his policy stick; the taste for blood among the Roman spectators prevailed, and later "games" presented in Nero's reign were bloody enough. But he appears to have bowed to public pressure rather than to his own inclinations.

Many Romans were appalled at the gladiatorial games, incidentally, and spoke out strongly against them.

golf ball, moved. A golf ball can move and still not be regarded as having moved—paradoxical as this sounds. The rules define a moved ball as one that leaves its position *and comes to rest in any other place.* A ball partially embedded might thus be touched and moved; but if it settles back into its original position it hasn't moved, according to the rules.

golf clubs in a bunker. There is absolutely no rule against carrying two or more clubs into a bunker, though it is widely believed that there is. Indeed, the rules specifically permit laying one's whole bag of clubs down *in the hazard,* as long as doing so does not contribute to an improved lie or constitute testing the soil, or sand, in the hazard.

Perhaps even less known to many golfers is that the "unplayable lie" rule can be invoked in a bunker, just as it can anywhere on the course except in a water hazard. The rules permit a ball to be declared "unplayable" at the sole option of the player. That is, the player may pick up and drop his ball within two club heads of where it lay but not nearer the hole, or at any point on the line of flight to the hole behind where it lay. It involves a one-stroke penalty; but many a duffer, caught under the overhanging lip of a bunker, has wasted half a dozen strokes trying to get it out of there—when all he has to do, at the cost of only one stroke, is to move it to where he has a fighting chance. (He cannot, however, move it so far as to be out of the bunker; a ball declared unplayable in a bunker must be dropped in it.)

"Good fences make good neighbors." This phrase, so thoroughly identified with the American poet Robert Frost (1874–1963) that it was placed on the postage stamp issued in his honor, is often misapprehended. It is from one of his most famous poems—"Mending Wall," written (in Great Britain, incidentally) in 1913—but it does not express Frost's sentiment: quite the opposite.

In "Mending Wall" Frost describes the New England custom of neighbors' walking on either side of a fence line to replace any fallen stones. It is not the narrator, but the neighbor, who makes the remark; he is compared to "an old-stone savage armed" and seems to the narrator to move in darkness; he will not "go behind his father's saying" that good fences make good neighbors. The poem's point is that good fences do not necessarily make good neighbors at all —"Before I built a wall I'd ask to know/What I was walling in or walling out," as the poet-narrator says. Assuming that it represents Frost's point of view is to fail to grasp the whole intent of the poem.

Grand Central "Station" (New York). Why the quotation marks? Because there isn't any such place, that's why. Well, there is; but chances are it's not the place you think it is. What almost everybody calls Grand Central Station is really Grand Central *Terminal*. However, as *The New Yorker* for August 6, 1979 (page 26), reminds us, there really is a Grand Central Station in New York; it's where the I.R.T. Lexington Avenue subway stops, close by.

Grand Tetons. One must assume that the shades of more than one French trapper-explorer of the old days in Jackson Hole now and then smile in amusement at the cartological enshrinement of this name for these most awesome mountains south of Yellowstone Park. For surely it must have been a kind of male-chauvinist joke, originally; it translates as "Big Tits."

Gray, Pearl Z. Yes, that was Zane Grey's name. The "Z," true, is for "Zane"; he was born in Zanesville, Ohio, named by his grandfather Colonel Ebenezer Zane. In the context of his time and his writings, it is easy enough to see why Grey chose to drop the "Pearl," though why he changed the spelling from "Gray" to "Grey" is less certain.

A dentist as his father had been, Grey, or Gray, was by no means a product of that Old West he was to romanticize in so many of his books and stories—89 of the former, 213 of the latter. The man whose books, so it has been said, made the West famous created, like Gatsby, his own Platonic image of himself. He had the help of his wife; after he published at his own expense, with money borrowed from a patient, his first book, *Betty Zane* (1903), he married, quit dentistry, and wrote while living on his wife's money. To his credit, he did not—as sometimes happens—abandon her when he achieved success; they were always very close, according to Frank Gruber's *Zane Grey: A Biography* (1970).

Once he had gained a measure of fame, his early interest in the outdoors was expanded to include hunting and fishing trips in many parts of the world. But he maintained enough interest in the trappings of civilization to acquire five residences—three in California, one each in Arizona and Oregon—and to indulge his fascination for big cars; he once bought, says Gruber, not one, but two Lincolns—for cash.

An interesting and little-known sidelight is that, according to Norris F. Schneider's *Zane Grey* (1967), in 1930 he suddenly changed his attitude toward hunting, although he had pursued many animals on his various trips and expeditions. He called for conservation and stopped killing game. He died in 1939.

Great Wall of China as only man-made object visible from moon. A persistent popular notion, perhaps springing from a "Ripley's Believe It or Not!" of many years ago, is that the Great Wall of China is the only man-made structure that can be seen from the moon with the naked eye.

Disturbed that no lunar astronaut had mentioned being able to see the Great Wall, Doug Baker, columnist for the Portland *Oregon Journal,* referred to this popular belief in his column in 1971. Shortly thereafter he got a definitive answer from Captain Alan Bean, the astronaut:

Dear Mr. Baker:

The only thing you can see from the moon is a beautiful sphere mostly white (clouds), some blue (ocean), patches of yellow (deserts) and every once in a while some green vegetation. No man-made object is visible on this scale. In fact, when first leaving earth's orbit and only a few thousand miles away, no man-made object is visible at that point either.

And so it appears, on the best possible authority, that Robert Ripley was wrong.

gunpowder and armored knights. That the introduction of gunpowder into Europe in the thirteenth century spelled the doom of knights and armor and particularly their mounted attacks en masse is a persistent myth. It bears no relationship whatever to the facts.

It was not gunpowder but the longbow that first destroyed the military effectiveness of the armored and mounted knight. Though not, as usually thought, a native English weapon (the Welsh originated it), the longbow was first put to use by the English in a major battle: Morlaix, in France. (Not Crécy, as often said, though it was at

Crécy that the longbow fully proved its mettle.) And it was a fearsome weapon. It still is, as those who have seen it used at target practice in Britain can affirm.

Some of the confusion over the role of the longbow in medieval times may result from the use of the word *artillery* by medieval writers. Froissart, in fact, uses it in his account of the Battle of Crécy in 1346, when Edward III of England routed the French King Philip VI's much larger force. But Froissart meant, as was commonly meant then, crossbows and similar weapons. There were a few English guns at Crécy, more noisy than dangerous; but Froissart refers to them as "kanons."

The longbow owed its effectiveness principally to two factors: the mobility and expertise of the yeoman who wielded it, and its firepower, to use the modern term. The crossbow shot its bolt with great force but was much slower to reload. According to Donald Featherstone, author of *The Bowmen of England* (London, 1967), an English archer could get off as many as twelve shots a minute with a longbow—at an extreme range of 350 yards. (The *Britannica* claims twenty aimed shots a minute; Featherstone is somewhat more conservative in his estimate.)

And this was with an accuracy capable of severing an anchor line, or rope, with four shots at 200 paces, according to one account. When the massed French forces attacked at Crécy, the deadly shower of English arrows disabled and demoralized men and horses. It also made them easy prey as the bowman moved in on his secondary assignment: battering with his sledgehammer-like maul, or carving up with his sword, the helpless fallen warriors.

The cumbersome armor worn by the knight was not much help. There were arrows capable of piercing even plate armor; the commonly employed chain mail offered practically no protection. After Crécy, armor was improved so that it did a better job of deflecting the arrow. But suits of armor still had to be articulated at the joints; these were weak spots. When the fearsomely howling clouds of arrows descended even from a distance, many of them found their way into the vulnerable jointings at shoulder and neck. And many found their way into the horses, who could not be completely armored. A battle horse with an arrow in him, plunging and rearing in agony, is, to say the least, a highly disruptive force.

In terms of speed of firing, the longbow held its advan-

tage even into the nineteenth century. Says Featherstone at
one point (page 177), "It is not outside the bounds of
possibility to claim that the musket used at Waterloo in
1815 was inferior to the longbow used at Agincourt in
1415, both in range and accuracy." Only a few years
before Waterloo, in 1793, one Lieutenant Colonel Lee of
the 44th Regiment advocated the return of the longbow
on the ground that the longbow could discharge four arrows in the time it took to discharge one bullet.

Perhaps, had the American revolutionary troops pos-
sessed the longbow (and the physical prowess and skill that
went with it in medieval England), the British might have
been vanquished even sooner—and with the very weapon
they made famous.

The last recorded use of the longbow in battle, incidentally, was the killing, on May 27, 1940, of a German
soldier by Captain Jack Churchill, in France, with his own
100-pound-draw longbow made of—what else?—yew.

hamburger as German invention. Practically everybody
knows that credit for inventing the hamburger should go
to the good citizens of Hamburg. Not so. True, there was
a Hamburg *steak* (later called a Hamburger steak), and
it apparently originated in Hamburg during the latter part
of the nineteenth century. But incorporating it into a sand-
wich appears to have been an American innovation. And
what, after all, is a hamburger without a bun?

The euphemism "Salisbury steak," by the way, does not
appear to have arisen as an attempt to paint the lily but to
have been coined during World War I as a patriotic gesture,
akin to "Liberty cabbage" for the German "sauerkraut."
German measles even got called "Liberty measles" by a few
superpatriots.

Handel's *Messiah* as Christmas music. No musical work is
more closely associated with the Christmas season than the

soaring oratorio *Messiah*, by George Frederick Handel (1685–1759). It may thus come as something of a surprise that it had nothing to do with the Christmas season when it was composed. It will certainly surprise many that the full title of the work is merely *Messiah;* it is widely and incorrectly recorded as *"The* Messiah."

The composer was German by birth but became a naturalized Englishman in 1726. His name is customarily—and properly—spelled "Handel" in English, but "Händel" in German. The pronunciation "handle" is quite correct, although Germans—or those seeking, perhaps, to make an impression—say (approximately) "hendle."

Handel wrote *Messiah* in the summer of 1741, and it was first performed the following spring—and no, not in connection with Easter. Its premiere, in Dublin, was a benefit for prisoners in jail for debt as well as for a hospital and an infirmary. According to the noted music critic Herbert Kupferberg, enough money was raised to free 142 unfortunate debtors.

The story that Handel wrote his famous *Water Music* in order to get back into the good graces of George I of England is self-evidently false. The Elector of Hanover was Handel's patron in Germany; in 1712, with the Elector's understanding that it was to be a short visit, Handel left for England. But the short visit became, in effect, a desertion; Handel was still in England when, in 1714, his abandoned patron became George I. This may have proved an embarrassment to Handel. The tale is that when the new King planned a royal boating party on the Thames, Handel composed the *Water Music,* engaged some musicians and a barge, and, conducting the orchestra himself, followed the royal boat down the river. So delighted was the King, the story goes, that Handel was at once restored to his favor.

Charming as the tale may be, the fact is that the *Water Music* was not composed until 1717, though it is true that it was written for a royal picnic on the water. George I had long since forgiven Handel and, indeed, granted him a pension of 400 pounds a year, a substantial sum in those days.

harness, to die in. When Winston Churchill spoke of Franklin Roosevelt's death, he said that he "died in harness."

But "harness" here has no reference to horses; originally

it meant a warrior's armor. (Later in this same speech, delivered in the House of Commons in 1945, Churchill uses the expression *battle harness.*) To die in harness means to die with one's armor on, analogous to the Western expression, or at least the Western movie expression, "He died with his boots on." See *Macbeth* (act 5, P. 5, lines 51–52):

> Ring the alarum-bell! Blow, wind! Come, wrack ["ruin"]!
> At least we'll die with harness on our back.

Hawaii. That's the proper name for the fiftieth state to be admitted to the Union. But it also happens to be the name of the largest of the Hawaiian Islands. That is why a resident of Honolulu, on the island of Oahu, never speaks of "going to Hawaii," which is a bit ridiculous since he or she is already *in* Hawaii. Natives always call Hawaii "the big island"—which is not, thus, as sometimes thought, a linguistic affectation designed to separate the *malihini* (newcomer) from the *kamaaina* (one born and raised in Hawaii). Rather, it's simply to avoid confusion.

Hawaii and the South Pacific. Hawaii lies within the tropic zone, though just barely. But it's not in the South Pacific, although many think it is. It lies considerably north of the equator and is thus in the North Pacific Ocean, at about the same latitude as Cuba. Nor is Hawaii a sort of eastern outpost of the Pacific islands; it is west of Tahiti and more than a thousand miles west of the Marquesas.

health foods and additives. A vast amount of misinformation surrounds the current passion for "natural" or "organic" foods and the fear of "chemical additives." But eating only "natural" foods is certainly no guaranteed road to health. After all, a poisonous wild mushroom is about as natural and organic as you can get.

As for the fear of chemicals, Elizabeth M. Whelan, a public health specialist and coauthor (with Dr. Frederick J. Stare) of *Panic in the Pantry: Food Facts, Fads, and Fallacies* (1975), reminds us that all foods, natural or artificial, are composed of chemicals. Coffee, eggs, and melon for breakfast, Ms. Whelan reminds us, involve the consumption, among other things, of methanol, acetaldehyde, ovomucoid, zeaxanthin, succinic acid, anisyl propionate, and malic acid—a list that, if printed on a label, would be almost guaranteed to frighten off an advocate of natural foods.

There is good reason to adopt a healthy skepticism about additives and substances that have been shown to be dangerous. There is no reason at all to assume that just because it's a "chemical" it must be bad.

hens, roosters, and eggs. A surprising number of people believe that, without a rooster, a hen will not lay—lay eggs, that is. H. G. Wells thought so; in his *The Food of the Gods* giant hens live eggless without a rooster. But as Lysander Kemp of the Institute of Latin American Studies, University of Texas, reminds us, hens will lay eggs without a rooster—infertile, true, but eminently edible.

hi-fi, stereo. Although these two terms are often considered synonyms—hi-fi is a stereo is a hi-fi—they are not. "Hi-fi" is an obvious abbreviation for "high fidelity." It early arose in an attempt to distinguish between tuners, amplifiers, speakers, and other components that were designed and built, often by hand, in an effort to reproduce sound as accurately as possible. Such attempts were made long before "stereo," for "stereophonic," became a word in popular usage.

Stereo does not simply mean two (or more) speakers; many a cheap monophonic radio receiver has two speakers. And as early as the 1920s, monophonic high-fidelity equipment often made use of more than one speaker, each reproducing a part of the sound spectrum. Stereo involves two separate sources, or channels; in effect, it means separate circuits for each channel, as well as separate means of reproducing the sounds originally recorded by each channel.

A cheap stereo set may be truly stereo; but it may not even be close to high fidelity, which still depends on the care and skill of assembly and the selection of good component parts.

high blood pressure as disease of age. Not everything is known about hypertension, or high blood pressure; but the belief that it is exclusively a disease of age is false. It can occur in children, which is why some doctors think that a once-a-year blood pressure check is a good idea for the young—even those as young as three years of age.

Particularly among adolescents who may have, or be predisposed to, high blood pressure, salt is a problem. (Salt appears to be a strong contributing factor to high blood pressure; in areas where salt intake is very low, hypertension is rare.) One hamburger-with-potato chips may contain four fifths of the recommended daily intake of salt. There is enough salt naturally present in foods to take care of the body's needs.

Hindenburg disaster. Newsreel films and still photographs of the awesome, swift destruction of the *Hindenburg* have created a widespread impression that most, if not all, of those aboard the ill-fated dirigible perished with the airship. Surprisingly, despite the rapidly spreading fire and subsequent crash, many of the passengers and crew escaped with their lives: fifty-six of ninety-two survived the horror.

Perhaps by association with the *Titanic*, which was on its maiden voyage when it hit that iceberg, the *Hindenburg* is often thought to have burned after its first transatlantic trip. Quite the contrary; when the *Hindenburg* burned at Lakehurst, New Jersey, on May 6, 1937, it had made ten round trips.

Nor was the *Hindenburg* the first large airship to engage in regular passenger-carrying transatlantic service. The *Graf Zeppelin* had made 144 ocean crossings in nine years of successful commercial service between 1928 and 1937, when it was retired from service in favor of the new *Hindenburg*.

It's often said that the refusal of the United States to export helium gas, which is nonexplosive though not quite so buoyant as hydrogen, was a causative factor in the *Hindenburg* disaster. The United States had—and has—a natural supply of helium resulting from discoveries in the Midwest and Texas. Such a supply was so scanty anywhere else in the world that it amounted to a U.S. monopoly.

But the *Graf Zeppelin*, like all German airships, had used hydrogen for almost a decade without accident. As long ago as 1783 it had been used to inflate balloons. And it is widespread (as every schoolchild knows, water is H_2O —that is, a combination of hydrogen and oxygen), cheap, and easy to manufacture. There seemed no reason for the Germans to go to the expense of helium; many years of experience had evolved elaborate safety precautions thought to be—and demonstrated to be—quite adequate.

There were two *Graf Zeppelins*, actually: the first one, just referred to, and its successor. In spite of the *Hindenburg* disaster, the LZ-130 (the *Hindenburg* was the LZ-129, the first *Graf Zeppelin* the LZ-127; the LZ-128 never got past the blueprint stage) was pushed to completion in September of 1938. It too was named the *Graf Zeppelin;* and this one was, true, designed for helium. But the international situation had so much worsened by this time that helium was unobtainable by purchase from the United States. So the new *Graf Zeppelin* also flew with hydrogen —successfully enough, although it never got into commercial service.

As World War II became imminent, the German government abandoned its airship program. In April of 1940 both the old decommissioned *Graf Zeppelin* (the LZ-127) and the new *Graf Zeppelin* (the LZ-130) were dismantled for their duralumin and steel. The Zeppelin company went into the production of various war matériel. It was destroyed by Allied bombing in 1944.

Himmler, Heinrich, as founder of Gestapo. The notorious Himmler was head of the Gestapo (from *Ge*heim *Sta*ats *Po*lizei, or secret state police) for years. But he was not its first head, nor did he originate it. Hermann Goering was responsible for its creation in 1933, and he placed it under his own authority. It was a year later that Himmler took over direction of the Gestapo.

Hippocratic oath. This amiable and well-meaning antique has no legal status and is not required of those receiving the M.D. degree. Indeed, says Lawrence K. Altman, M.D., writing in the *New York Times* for May 1, 1979, many of today's accepted medical practices are inconsistent with the oath; for example, a strict interpretation would bar telling an insurance company a patient's symptoms and thus deny the patient reimbursement.

Nobody knows how many American doctors have taken the oath; in Sweden, it has not been taken by doctors since 1887 and, says Dr. Altman, as of 1964 only two British medical schools included it as a part of the graduation ceremonies.

"his name is mud." An American myth almost as persistent as the one that has display clocks reading 8:18 because that was the hour Lincoln died is that the expression "his name is mud" derives from Dr. Samuel Mudd, the physician who set John Wilkes Booth's broken leg.

The fact is that the expression "his name is mud" dates back to the 1820s and derives from an even older meaning of "mud," according to Eric Partridge—a dull fellow or a fool. Partridge cites an 1823 quotation: "And his name is mud!"

Samuel Mudd's grandson, Dr. Richard Mudd, has spent more than fifty years trying to rectify what he regards as the injustice shown his grandfather, who was found guilty of conspiracy to assassinate Lincoln and sent to a Florida prison. (He was later given a Presidential pardon for his heroism in fighting a prison epidemic of yellow fever.)

Hitler's victory jig. Countless millions of moviegoers saw, or thought they saw, Adolf Hitler dance a silly little jig after the French surrender at Compiègne in June of 1940. More millions have seen it in various reruns of World War II news films.

But it was—and remains—a fake. True, Hitler made what Laurence Stallings, who told the story in *Esquire* for October 1958, calls "a small leap of astonishment at himself" following the signing of the armistice. Allied propagandists, using Nazi film sources, "looped" the film; that is, they took that one little hop and ran it over and over again while duplicating the result. (A similar technique is well known to present-day TV technicians. Everyone has seen a controversial play in a football game "frozen" and then rerun, sometimes repeatedly. The process by which cats are made to appear to dance in a catfood commercial is another example.)

Stallings, coauthor with Maxwell Anderson of *What Price Glory?*, was editor in chief of the Movietone newsreel system when he saw the Hitler "jig." Like many other experienced technicians, he spotted the trick at once and later confirmed his observation by talking to the man responsible: John Greierson. The reason for the deceit is obvious: Hitler was made to look, again in Stallings's words, like "the sissiest, most ludicrous conqueror that ever lived."

"hoi polloi, the." Those who know Greek like to point out that the expression is correctly rendered simply as "hoi

polloi," since the Greek article *hoi* means "the." New
Mexicans sometimes make the same point with reference to
a well-known Santa Fe hotel, La Fonda, since *la* is "the" in
Spanish; thus to speak of staying at "the La Fonda" is
tautological. Those who err, or are believed to err, in the
first instance have one of the most scholarly of English
poets on their side: John Dryden. In his "Essay on Dramatic Poesy" he uses the term "the hoi polloi." Those who
err in the second instance have no one but tourists in their
corner. In any event, there are probably more important
things in the world to worry about.

"Home is the sailor. . . ." The last two lines of Robert Louis
Stevenson's poem "Requiem" are almost invariably misquoted. This is how they should read:

> Home is the sailor, home from sea,
> And the hunter home from the hill.

Stevenson did *not* write "home from *the* sea."

hot cross buns. Thoroughly identified though they may be
with the Christian celebration of Lent, hot cross buns are
of thoroughly pagan origin. Ancient Romans ate bread
marked with crosses—the *Britannica* suggests that the cross
might have been intended to suggest the four quarters of
the moon—at public sacrifices. The pagan Saxons also had
bread marked with a cross, as did ancient Mexicans and
Peruvians. So widespread was the custom that its adoption
by early Christians is simply another example of the common practice of adapting old pagan ritual and symbol to
Christian belief.

Those inclined to criticize such blending of the old and
the new should, perhaps, take a look at Romans 13:7:
"Render therefore to all their dues: tribute to whom tribute
is due; custom to whom custom. . . ."

I

ice cream and Martha Washington. A tale sometimes told is that Martha Washington was the first to serve ice cream to her guests. Sometimes it is said that she was the first to serve it in the White House; but neither Martha nor George ever lived in the White House, for the most obvious of reasons: it wasn't ready for occupancy until 1800 and George Washington's tenure as President ended in 1797. (Washington laid the cornerstone in 1792 after picking out the site; the first occupants were John Adams and his wife. Even after eight years, it still wasn't finished; it's said that Mrs. Adams hung her washing in the uncompleted East Room.)

In 1784 George Washington did order a "cream machine for ice," according to his expense ledger. If such a machine was available to him—and Martha—obviously others were already making and enjoying ice cream.

And Cynthia Wichmann reminds us that according to *Cooks, Gluttons & Gourmets: A History of Cookery,* by Betty Wason (1962), ice cream was introduced into the French court in 1533 by Catherine de Médics' Florentine cooks, who accompanied her when she moved to France to become the Queen of Henry II. (See MAJORETTES AS TWENTIETH-CENTURY INVENTION.)

Another authority, Paul Dickson, says, however, that something very like ice cream was served at the coronation feast of Henry V of England in 1413, more than a century earlier.

Ms. Wason says that Thomas Jefferson was "one of the first to serve ice cream at a state banquet. He learned to make ice cream while in France, writing down the recipe in his own hand. On one occasion he served for dessert at the White House crisp, hot pastry with a center of frozen ice cream." One wonders if he called it Baked Washington.

"If nominated, I will not run. If elected, I will not serve."
This is not what General William Tecumseh Sherman (1820–91) said. His actual words, spoken to the Republican National Convention on June 5, 1884, were, "I will not accept if nominated and will not serve if elected."

A kind of folk editing, sometimes for the better, seems to apply to famous remarks. Churchill's reputed "blood, sweat, and tears" is another example. His actual words were "blood, toil, tears, and sweat."

Even more famous is General Sherman's reputed remark, "War is hell." Sherman could not remember ever having uttered it. Some authorities think it comes from a speech Sherman made to a GAR convention at Columbus, Ohio, on August 11, 1880: "There is many a boy here today who looks on war as all glory, but, boys, it is all hell."

Bartlett, which gives the "War is hell" source as the *National Tribune* (Washington, D.C.) for November 26, 1914, says that Sherman used these words, or is supposed to have done so, in an 1879 graduation speech at Michigan Military Academy; Bartlett suggests a comparison with Robert E. Lee's remark, said to have been made in 1862. But Lee's words are more subtle, perhaps more sophisticated—and certainly more ambivalent: "It is well that war is so terrible, or we should get too fond of it."

igloo. Does not mean, and never has meant, only the kind of dome-shaped structure made of blocks of snow that most people associate with "igloo." Nor do Eskimos customarily inhabit such a structure; indeed, many Eskimos have never seen an "igloo," except, perhaps, in the movies. "Igloo" (Eskimo *iglu* or *igdlu*) simply means "house."

"I have seen the future, and it works." Not said by the American journalist and poet John Reed (1887–1920), though often attributed to him. Lincoln Steffens (1866–1936) said (note the actual phrasing), "I have been over into the future, and it works." His remark was in answer to a question from Bernard Baruch (1870–1965) about Steffens's visit to Russia in 1919.

impeachment. No legal term in the U.S. Constitution is more often misunderstood than the "impeachment" of a President. Though popular usage has led at least one reputable dictionary to accept impeachment and conviction as synonyms, in Constitutional terms they are anything but. The House of Representatives brings the charges: that's impeachment. The Senate tries the case; and just as the House has sole power to impeach, so only the Senate can convict.

In spite of numberless statements to the contrary, Andrew Johnson did not "escape impeachment by only one vote." He most certainly was impeached and by a very large (and straight-party) vote of the House: 126 to 47. A simple majority of a quorum is all that is required for impeachment; another common misconception is that impeachment requires a two-thirds vote.

What President Johnson did escape, and by only one vote, was *conviction*. Conviction does require a two-thirds majority—not, however, of all members but only of those present. Those present must, of course, constitute a quorum; but since the Constitution defines a quorum as a majority, it would be possible for conviction to result if only a third of the total Senate membership voted the defendant "guilty." (Total members, 100; quorum, 51; two thirds of 51, 34.) Impeachment, as a matter of fact, could be accomplished by only a *quarter* of the total membership of the House, since it requires only a majority of a quorum (total House membership, 435; quorum, 218; majority of quorum, 110). Admittedly, however, it is not likely that very many, if any, Senators or Representatives would absent themselves from such important proceedings.

The vote for Johnson's conviction in the Senate was 35 to 19, one short of the necessary two thirds. Ironically, Andrew Johnson himself misused the word "impeachment." In a letter, he spoke of the vote on impeachment as a close one. As just noted, it was anything but that. The vote to convict was close, all right; it could not, in fact, have been closer.

It is often said that the late Senator Joseph McCarthy was the subject of an impeachment attempt. He was not. There was an attempt to expel him from the Senate, the Constitutional right of both Senate and House. Expulsion requires a two-thirds vote. But this is not the same as impeachment. However, McCarthy did not go scot free, he was censured by the Senate.

Another common misapprehension is that impeachment and conviction automatically carry with them some kind of criminal penalty. They do not; the consequences are simply removal from office and, in the words of the Constitution, "disqualification to hold and enjoy any office of honor, trust, or profit under the United States." However, the Constitution specifically notes that impeachment and conviction do not exempt the person convicted from further "indictment, trial, judgment and punishment, according to law." So specious were the politically motivated charges against Johnson that it is highly doubtful that, even had he been convicted, any further legal processes would have ensued.

"I must get out of these wet clothes and into a dry martini." Attributed by Bartlett to Alexander Woollcott (1887–1943), though with uncharacteristically incomplete documentation ("From *Reader's Digest*").

But if Woollcott said it, he got it from Robert Benchley (1889–1945), who in turn heard it from a press agent. Benchley liked the line, said he wished he'd said it—and so he did, in one of his films.

income tax, origin of. It is certainly true that "a heavy progressive or graduated income tax" is one of the measures proposed by Marx and Engels in the *Communist Manifesto* (1848). It is certainly untrue that this is where the proposal was first advanced. As a matter of fact, William Pitt (1759–1806), the brilliant—and titled—British Prime Minister, both proposed and succeeded in implementing an income tax in 1798. It was not repealed until 1815.

And in 1842, another notable Prime Minister, Robert Peel (1788–1850), also titled, revived the income tax. So don't blame the *Manifesto*, come April 15; William Pitt and Robert Peel got there first.

Index Expurgatorius. As Fowler reminds us, often used loosely to mean the list of books that the Roman Catholic Church forbids its members to read, or allows Roman Catholics to read only in expurgated form. However, what most people call the Index Expurgatorius is properly Index Librorum Prohibitorum ("List of prohibited books"); the Index Expurgatorius lists the offending *passages*.

Indians and alcohol. An old—and still common—belief is that American Indians cannot tolerate alcoholic beverages as well as whites can. In Western folklore, only somewhat higher on the scale than the frontier renegade who took up with a squaw and sold out to the redskins was the frontier renegade who risked driving the hostiles into orgies of insane rapine by selling them firewater.

However, a recent study by Lynn J. Bennion, M.D., and Ting-Kai Li, M.D., disputes the assumption that there are racial differences between American Indians and whites in terms of the rate of alcohol metabolism. (The faster alcohol is metabolized, which is to say "digested," the more tolerance an individual has for it.)

What the doctors found is that there is no difference in the rate of alcohol metabolism between American Indians and American whites. Their results were published in the *New England Journal of Medicine* for January 1976 (vol. 294, no. 1, pages 9–13). Entitled "Alcohol Metabolism in American Indians and Whites: Lack of Racial Differences in Metabolic Rate and Liver Alcohol Dehydrogenase," the study was sponsored in part by the U.S. Public Health Service. Cooperating were the Phoenix Clinical Research Section of the National Institute of Arthritis, Metabolism and Digestive Diseases, and the departments of medicine and biochemistry of Indiana University.

The U.S. Department of Health, Education, and Welfare (HEW) estimated in 1971 that the prevalence of alcoholism among American Indians is at least twice the national average. If this is so, other causes than any inherent inability to tolerate alcohol would seem to be involved.

"I rob banks because that's where the money is." Attributed to Willie Sutton, the most publicized bank robber since Jesse James, this remark was not made by him. According to the CBS program "60 Minutes" (August 8, 1976), Sutton said that a reporter made it up and attributed it to him.

"It is a far, far better thing that I do, than I have ever done; it is a far, far better rest that I go to, than I have ever known." These are the final words of Charles Dickens's *A Tale of Two Cities,* and—perhaps with one exception—the best-known quotation from it. The exception is the opening; *A Tale of Two Cities* is unusual in that both its opening and its closing words are famous. (It opens, "It was the best of times, it was the worst of times, it was the age of wisdom, it was the age of foolishness, it was the epoch of belief, it was the epoch of incredulity," and so on, oxymoronically, to the end of the paragraph.)

The closing words are spoken by Sydney Carton, right? Wrong. They are not really spoken by anybody, in spite of the fact that they are in quotation marks in the novel. Here is the paragraph that introduces the "remarks" which end the book. Carton has just been guillotined (the "axe"):

> One of the most remarkable sufferers by the same axe —a woman—had asked at the foot of the same scaffold, not long before, to be allowed to write down the thoughts that were inspiring her. *If he* [Carton] *had given any utterance to his, and they were prophetic, they would have been these* [italics added].

Perhaps the fact that Ronald Colman, in the old and memorable film of *Tale,* does speak the words has helped perpetuate the mistaken belief that they were actually said by Sydney Carton.

"It is later than you think." Carved on countless sundials of the sort sold by roadside vendors who feature mama goose and her goslings cast in concrete, this phrase was originated by Robert W. Service. Yes, the same Robert W. Service, beloved of millions if never found in college anthologies, who gave us the gunned-down Dan McGrew and the incinerated Sam McGee.

As Ben Woodhead, whose column in the *Beaumont* (Texas) *Journal* ("Who Said That?") is a popular feature, points out, Service was capable of reasonably profound thoughts now and then. The full quotation, the famous second line of which is also the poem's title:

> Ah! the clock is always slow.
> It is later than you think.

J

Jackson, Rachel, and her corncob pipe. If Mrs. Andrew Jackson smoked a corncob, she didn't do it in the White House, in spite of the American myth that has her doing so. She died before Jackson was inaugurated.

Jacobites. Many are puzzled as to why supporters of the Stuarts, notably of James II and the "Old Pretender" James III of Scotland in the eighteenth century, were known as Jacobites. The term derives from the Latin for "James": Jacobus.

Japanese as clever copycats. When the Japanese first entered Western markets, they copied everything from beer to violins. This gave rise to the myth that they could only imitate the work of others. This myth surely had something to do with the problems American fliers encountered during World War II in the Pacific. The Japanese Zero fighter plane was, in fact, so far from being a copy of any American or other design that it was not at first taken very seriously; by American standards it was underarmored, far too light, and thus, by implication, too fragile to stand up to American aircraft. These very factors, however, were responsible for the maneuverability and speed that made the Zero so unexpectedly formidable in combat. It would have been better if the Japanese *had* copied an American design. As it was, the Zero was a very successful original. (In the long run, obviously, not successful enough. But it took a while for American pilots to learn that here was an opponent to be feared, and a good many lives must have been unnecessarily lost because of the persistence of the myth.)

With the advent of Japanese cars, cameras, and electronics, this myth has reached the vanishing point.

Jonah and the whale. Nowhere in the (King James) Bible is there any reference to Jonah's being swallowed by a whale (see Jonah 1 and 2). Whatever swallowed Jonah—who gets tossed into the sea at his own suggestion, by the way —is described as a "great fish."

K

kangaroo rat. Neither kangaroo nor rat, this small Western rodent of the family Heteromyidae is, rather, a mouse with a difference. The difference, and what gives rise to the popular name, is that the kangaroo rat travels in leaps and bounds on oversized rear legs, using its tail for balance.

Kipling, the Whiffenpoof Song, and Mandalay. If there are Yale men or women who have read Kipling's *Barrack-Room Ballads*, they are surely aware that "The Whiffenpoof Song" is a fairly direct steal from "Gentlemen-Rankers." If they are ever subjected to garden-party baritones belting out "The Road to Mandalay," they should also be made aware that Kipling did not know whereof he spake. Or so at least says Paul Theroux in his fascinating book *The Great Railway Bazaar* (1975):

> . . . the fact is that Kipling never set foot in the place [Mandalay], and his experience in Burma was limited to a few days in 1889, when his ship stopped in Rangoon.

koala bears. The cuddly koala is not a bear. Like the kangaroo, it's a marsupial. Its diet, rather charmingly, is eucalyptus leaves.

"kudos." *Time* magazine did not invent this word—far from it. Kudos is Greek, straight out of Homer, to whom it meant "glory," as in "the great glory of the Achaeans." Early nineteenth-century British university students used it as slang, in the way that *mater* for "mother" and *pater* for "father" became part of student talk.

"Kudos" is not, as almost everyone seems to think, a plural; it just happens to end in "s," like "homotaxis." So although it may sound a bit strange, "Kudos is due Leslie Botz" is the correct form when you want Leslie to take a bow.

L

"Lafayette, we are here." General John Pershing, to whom this famous remark is almost always attributed, wrote in 1931 that he could not recall having said it. It was certainly said (on July 4, 1917) by Charles E. Stanton, chief disbursing officer for the American Expeditionary Forces in France, whom General Pershing had sent to speak on behalf of the AEF in ceremonies held at the Tomb of Lafayette in a Paris cemetery. Stanton said it again on Bastille Day (July 14) of the same year.

An American correspondent, Naboth Hedin, maintained, however, that he had himself heard Pershing say "Lafayette, we are here" when Pershing visited the tomb on June 14, 1917. A possible explanation of the discrepancy is that the remark was current at the time of Pershing's arrival in Paris; it was the kind of comment that would occur to a good many. It would not be the first time that an apt saying has been attributed not to its unknown or obscure originator but to someone of note.

"Lance," the superpoison. A fascinating case history of how misconceptions are born, grow, and spread is revealed in a story from the (Portland) *Oregon Journal* for February 3, 1977. This is what happened.

In Killeen, Texas, the police got a tip from a drug addict under treatment for an overdose of cocaine. The addict said that a deadly substance called "Lance" was being used to "cut" heroin and cocaine. The Killeen police passed the tip along to an Arizona Customs Service border investigator.

From there, apparently, the story was relayed to the customs office in St. Louis. Then the *Oregon Journal* received a UPI story containing a customs service version of the tale; the story said that the St. Louis customs people had learned that "Lance" was being used to cut heroin and

118

cocaine—and added it was so deadly that agents should not even open bags of narcotics but should send them sealed to laboratory specialists.

Next, in apparent confirmation, the *Journal* heard from the chairman of the Multnomah County Board of Commissioners, whose headquarters are in Portland. County officials, said the chairman, had been warned to be on the lookout for Lance, which was being mysteriously mailed to various government offices; the chairman said it was a powder, like talc, that would instantly kill anyone tasting it and would damage the brain irreversibly even if it was merely smelled. The warning, said the chairman, had come from federal sources.

Sources? Were other "sources" than the Customs Service involved? The *Journal* called the federal Food and Drug Administration. No, it wasn't the FDA. However, the FDA did relay a Postal Service internal message, addressed to Postal Service officials, saying that Lance was being mailed to government officials.

But the Postal Service had not based its message on what came out of Texas by way of Arizona and St. Louis; it had got *its* tip from the customs office at Rochester, New York —which, presumably, had heard from St. Louis. Nobody, as the story grew with each relaying, bothered to check its authenticity, except for the *Oregon Journal*.

The first Portland warning went out on Tuesday. By Thursday it was ended: the FDA, the Postal Service, and the U.S. Customs Service repudiated their warnings. It was all a false alarm.

Turned out that there is, true enough, something called "Lance." But it's not some kind of deadly nerve gas, or anything like it; it's a crowd-control substance available on the commercial market.

So it all started with the obviously unverified remark of a drug addict under treatment. See Bartlett, under either "Acorns" or "Oaks."

laws, "funny." The publication of Dick Hyman's *The Trenton Pickle Ordinance and Other Bonehead Legislation* in 1976 revived an interest in laws that on their faces seem absurd.

But many laws that seem foolish (especially when put into summary form) have, or once had, a good reason.

One of Mr. Hyman's entries points out that it is illegal to hunt elk on Main Street in Ouray, Colorado.

A prohibition against hunting elk on Main Street may seem amusing to those who live in White Plains. But many a Western town, like Ouray ("You-ray"), is so nestled in wilderness that elk—or deer, bear, and bobcats for that matter—may well appear on Main Street occasionally. Some hunters are trigger-happy; hence, no doubt, the law.

Fortunately Lewiston, Idaho, has never had a law on its books, so far as is known, prohibiting the shooting of elephants on Main Street. Otherwise the mayor of Lewiston, many years ago, might have spent some time in the pokey. For he did indeed, to the certain knowledge of this writer, who was there at the time, shoot an elephant on Main Street. The unhappy creature had escaped from a visiting circus and rampaged, probably because of heat and thirst. (Temperatures as high as 115° have been recorded in Lewiston.) The mayor was a physician and big-game hunter; his was the only elephant gun in town. One can only speculate on what might have happened had the elephant gone wild in Walla Walla.

"It is a criminal offense in Massachusetts," reads another of Mr. Hyman's items, "to wear a costume while collecting a debt." Though the image of Harlequin pursuing a reluctant debtor is not without its amusing aspects, it seems fairly certain that this law has a point. It is no doubt designed to prevent bill collectors from dressing like sheriffs or deputies, the better to frighten the hapless. Mr. Hyman also mentions that it is illegal to use dynamite for the purpose of catching fish in Illinois. As a matter of fact, it is illegal just about everywhere. And with every reason; devices designed to explode underwater will stun or kill, and bring to the surface, every fish within range, as criminal poachers know well.

Sometimes absurd laws get onto the books because someone's original purpose went awry. An interesting example is one of the most often quoted of legal absurdities: the Kansas law that reads, "When two trains meet at a crossing, both shall come to a full stop, and neither shall proceed until the other has gone." According to Mr. Hyman, this was deliberately added as a rider in order to kill a bill. Unfortunately, the bill passed; and, thus, so did the rider.

A local South Carolina ordinance requires horses to wear pants. Ridiculous, no? But as a matter of fact, a local

regulation in Oregon requires horses to wear "diapers" within certain areas of the high forest drainage basin that supplies Portland with its drinking water.

The habits of horses are not such as to bring delight to those in charge of ensuring a supply of unpolluted water to a major metropolitan area. Someone had seen the diaper-like devices used on horses in Tennessee (or, perhaps, South Carolina). They did the job, so they were installed on the Portland watershed horses; and they are still used when horses help with the logging. Those who drink Portland's water would not have it otherwise.

lemmings, death march of. As useful metaphorically as the mythological ostrich with head in sand, the suicidal lemming lives in legend. Lemmings want to survive, however, just like other creatures. What apparently happens is that periodically the lemming, which is fecklessly fecund, over-crowds its habitat and outeats its food supply. So, like any sensible animal, it leaves the hills of Norway and Sweden for greener, or at least better, pastures in the tidelands. On the way, the lemmings frequently swim across small streams. A good many of them apparently misjudge the ocean, if and when they reach it (not many do; most die along the way) and simply go out too far to make it back to shore. People sometimes do that too, but without becoming metaphors.

lighting a cigar with a $100 bill. Or a thousand-dollar one, for that matter. This grandiose gesture can be accomplished at no cost whatever. U.S. paper money that has been burned or otherwise damaged can be redeemed at any Federal Reserve bank—if, that is, more than half the original bill survives in recognizable form. So just be certain to blow out the flame in time. Nor is there anything illegal about it; no law forbids setting money afire.

lights dimming at moment of electrocution. Fixed in American mythology is the notion that when the switch is thrown and the first jolt hits the condemned man, the lights all over the prison dim.

Dramatic, yes; true, no. An electric chair takes over 2,000 volts, at amperages varying from four to eight. It has to have its own power supply, apart from the lighting circuits.

What the electric chair does, in effect, is to create a deliberate short circuit, not fused. Hence it would not be possible to connect it to the fused circuits that supply regular power. Further, penologists point out that few situations would be more likely to induce terrible tensions and anxieties, with all their potential for trouble, than to have a prison full of inmates sitting around waiting for that fateful dimming of the lights. In any case, it doesn't happen, no matter how many times you may see it on the silver screen or the TV tube.

"little band of willful men . . ." Woodrow Wilson said something *like* this, but he was not referring to those who opposed U.S. participation in the League of Nations, although this is commonly believed. He was actually talking about a "group" of eleven Senators who filibustered against a bill authorizing the arming of U.S. merchant vessels before America's entry into World War I. His complete remark was "A little group of willful men, representing no opinion but their own, have rendered the great Government of the United States helpless and contemptible."

These "willful men" were led by Senators Robert La Follette and George Norris.

"live" TV and radio call-in talk shows. Almost everyone knows that most big television shows are taped rather than live. But many are unaware that "call-in" shows on TV or radio—that is, programs during which listeners are invited to telephone the host or guests with on-the-spot questions —are not so "live" as they appear to be.

Because of fear that a caller may use language not regarded as suitable or that may invite a lawsuit for slander, almost all such programs use a "tape delay." In radio, the caller's comments are put on tape which, by a process analogous to "looping" (see HITLER'S VICTORY JIG), is held back for some five to seven seconds before being put on the air.

A technician or director in the control booth can thus hear what is said before it gets on the air and invoke such censorship as is deemed expedient. Television call-in shows achieve the same result by slightly different means: two machines, one of which does the recording and then feeds the program material, after the requisite delay, to the machine that broadcasts it.

Those who have called such programs and have wondered why they are always asked to turn off the radio or television set while they are talking now know the real reason. It has nothing to do with "audio interference" or "feedback" in the usual senses. Rather, a person watching or listening to himself or herself saying on the air what has actually been said several seconds before is likely to become so disoriented as to lapse into incoherence.

"lynch"—origin of term. "Lynch" is almost universally regarded as eponymous—that is, the common noun "lynch" comes directly from the proper noun for a person named Lynch, just as BOYCOTT (which see) comes from Captain Charles Boycott. But there are so many claimants for the "honor" of being the one whose name gave us "lynch" that it seems difficult, if not impossible, to determine exactly which Lynch it was—if any.

Was it Charles Lynch, a justice of the peace in Bedford County, Virginia, who in the 1780s more or less took the law into his own hands? Or William Lynch of Pittsylvania County, Virginia, senior justice of the Pittsylvania county court? Or even a fifteenth-century Irishman named Lynch who shows up in various old legends involving summary "justice"?

Both Mencken and the *Oxford English Dictionary* believe that the weight of evidence favors the Pittsylvania Lynch, William. But whether William or Charles, the fact is that neither behaved in the manner associated with lynch mobs. Both are said to have acted out of necessity when roving bands of thieves, aided by Loyalists (or Tories) and the British Army, made life miserable for the law-abiding in parts of Virginia during pre-Revolutionary and Revolutionary times. In each case, the difficulty of getting prisoners to trial at the nearest court—they were usually intercepted and freed by their friends, by Loyalists, or by English troops—led to quasi-legal trials by the arresting magistrates. But apparently legal formalities were strictly observed; there were no "lynchings" in terms of what the word came to mean.

There is another problem in attempting to assess the origin of "lynch." An old English word often spelled "linch" and going back at least to 1600 meant to punish by whipping or flogging. And this punishment was sometimes imposed by the lynch "courts" of Virginia. So it may be that "lynch" goes back much further than either of the two persons named Lynch who are almost always said to have been responsible for the word.

M

macadam. This common noun, derived from John Loudon McAdam (1756–1836), Scottish inventor and engineer whose pioneering ventures into roadbuilding were mostly in England, is not a synonym for "asphalt" or "asphalt surfaced," as is very commonly believed. "Macadam" is a method of construction, not a building material.

McAdam rejected the large stones and loose earth often characteristic of roads before his time; he used a 1-foot layer of broken stone, as cubical as possible and of such dimensions as to pass through a 2½-inch ring but not a 2-inch one, placed on a very firm subsoil.

It is the practice of using asphalt or similar material as binder on the surface of a macadam road that has no doubt led to the incorrect assumption that "macadam" and "asphalt" mean the same thing.

McCoy, the "real." In spite of popular belief, the expression "the real McCoy" did not originate in connection with the fighter Kid McCoy (welterweight champion 1896; real name Norman Selby). McCoy himself helped to spread the story. He said that once, when he was having a drink with a lady friend in a saloon, a drunk started annoying the lady. McCoy tried to warn the drunk, who would not believe he was being menaced by the Kid himself. So McCoy finally tapped him one, or so he said. When the stranger came back to his senses, he remarked, "It's the real McCoy, all right."

It seems clear, however, that McCoy's name became associated with an expression that was common long before he gained fame as a boxer. *The Scottish National Dictionary*

(1965) says that Messrs. G. Mackay, whisky distillers of
Edinburgh, touted its product as "the real Mackay" beginning in 1870, and deduces that the expression was current
before that date. (The application to allegedly first-rate
booze certainly endured for decades: during the years of
Prohibition in the United States "the real McCoy" or just
"the McCoy" was the most common assurance made for
suspect liquor.)

Some believe that "real" is a corruption of Reay, in
Sutherland, Scotland. The Mackays of Reay laid claim to
being the principal branch of the family, and it is suggested
that there was a gradual transition from "the Reay Mackays" to "the real Mackay."

On the other hand, the phrase is found with other names
and spellings—McKie and Macoy, for example—and the
search for the *real* McCoy continues.

Mack Sennett as originator of pie in the face. It was not
Mack Sennett who invented the comic, or presumed to be
comic, pie in the face. Nor was it Charlie Chaplin, although he was indeed, by his own account, the first to deliver a pie in this fashion. Willie Hammerstein, son of
the first Oscar Hammerstein, originated the idea. The story
is told by Lillian Ross in the May 22, 1978 issue of *The
New Yorker* on page 102 of her "Reporter at Large" story
about Chaplin, whom she quotes as remarking that when
he was with the Fred Karno troupe in 1911, he acted the
part of a disruptive drunk in a box in the audience.

At one point, as part of his act, Chaplin would knock
over another actor, a boy, in the box. Willie Hammerstein
suggested doing it with a pie. Chaplin did; it got a big
laugh and became a comic fixture later made famous by
Sennett, for whom Chaplin went to work after leaving the
Karno troupe.

Maginot Line, the. Named for André Maginot, yes; but not
his idea. Maginot, Minister of War in 1929, merely has-
tened the implementation of the ill-fated defensive fortifications that had first been proposed in 1925 by Paul Pain-
levé.

majorettes as twentieth-century American innovation.
Catherine de Médicis (1519–89), Queen of France, is remembered for her part in planning the notorious St. Bar-

tholomew's Day massacre in 1572. Those looking for her brighter side might like to know that she also seems to have been responsible for the first majorettes: a troupe of young ladies who performed various majorette-type maneuvers at the court of the Louvre.

manna from heaven. Whatever the "manna" of the Old Testament was—and a good many scholars have spent a good deal of time trying to puzzle it out—its use as a synonym for unexpected good fortune of the highest order needs an important qualification. The Israelites got mighty tired of it in fairly short order, as is evident from Numbers 11:5–6:

> We remember the fish, which we did eat in Egypt freely; the cucumbers, and the melons, and the leeks, and the onions, and the garlick:
> But now our soul is dried away: there is nothing at all, besides this manna, before our eyes.

To which complaint the Lord is less than sympathetic (18–20):

> . . . the Lord will give you flesh, and ye shall eat. Ye shall not eat one day, nor two days, nor five days, neither ten days, nor twenty days;
> But even a whole month, until it come out at your nostrils.

Perhaps the Lord's comment above is the ancestor of a common saying: We ate that stuff until it came out our ears.

marathon. Everybody knows that the Olympic marathon derives from the ancient Greek games, which featured such a race, something over 26 miles long. The Greeks were commemorating the valiant Pheidippides, or Philippides, who in 490 B.C. ran from Marathon to Athens, gasped out news of the glorious victory of the Greeks over the Persians, and then fell dead.

Not any of this is true—if we take the word of the only contemporary, or nearly contemporary, account, that of Herodotus, who was born just before the war with the Persians. Herodotus says that Pheidippides ran 150 miles from Marathon to Sparta, not 26 from Marathon to Athens; his purpose was to ask the Spartans for help against the common enemy. They agreed but got to Marathon too late; Miltiades, the Greek general, had already managed to defeat the Persians on his own.

The story that Pheidippides ran to Athens from Marathon and then dropped dead arose long after the date of the (itself even more remarkable) 150-mile race described by Herodotus. More than five hundred years later, Plutarch (c. 46–120) was to tell the story of a runner named Eucles (not Pheidippides) who expired after the Marathon-to-Athens run. Lucian (c. 125–180) also tells the tale—but attributes the feat to one Philippides, which may or may not represent a misspelling of Pheidippides.

Nor is this all. According to John Hopkins's *The Marathon,* published in London in 1966, the Greeks didn't even care very much for long-distance running; in the ancient Olympic games, in fact, no such races were included, the longest being about 2¾ miles. Hopkins remarks that Ladas, one of the winners of this "long" race commemorated in Greek verse, fell dead at its completion—no great argument, says Hopkins, for Greek stamina or training.

"Marie" Celeste, mystery of. The most famous unexplained disappearance at sea took place in 1872—and nowhere near the Bermuda Triangle, incidentally. But the ship involved was not the *Marie Celeste,* but the *Mary Celeste.* As Lawrence Kusche, author of *The Bermuda Triangle Mystery—Solved,* points out, not only the name "Marie" but many of the "facts" about the mysterious disappearance of all persons aboard derive not from the event itself but from a work of fiction based on the event called "J. Habakuk Jephson's Statement." The story, first published anonymously, appeared in the January 1884 issue of the *Cornhill Magazine* some twelve years after the disappearance of the *Mary Celeste.* In the story, the name of the ship was given as the *Marie Celeste.* Its author was a young unknown. He was not destined to remain unknown, however; his name was Arthur Conan Doyle.

"Mark Twain." It is usually assumed that this most famous of American pseudonyms originated with Samuel L. Clemens, who made it his own. Clemens, however, did not take the credit for this pen name; according to his account in Chapter 50 of *Life on the Mississippi* (1883), it had originally been used by a Captain Isaiah Sellers, an old riverboat pilot who wrote a rather ponderous column for a New Orleans paper. Clemens wrote a parody of the column, which apparently hurt the old man's feelings. Perhaps partly in expiation, Clemens adopted the name following the old pilot's death.

However, it should be added that Milton Meltzer, in *Mark Twain Himself* (1960), maintains that Sellers never used the name "Mark Twain," although Clemens himself obviously thought that he had.

The name derives from a term used by the leadsman on a Mississippi steamer whose job it was to take soundings with a line attached to a lead weight (hence the name "leadsman"). When the leadsman called out "by the mark, twain," he was saying that, according to the indication ("mark") on his line, there were a comfortable two fathoms ("twain") of water, or 12 feet—more than enough for even the largest steamer and a welcome cry to the pilot.

Mark Twain and his white suits. Hal Holbrook and almost universal public belief to the contrary, Mark Twain never lectured in a white suit. He did not come to the costume with which he is now so thoroughly identified until he was in his seventies and had long since given up the lecture platform.

What he customarily wore during most of his adult life, as contemporary portraits confirm, was quite the opposite: *black* serge and, in the words of his long-time friend and literary colleague William Dean Howells, of a "truly deplorable" cut.

Howells, in *My Mark Twain* (Harper and Brothers, 1910, page 96), says that

the first time I saw him wear [white] was at the authors' hearing before the Congressional Committee on Copyright [this would have been in 1906—T.B.]. Nothing could have been more dramatic than the gesture with which he flung off his long loose overcoat, and stood forth in white from his feet to the crown of his silvery head. It was a magnificent *coup,* and he dearly loved a *coup.*

Twain came to love his white serges, as he loved the spectacular scarlet and lavender robe that accompanied the honorary degree granted him by Oxford in 1907. But his rebellion against the sober black he had worn for so long was very late in developing.

martini, "bruising" it by shaking. Ah, the mystery—and the mystique—of the martini! Swirling clouds of argument surround its origins, its proportions, its ingredients (lemon peel or not?), and its construction (swipe the peel around the inside of the glass or twist it and drop it in?). But almost all agree on one thing: it must never, never be shaken, always stirred; else it will be "bruised."

There is, so far as is known, no case on record of a black-and-blue martini. But "bruised" is the word; passionate martini drinkers—or more accurately, perhaps, those passionately devoted to the martini—invariably express horror at the thought of a martini banged back and forth in a closed container like a can of paint being homogenized at a hardware store.

But let us take a small excursion into history. On page 25 of *The Bar-Tender's Guide or How to Mix All Kinds of Plain and Fancy Drinks,* written by one Jerry Thomas and first published in 1862, appears the following recipe for a "Martinez" cocktail (though author of a minor work on the subject now long forgotten, this writer will make no attempt to account for this early spelling):

> 1 dash Boker's bitters
> 2 dashes maraschino
> 1 pony Old Tom gin
> 1 wine-glass vermouth
> 2 small lumps ice

Shake thoroughly [italics added] and strain into glass. Add slice lemon.

If, indeed, this is the ur-martini, one can only quote a popular saying: You've come a long way, baby. Boker's bitters? Maraschino? A whole wine glass of vermouth? And where is the essential olive? Still, the basics are there: the gin and the vermouth. And, of course, the ice, though rather parsimoniously provided. Those who know Darwin are well aware that evolution and progress are not necessarily synonymous. Here, perhaps, is the exception.

But as for that "shake thoroughly." In an attempt to track down once and for all the authority, if any, that demands stirring rather than shaking, Patricia Cooper of this writer's research staff[1] undertook to consult with Kobrand Corporation and the Joseph Garneau Company, importers respectively of Beefeater gin and Noilly Prat vermouth.

Here, in part, are the responses. First, from Mr. Stephen Rineberg, director of administration for Kobrand:

> While we are unable to find any scientific basis for the belief that one should not shake, but instead stir, a fine martini, there are, nevertheless, valid reasons for this practice.
>
> A fine martini is truly a delicate and personal cocktail. The only universal agreement as to its formulation is that only the finest imported English Gin and only the most delicate vermouth are used and that the martini is served cold. The exact proportion of Gin and vermouth and the exact degree of relative coldness and the methodology of reaching this degree are very personal and the result of an interrelationship of one's own sight and experience.
>
> To shake a cocktail is without delicacy and proportion. To stir a martini in a fine glass pitcher allows the observance not only of the marriage of its ingredients, but also of the chilling process. A fine martini needs this personal attention of its creator.

W. E. Juckett of the Joseph Garneau Company had this to say:

> This is in response to your letter inquiring about the custom of stirring rather than shaking a martini cocktail.
>
> We have not been able to find a reference book explaining this custom; however, some of our own in-house "experts" say it is because shaking causes a "cloudy" or "milky" appearance which is undesirable in this cocktail. In other words, the basic ingredients are crystal clear and should remain so.

Perhaps this process would be called "bruising" by

---

[1] It would be less than honest not to admit that Patricia Cooper *is* this writer's research staff.

some experts, take it whichever way you like. The net result is that cocktails made with spirit base products, such as bourbon, gin, rum, vodka, or Scotch, are always stirred while those cocktails made with sugar, milk, cordials, or fruit juices can be shaken. I am sure there are many exceptions to this rule; however, this seems to be the best answer available on the subject.

So now we know. Or do we? Since dedication to the spirit of scientific inquiry should recognize no bounds, the writer conducted the obvious experiment: the construction of two martinis, both made with the ingredients imported by Kobrand and Garneau: Beefeater gin and Noilly Prat vermouth. One was carefully stirred, the other rather roughly shaken. The bruised and shaken martini showed no sign of milkiness. And a blindfold test involving the writer's wife, whose sense of taste is unparalleled, was completely inconclusive. She found them equally delicious.

"meat and drink." Those who, on encountering this phrase in biblical, medieval, and even later references, worry about the excessively carnivorous appetites of our forebears should be aware that until recently "meat" was a common synonym for food in general (as opposed to "drink").

miles per gallon. Those inclined to braggadocio about the "mileage" they achieve should know that even 60 miles per gallon is not a very impressive figure, when compared with what certain vehicles have achieved in Great Britain and Germany. A contest sponsored by Shell Oil in the United Kingdom recently turned up a winner that got over a thousand miles—that's right, 1,000 miles—per gallon. Shell's own unofficial entry did even better: it got 1,298 miles to the gallon.

Admittedly these were Imperial gallons, which are 20 percent larger than the American gallon. But even converted into American figures, the results are impressive; Shell's entry would have covered about 1,081 miles on a United States gallon.

True, the vehicles were scarcely your average family sedan. They carried just one passenger, the driver; and they ran heavily to bicycle wheels and extremely light frames. The winning entry, which was sponsored by the Cranfield

Institute of Technology in Bedfordshire, was shaped like a
cigar and, according to *Road and Track* magazine for
November 1977 (page 123), was made largely of washing-
machine parts.

No sails or similar devices were permitted, although the
competitors were allowed freedom in design just so long
as the basic fuel was gasoline. An entry from Tampere
University in Finland combined a tiny gasoline engine with
a steam unit; it placed third, getting only 814 miles to the
(Imperial) gallon. But it did win a prize for its innovative
design. Each vehicle had to be capable of averaging 10
miles per hour.

In a similar experiment, this one under the sponsorship
of a German magazine, a diesel-powered vehicle built by
students at the Mercedes-Benz apprentice school managed
to achieve 1,585 miles per gallon at 25 miles per hour. But
then, everyone knows that diesel engines get better mileage.

"Mind your p's and q's." Often earnestly explained as deriving from old alehouse tallies: "p" for "pint" and "q" for
"quart." The fact is that no one knows how the expression
originated. The most obvious explanation (and thus, one is
tempted to say, the least likely to be accepted) is that the
letters "p" and "q" look so much alike that a child learning
to write might well be admonished to mind his or her "p's
and q's."

"Molotov cocktail." Neither the term nor the object it describes arose out of World War II. According to Veikko
Väänänen, in the Finnish scholarly journal *Neuphilo-
logische Mitteilungen* (Nov. 4, 1977), the Molotov cocktail
was invented and named by the Finns during the 1939–40
Finnish-Russian War.

mongoose. Persons looking up "mongoose" in the dictionary are sometimes puzzled that no plural form is given. Is
it "mongeese"? But dictionaries do not ordinarily list
plurals formed in the regular way; that is, by adding "s" or
"es." Since the goose in mongoose has nothing to do with
the bird many English families like to roast for Christmas,
its plural, unlikely as it may sound, is "mongooses."

"Mongoose" is the English version of a Hindi word
māgūs, from Prakrit *Manguso,* the name given to the small

ferret-sized animal of India and elsewhere that feeds on
snakes and rodents.

Monitor and Merrimack as first ironclads. Neither the
Monitor nor the so-called *Merrimack* (actually, the *Virginia;* the South had raised the sunken Union ship, armored
it, and renamed it) was the first armored ship. Koreans believe that one of their vessels was armored in 1592.
Whether or not this is the stuff of fact or the stuff of legend, it is certainly true that in 1859, three years before the
Monitor-Virginia standoff, the French launched the *Gloire,*
which, according to Nathan Miller (*The United States
Navy: An Illustrated History,* 1977), had 4-inch-thick iron
plates down to 6 feet below the waterline.

Mormons. Those persons who, in an excess of Gentility, refer to Jews as "Hebrews" sometimes think that "Mormon"
is a term not favored by members of the Church of Jesus
Christ of Latter-day Saints, the "official" name of the Mormon church. But just as Jews do not mind being called
Jews, so Mormons have no objection to being called Mormons. The name, after all, derives, in Mormon belief, from
the writer and prophet (and father of the angel Moroni
whose statue tops the famous temple in Salt Lake City)
who was in charge of the records on the Hill Comarah revealed by Joseph Smith in the early nineteenth century.
    Surprisingly, a good many people are unaware that Mormons are Christians. But of course they are, accepting the
Bible, with the Book of Mormon, as the word of God. A
church that calls itself the Church of Jesus Christ of Latter-day Saints could scarcely be other than Christian.
    Mormons use the word "Gentile" for any person who is
not a Mormon. Jews (like Roman Catholics, Episcopalians,
and Presbyterians) are thus, to Mormons, Gentiles. Mormons are likely to be thought of as "Protestants" by those
who are not members of the church, but this is not correct.
Since they took no part in the various movements from
which the Protestant Reformation gets its name, Mormons
do not consider themselves Protestants.

motion to adjourn not debatable. Commonly believed by
countless clubs is that a motion to adjourn is never debatable or subject to amendment. This is not true. The bible
of parliamentarians, *Robert's Rules of Order,* makes it plain

that a motion to adjourn *can* be debated or amended—if no time has been set for another meeting.

Mozart as underpaid genius. Everyone knows that Wolfgang Amadeus Mozart died in need. Not so many know that according to a West German historian, Uwe Kraemer, he died in poverty largely because he loved cards and billiards, played both quite badly, but could not resist betting inordinate sums on his only too deficient skill.

The composer and musician many believe to have been the greatest ever to have lived actually made quite a lot of money. At one time (1783–86), Kraemer says, Mozart was raking in some 10,000 gulden a year for his concerts alone. In today's terms, that's over $100,000—a pretty fair income. And that doesn't count what he made composing and giving music lessons.

All this contrasts sharply with the popular image of the exploited but underpaid genius struggling to make ends meet. Kraemer, who dug into the Mozart household records, says that though Mozart's ill wife had expensive medical bills, Mozart still would have been in good financial shape if he had not spent large sums on clothes, expensive dwellings, and wagering for high stakes.

Muhammad Ali as Olympic heavyweight champion. Muhammad Ali, then known as Cassius Clay III, did not win the gold medal for heavyweight boxing at the 1960 Olympics. The heavyweight champion was Franco de Piccoli of Italy. What Muhammad Ali, or Cassius Clay, did win was a gold medal in the *light* heavyweight competition.

Mussel Shoals, Tennessee. Nope. It's "Muscle," not "Mussel"; and it's not Tennessee but Alabama. True, these shoals of the Tennessee River play an important part in the history of the vast complex known as the Tennessee Valley Authority, or TVA, which accounts for their frequently being misplaced in the public mind. (The shoals are now totally submerged because of dams at either end.)

In spite of the spelling, the name does come from the presence of mussels in that stretch of the river. How "mussel" got to be "muscle" is an interesting story. More accurately, "mussel" never did get to be "muscle," really; the name given to the shoals was historically "Muscle Shoals," though there have been many attempts in the past to "correct" the spelling.

But these attempts are themselves based on an incorrect premise. The mussels in the shoals area—they were once an important source of raw material for the pearl button industry—were quite different from the small edible mussels that are commonly found along the seashore and that belong to the family Mytilus. Those found on the Tennessee are large and clam-shaped, genus *Anodonta,* and they may measure 10 inches or even more. They were named "muscle shells" by early settlers in the South and Midwest because of the extremely tough and powerful muscles that hold the valves together, making them difficult to open. (A bit of pioneer punning may have been involved.)

Mussolini and his "Brown Shirts." Mussolini's personal bodyguard was not known as the Brown Shirts, but the Black Shirts. Mussolini did not, however, originate the black shirt as part of a uniform: it was originated by Gabriele D'Annunzio (1863–1938), the Italian writer and soldier who was an early convert to fascism. In the fall of 1919, troops under his leadership wore black shirts. Later the term came to be applied, loosely, to all Fascist Party militants.

N

nail, rusty, as cause of infection. Rust itself is harmless enough and not a cause of infection or its most dreaded result, tetanus. It's the fact that a rusty nail is also likely to carry germs, if it's stepped on in other than laboratory conditions, that makes it potentially dangerous.

Nero fiddling while Rome burns. Fiddles were completely unknown to Nero; it would be at least a thousand years before their first primitive medieval ancestors would emerge.

There is some evidence—or contemporary gossip, at any rate—that Nero, who was very much the ham, did sing and play against the flaming background of the great Roman fire of A.D. 64. But if he did, it was the lyre he employed. Nero studied the lyre, as he also studied singing and acting. He would no more have known what to do with a fiddle than what to do with a saxophone, another instrument of the (even more) distant future.

New York City. It may come as something of a surprise to some millions of people that there is no such place, but it's true. The official name is The City of New York or, in the short form, just New York. (But the postal identification New York, N.Y. refers specifically to the borough of Manhattan.)

Those who know Mexico often point out that the country's capital is simply Mexico, or, more completely, Mexico, D.F. (for District Federale)—not Mexico City. But you can feel free to refer to Salt Lake City; the "City" here is properly part of the name.

Nez Perce [Indians], pronunciation and spelling. Many reference works, and people as generally knowledgeable about the West as the late Bernard DeVoto and Dee Brown among countless others, insist upon spelling "Nez Perce" in the French fashion, with an accent ("Nez Percé"). Obviously this also assumes a French pronunciation: "Nay Pairsay."

Well, it may not be a war as big as the one Chief Joseph and his doomed band finally lost, but it does seem a shame that the Nez Perces should also lose this admittedly minor (except to the Nez Perce) skirmish. For Nez Perces have never spelled or pronounced the name imposed on them in the way everybody else seems to prefer. *They* say "Nezz Purse." And they spell it without the accent.

Clearly the term itself is, or once was, French; equally clearly, it "means" pierced nose, at least with that accent. Lewis and Clark refer to the "Chop - pun - nish or Pierced nose Indians" (describing them, incidentally, as "Stout likely men, handsom women, and verry dressey in their way [sic]"). Dee Brown, in *Bury My Heart at Wounded Knee* (1971), says that French trappers observed the "Nez Percés" wearing shells in their noses. But Dee Brown is neither Nez Perce nor, in fact, Indian; and Nez Perces themselves deny that either nose piercing or inserting shells through the septum was ever practiced.

Why, then, the name? According to Richard Halfmoon, of Lapwai, Idaho, member for twenty-three years, and chairman for sixteen of those years, of the Nez Perce Tribal Executive Committee, "Nez Percé" is "all wrong." And, says Mr. Halfmoon, it very likely arose out of a white man's misunderstanding of the sign by which Nez Perces once identified themselves: a hand motion across the face that someone, perhaps one of those French trappers, completely misunderstood, taking it to be a kind of simulation, or imitation, of piercing the nose.

Like anyone who is a Nez Perce or has spent time among them, Mr. Halfmoon, though evidently outnumbered, continues to wage a linguistic battle against the accent. At least one standard reference work has conceded the point, in part anyway: the Merriam-Webster unabridged dictionary now allows "Nez Perce" as a variant.

But it's no variant to the Nez Perces; it's the only way.

"nicotine-stained" fingers. It's not the nicotine that stains the fingers of cigarette smokers; nicotine is colorless. The stain comes from the combustion products of the paper and the tobacco, often called "tar."

nightingale, song of. Ah, Philomela! How beautiful her song! Many know, and love—as they should—John Keats's marvelous "Ode to a Nightingale," perhaps the greatest of the many tributes to the bird whose song, once heard, is never forgotten. We know something of how Keats got his inspiration. In the words of Charles Brown, with whom Keats was living at the time in Hampstead:

> In the spring of 1819 a nightingale had built her nest near my house. Keats felt a tranquil and continual joy in her song; and one morning he took his chair from the breakfast table to the grass plot under a plum tree, where he sat for two or three hours. When he came into the house, I perceived he had some scraps of paper in his hand, and these he was quietly thrusting behind the books. On inquiry, I found those scraps, four or five in number, contained his poetic feeling on the song of our nightingale.

Notice anything wrong? Clue: "a nightingale had built her nest near my house. Keats felt a tranquil and continual joy in her song."

In fact, and in spite of countless references—Sophocles to Shakespeare to T. S. Eliot, among many others—that speak of the full-throated nightingale's song as "hers," only the male nightingale sings.

Nobel, Alfred, and nitroglycerin. Alfred Nobel did not invent nitroglycerin, although it is frequently said that he did. Nitroglycerin was first invented, or synthesized, by an Italian, Ascanio Sobrero, in 1846. True, Nobel *manufactured* nitroglycerin and was to expand greatly its practicability; in 1867 he was granted a patent for combining nitroglycerin, a dangerously unstable product, with an inert ingredient. The result was dynamite.

And dynamite is usually regarded as Nobel's most important invention. However, it was not, according to many experts; more important still was Nobel's invention of the detonator, or blasting cap, which E. Bergengren (*Alfred Nobel: The Man and His Work*, 1960) says has been repeatedly described by scientists as the greatest advance in the science of explosives since the invention of gunpowder.

First attempts at a blasting cap involved a gunpowder charge into which a fuse was inserted; Nobel finally hit upon a metal cap charged with fulminate of mercury. Without the blasting cap, dynamite would, in fact, be virtually unusable. Though it is not true that dynamite will merely burn if ignited (a small quantity may but if the mass heats up to about 360° F. it will explode), it takes a blasting cap to ensure an explosion at the desired time and at will.

A common myth about Nobel's invention of dynamite is that it was an accident resulting from Nobel's inadvertent mixing of nitroglycerin and a collodion solution; another version has nitroglycerin leaking into the substance (called kieselguhr, a form of diatomite) in which the nitroglycerin was packed for shipment. There is no truth to any of this; Nobel worked long and hard to devise a means of combining nitroglycerin with a suitable inert substance.

Nobel developed dynamite because of the highly dangerous nature of nitroglycerin when mishandled. One disaster, a ship explosion in Panama on April 3, 1866, killed forty-seven men. Similar accidents led to much public censure of Nobel—and considerable damage to the family business.

noisome. Not loud, but smelly. Sometimes mistakenly thought to refer to "noise," which it does not, "noisome" is related to "annoy" and is commonly used to describe a bad odor. The etymology of "noise" is not clear, but it is not cognate with "annoy."

"normal" body temperature. That any departure from 98.6° Fahrenheit is an indication that something is wrong is quite erroneous. The figure 98.6° is a mathematical abstraction that approximates the temperature of a healthy human being. It may vary from one person to another, and most certainly often varies in any one person depending on the time of day and other factors.

"normalize." Looks for all the world like the kind of Madison Avenue coinage that drives such critics as John Simon and Edwin Newman up the wall, but it isn't. The *Oxford English Dictionary* lists it in a quotation dated 1865.

O

oil gushers. Hollywood sagas of the oil fields have conditioned us to expect a climax in which the drilling crew, releasing long-pent tensions, gambols around a derrick that has suddenly exploded into a fountain of oil and natural gas. That's how it used to be, but nowadays a crew that found itself taking an oil shower would be glumly, if not desperately, trying to figure out what had gone wrong. For drilling is now done with great care and with equipment so sophisticated that the gusher has become a very rare accident. Modern drillers know when an oil strike is near and have everything in readiness to prevent the gushers which, in earlier days of the industry, sometimes spouted wastefully for days on end.

oldest seat of government in U.S. New Englanders accustomed to thinking of the Northeast corner of the United States as where it all started should know that the Governor's Palace in Santa Fe, New Mexico, away out there in a state which wasn't even admitted to the Union until 1912, was built in 1610, ten years before the *Mayflower* landed. Santa Fe itself is, as a matter of fact, the oldest seat of government in the United States.

old oaken bucket, the. Samuel Woodworth (1784–1842) wrote "The Old Oaken Bucket." But he didn't say "How dear to my heart are the scenes of my childhood," no matter how many of us sing it that way. Apparently sensitive to repetition, what he really wrote was "How dear to *this* heart are the scenes of my childhood" (italics supplied).

"Old soldiers never die; they just fade away." So thoroughly identified with the late General Douglas MacArthur is this phrase that many think he originated it. He did not, nor did he pretend to. This is what he said when addressing a joint meeting of Congress on April 19, 1951: "I still remember the refrain of one of the most popular barracks ballads of that day, which proclaimed most proudly that old soldiers never die; they just fade away. I now close my military career and just fade away."

"Of that day" refers to the time of World War I; a British army song of the period contains the lines "Old soldiers never die; they only fade away," according to Bartlett. Bergen Evans has it "simply fade away." MacArthur, always something of a stylist, evidently preferred "just" to either "only" or "simply" as more suitable to the rhythms of prose.

"olympiad" as synonym for "Olympic games." Strictly speaking, "olympiad" means the four-year span *between* the games, used as a measurement of time in ancient Greece. Sportswriters, sometimes addicted to what Arthur Quiller-Couch (1863–1944) called "elegant variation" ("initial sack" for "first base," e.g.), have, however, turned it into a synonym for the games themselves.

optician, oculist, ophthalmologist, optometrist. Not surprisingly, these terms are often confused. The confusion is not alleviated by the fact that the term *oculist* is still around; it still means a physician specializing in eye cases.

An *optician* is trained to grind lenses and fit spectacles and is primarily a prescription-filler, like a pharmacist. An *ophthalmologist* is a physician (M.D. degree) with special training. An *optometrist* (O.D. degree) is not a physician but has graduated from a college of optometry, where he or she has concentrated on what might be called the "visual" (i.e., fitting of glasses) aspects of the eye.

Both ophthalmologists and optometrists examine eyes and write prescriptions for corrective lenses. But only ophthalmologists are trained both to diagnose and to treat diseases of the eye or to operate, if necessary—as in removal of cataracts. The major difference is that the ophthalmologist is a doctor of medicine, the optometrist is not.

Generally speaking—it depends on state or local law—optometrists may advertise. Ophthalmologists follow the same practice as other physicians with respect to advertising—which is to say, they don't.

"ox, strong as an." Most men would take this simile as a compliment; those who know how oxen are created might prefer another.

oxtail. Oxen have tails, but they aren't what go into oxtail soup or stew. "Oxtails" are actually the tails of beef cattle.

P

Pall Mall, pell-mell. Those who know that the name of the London street called Pall Mall is usually pronounced "pell mell" often assume that the pronunciation comes from some past association with hurrying crowds. Not so; in fact, the adjective "pell-mell" comes from a quite different source and has nothing to do with the pronunciation of Pall Mall.

It is easy—well, fairly easy—to explain how the confusion arises. A game called "pall mall" was popular in

seventeenth-century London. Earlier played in Italy and
France, it got its name from Italian *palla* or *balla,* "ball,"
and *maglio,* "mallet," from Latin *malleus.* As might be
guessed, the game involved striking a ball with a mallet, or
maul. The objective was to put a wooden ball through
an iron ring suspended above the ground in a street or an
alley. For whatever reason—perhaps because of various
early spellings, among them the French *paille maille*—the
name of the game was pronounced "pell mell" in England.

Both The Mall, the wide street leading to—or from—
Buckingham Palace, once a tree-bordered walk very fashionable in the seventeenth century, and Pall Mall, the nearby London street paralleling The Mall, derive their names
from the game called "pall mall" and pronounced, as explained above, "pell mell." Pall mall was played on
these two streets in earlier days; hence their names.

It should surprise no one aware of the inconsistencies
of the English language that Pall Mall customarily retains
the pronunciation derived from the street game once played
there, whereas The Mall does not (nobody calls it "The
Mell").

"Pell-mell," the adjective, is related to "melee" and is
pronounced as spelled. (It has been speculated that the
throngs of promenaders and game players in seventeenth-
century London may have led some to apply the adjective
"pell-mell" to the crowds associated with the games.
Whether this simplifies or confuses the question of pronunciation is left up to the reader.)

Presumably the American cigarette called Pall Mall was
named after the London street to add an air of class. Its
TV and radio pronunciation—the British-sounding "Pell
Mell"—back in the days when radio and TV carried cigarette advertising was clearly an attempt to class it up even
more.

"Pap" test. First developed in 1943 by the Greek-American
physician Dr. George Papanicolaou (1883–1962), the Pap
test is usually thought to be useful only in the early detection of uterine cancer. Not at all; Dr. Papanicolaou's technique involves staining and evaluating cells from various
parts of the body, as J. N. Tarro, M.D., of Lake Oswego,
Oregon, reminds us.

True, it is commonly employed in connection with ex-
aminations of the female genital tract. But it is also useful

in such other areas as the respiratory tract, urinary tract, body cavities, and breast.

Because "pap" is an old word for "nipple," some have thought that the Pap test involves only examination of the breast. Obviously this is not true.

pasta, discovery of, by Marco Polo. Still current, as a reference in *Natural History* for January 1979 confirms, is the belief that in the thirteenth century Marco Polo discovered pasta in China and brought it back home to Italy. And every time Gary Cooper's 1939 *The Adventures of Marco Polo* is shown on television, the story is given new impetus: Cooper as Marco Polo is shown slipping samples of pasta from Cathay into the purse given him by his father as a repository for such small treasures as he might find.

The tale is utterly false; pasta is as old as wheat, and that's very old indeed. No doubt the Chinese knew a variety of it; but so did the ancient Romans (the Etruscans had it at least as early as the fourth century B.C.), the Greeks, and the Egyptians, thousands of years ago.

How the Marco Polo tale apparently originated is told, in most interesting fashion, by Gertrude Harris in *Pasta International,* published in San Francisco in 1978. Like H. L. Mencken's famous bathtub hoax, which still surfaces periodically even though Mencken repeatedly tried to disown it, the tale of the pasta seems to have started as a bit of good-humored spoofery.

In October of 1929, a trade magazine called *The Macaroni Journal* told how Marco Polo had encountered pasta in Cathay and had taken it back to his ship in dried form only to discover that it was inedible. A sailor explained that the pasta had to be boiled first, as he had seen a Chinese girl do. And so it was, and it was delicious. The sailor's name? Spaghetti! This clue alone ought to be enough; for "spaghetti," as anyone with even minimal Italian knows, is simply the diminutive of *spego,* the Italian word for "cord" or "string."

As both Ms. Harris and the *Natural History* story point out, there is a reference to pasta and the Chinese in an early sixteenth-century copy of Marco Polo's account of his travels, but the reference is a casual one, pointing out that the people of Cathay do not eat bread, but rather vermicelli and lasagna, words that would not have been used unless they were already familiar to his readers.

Interestingly enough, Marco Polo's memoirs were written not by him—he seems not to have been much of a writer—but, in collaboration, by one Rustichello or Rusticania, known for his romantic fiction and said to have been an authority on chivalry. The original title was *Divisamente Dou Monde* ("Description of the World").

petard. When Hamlet speaks of one's being "hoist with his own petar," or "petard," it is quite true that his reference (act 3, P. 4, lines 205 ff.) is not to a type of derrick but to some kind of bomb or mine. But there is more to it than that.

For the word "petard" derives, as even the august *Oxford English Dictionary* reveals, from a medieval French word for "fart" or "farting." Indeed, "petard" for various kinds of artillery pieces, including the device Hamlet has reference to, appears to derive from the old word for breaking wind. (The modern French noun for "fart" is *pétarade*, obviously a direct descendant of the medieval word. Modern French *pétard* means, not all that surprisingly, "firecracker"; in familiar usage, it stands for "backside.")

Hamlet's remark thus carried a double meaning to Shakespeare's audience. One can be certain that the secondary, and coarse, implications were fully appreciated by the playgoers, including some who would only a few years later laugh at the remark by a character in Ben Jonson's 1609 comedy-farce *Epicoene, or The Silent Woman:* "He has made a petarde of an old brasse pot, to force your dore" (act 4, sc. 4, line 270).

"pig" for "police officer." "Pig" as a pejorative slang term for the police did not originate with the "hippies" and young radicals of recent years. It goes back at least to the early nineteenth century; later, according to Partridge, it came to be applied primarily to plainclothesmen in London.

Pilar. Many are under the impression that Ernest Hemingway named his beloved fishing boat the *Pilar* after the remarkable woman in his 1940 novel *For Whom the Bell Tolls.*

But the reverse is the case. The woman is named for the boat. Ernest acquired the *Pilar* in 1934, years before he started writing *For Whom the Bell Tolls.* It was a diesel-powered twin-screw 38-footer. Hemingway bought it for

$7,500 (it would cost at least ten times that today). On the other hand, Hemingway, though he was certainly by this time one of America's best-known authors, not only could not afford the price; he had to get a $3,300 down payment from Arnold Gingrich of *Esquire* magazine as an advance against future contributions.

Ernest chose *Pilar* (Spanish for "pillar") in honor of a shrine in the Spanish city of Zaragoza and also, Carlos Baker says, for his (then) wife Pauline, who had used it as a nickname for Ernest.

"piping hot." This old expression (Chaucer uses it in *The Miller's Tale*) has naught to do with piping the food to the table while it's still smoking. It merely expresses symbolically the "piping" sound very hot food makes as it hisses or boils.

pirates and the plank. That victims of pirates were commonly made to walk the plank is not true. In the words of Hugh F. Rankin, author of *The Golden Age of Piracy* (1969), it "appears to have been a fabrication of later generations." When pirates wished to dispose of their captives, they simply threw them over the side.

pitch, changes in, as determining meaning. Many English-speaking persons who have heard that Chinese involves changes in pitch that can change the meaning of words wonder how this can possibly be ("What about monotones like me, who can't even carry a simple tune—how could they ever learn Chinese?"). But spoken English provides a good many examples of changes in pitch to change meaning. "You are going tomorrow," for example, is a statement if the pitch of the last syllable of "tomorrow" slides downward, a question if it slides upward—quite a difference in "meaning."

"Oh, yeah?" represents a sardonic rejection or a simple "Yes, indeed"—again, depending on the pitch changes in "yeah." And stress, or "accent," very often involves not merely variations in loudness but also in pitch. Compare "contract," meaning "legal document," with "contract" as in "Are they likely to contract the disease?" There are many more pitch variations in English than most of us realize, and they cause no trouble to monotones.

"Please don't shoot the piano player; he's doing the best he can." Few would associate this statement, so redolent of Wild West saloons, dance halls, and brothels, with Oscar Wilde. Yet it was Wilde who gave the remark its currency.

Wilde first came to the United States in 1882 for a nationwide lecture tour. Surprisingly, he got along fine in the mountains and mining camps; according to H. Montgomery Hyde's *Oscar Wilde* (1975), Wilde said he "had a delightful time all through California and Colorado," though he did admit that there was but "infinitesimal" knowledge of art west of the Rockies. (Wilde apparently took seriously the tale of an ex-miner patron of the arts who sued the railroad company because a plaster cast of the Venus de Milo arrived without its arms—and won his case.)

It was at Leadville, so high in the Colorado mountains that its climate has been described as "ten months of winter and two months mighty late in the fall," that Wilde saw what he was to call "the only rational method of art criticism I have ever come across," the sign reading (as Wilde reported it):

PLEASE DO NOT SHOOT THE PIANIST
HE IS DOING HIS BEST

Polonius, advice of. Generations of schoolchildren have memorized Polonius's famous speech to his son, Laertes, in *Hamlet* (act 1, sc. 3, lines 55 ff.)—the one that ends as follows:

This above all: to thine own self be true,
And it must follow, as the night the day,
Thou canst not then be false to any man.

Admirable sentiments, certainly. But it is equally certain that Shakespeare was fully aware of the irony implicit in the fact that these words are delivered by a tedious old fool (as Hamlet himself called him), a busybody who, far from being "true to himself," engages in a rather shabby plot, using his daughter Ophelia as bait, to entrap Hamlet while at the same time pretending friendship; and who is ultimately killed by Hamlet while trying to spy on him.

Some of the most savagely sardonic lines in Shakespeare

are, in fact, those Hamlet speaks (act 3, sc. 4, lines 31 ff.)
after he realizes that it is Polonius he has stabbed through
the curtain, or arras, behind which Polonius is hiding
(Hamlet thought the person behind the arras was King
Claudius—"I took thee for thy better"):

> Thou wretched, rash, intruding fool, farewell!
> I took thee for thy better; take thy fortune;
> Thou findst to be too busy is some danger.

True, not always are noble words the product of noble
minds:

> If an idea is right in itself, and if thus armed it em-
> barks on the struggle in this world, it is invincible and
> every persecution will lead to its inner strengthening.

You can find this exalted sentiment in the first volume
(Chapter 12) of *Mein Kampf* by Adolf Hitler.

porcupines, birth of. Analogous to the old joke about how
porcupines make love ("very carefully") is the folk belief
that porcupines are always born head first to avoid injuring
the mother. But not to worry; it's true enough that porcupines are born with their quills, but like most other mammals they are born in a sac or membrane that adequately
protects the mother no matter how things come out.

Postal Service, U.S., motto of. Contrary to popular belief,
the U.S. Postal Service has no official motto. What most
people take to be the motto of the postal service is, rather,
this famous inscription on the General Post Office in New
York: "Neither snow nor rain nor heat nor gloom of night
stays these couriers from the swift completion of their appointed rounds. Herodotus."

The inscription was supplied by William Mitchell Kendall
of McKim, Mead & White, the architects who designed the
New York General Post Office. It has reference to a system
of mounted postal couriers used by the Persians when the
Greeks, about 500 B.C., mounted an expedition against the
Persians.

It is interesting to compare the inscription on the Washington, D.C., City Post Office:

Messenger of Sympathy and Love
Servant of Parted Friends
Consoler of the Lonely
Bond of the Scattered Family
Enlarger of the Common Life
Carrier of News and Knowledge
Instrument of Trade and Industry
Promoter of Mutual Acquaintance
Of Peace and of Goodwill
Among Men and Nations.

According to the U.S. Postal Service *News,* from which the foregoing is taken, the Washington inscription was written by the famous Dr. Charles W. Eliot (1834–1926), President of Harvard 1869–1909. Originally called "The Letter," Dr. Eliot's creation, according to the Postal Service *News,* was subjected to "some slight changes in the original text" before it was carved into the white granite of the postal building. His editor was President Woodrow Wilson.

The Washington inscription is somewhat more than twice as wordy as New York's. Make of this what you will.

Post Office Department seal. Until the 1970 Postal Reorganization Act, when a new seal was adopted, the U.S. Post Office Department showed on its official emblem a horse with mailbags and rider. Almost everyone took this to be a representation of the Pony Express, but it was not. The Pony Express service did not come into existence until 1860; the seal was adopted in 1837, and it depicts an intercity Post rider.

potato peels and vitamins. "Don't throw away the potato peel—that's where all the vitamins are." This common bit of folk wisdom shares with a considerable body of folk wisdom a common characteristic: there's not a word of truth in it.

Dr. Jorg Augustin, who as a biochemist at the University of Idaho ought to know his potatoes, points out that not only does the peel amount to a very small fraction of the whole, but that two vitamins (thiamine and niacin) are actually present in greater concentration in the flesh than in the skin. Another, vitamin C, is present in approximately the same amounts in potato flesh and skin. That most of the nutrients of the potato tuber are in the peel is thus a falsehood.

potholes and test tracks. Not long ago, a good many newspapers in England and America, including the august *Manchester Guardian* and the august *Wall Street Journal*, revealed that a new nine-million-dollar automobile test track, to be built by a British manufacturer, would incorporate potholes. The potholes were to be reproductions of some of the most notable found in New York City streets.

Before the story ran its course, it was reported that someone with a bucket of plaster of paris and a New York street map was seeking potholes; he would make casts and ship the "holes" to England, where they would be conscientiously reproduced in the new test track.

But the whole thing started, as such items not too uncommonly do, as a press agent's little joke. Martha Lorini tells the story in the March 1979 issue of *Car and Driver* magazine. An account executive with the British manufacturer's American public relations firm tapped out a phony "press release" suggesting that New York potholes ought to be included in the new test track. It was sent, as a joke, to the British firm which, tongue in cheek, put the item in its house organ.

The *Guardian* got hold of the item and printed it. And from there on, it was off and running: from *Guardian* to *Express* to *Star* to *Wall Street Journal*, with inquiries along the way from CBS and NBC. The *Detroit News* editorializes that Detroit's potholes would make Manhattan's look like baby footprints. The *San Diego Daily Transcript* suggests that America could be to potholes what Saudi Arabia is to oil.

NBC-TV, on its local New York city news show, covers the story. Before long, some forty to fifty newspapers have picked up the "news item." As for the press agent who started it all, he said that it was the easiest publicity he'd ever got. And then he added, apparently a captive of his own creation, that he thought maybe potholes in the test track weren't such a bad idea, at that!

practice swing, golf. "Locker-room lawyers" sometimes impose, or attempt to impose, a penalty on the opposition for taking a practice swing in a hazard or the "rough." But there is nothing in the rules of golf that prohibits a practice swing anywhere on the course; indeed, it is specifically permitted without penalty by a special note to Rule 8, as long as the player does not otherwise violate the rules. (Grounding a club in a hazard, for example, would call for a penalty if the swing were "practice" just as much as if it were not.)

A practice *stroke* is another matter. It is no doubt a failure to recognize the difference between a swing and a stroke that causes the confusion. A "stroke" in golf involves either the actual hitting of the ball or an attempt to do so. Practice strokes are always forbidden during the play of a hole. (Between holes, a player may legally take a practice stroke on or to the putting green of the last hole played. Those who do so, however, especially on a crowded course, violate the etiquette of golf and will no doubt arouse the ire of other players waiting to approach the green.)

pregnancy, weight, and diet. Doctors for several decades have warned the newly pregnant about the hazards of gaining weight. Ten to fifteen pounds in the entire nine months was what they allowed, and many a mother-to-be trembled in expectation of a stern lecture from her obstetrician when she stepped on the scales for the weigh-in. Some starved themselves before their visits; others suffered to term on irksome diets.

Recent studies of maternal nutrition have shown that the weight taboo is largely hogwash.

The entire nutritional picture is complex, of course, but the consensus now is that if a woman starts pregnancy at the normal weight for her frame and eats a well-balanced diet, she'll best ensure a safe birth and the health of the baby if, by the time she delivers, she gains from twenty-four to twenty-seven pounds—up to three pounds the first three months, and about one every nine days after that.

The story is quite different for those who start off with a pounds problem, whether it be under or over. Skinny women who conceive may have dangerously small babies even if they do eat correctly and put on weight normally; they ought to gain up to thirty pounds. Heavyweights run risks (as of high blood pressure and difficult births) that endanger both mother and child. Once a heavy woman is pregnant, however, it is desirable that she put on *some* weight with the proper food: her baby has a far better chance of surviving (50 percent better, according to one national study) than the child of an obese mother who gains little during pregnancy.

Dieting to shed pounds during pregnancy is especially hazardous because it may deprive the fetus of nutrients essential to proper development of brain and body, and weight loss that causes a breakdown of fat also releases ketone bodies that are toxic for a developing baby.

The simple truth—what practically all mothers-to-be recognize instinctively—is found in the received wisdom of less sophisticated times: the pregnant woman must "eat for two." That means the right foods, and enough of them, to ensure the health of the fetus, help the mother through the stresses of pregnancy and birth, and then enable her to care for and nurse the newborn baby. It means, inevitably, a gain in weight far more substantial than most doctors allowed in the past.

Another alleged hazard of pregnancy, salt intake, has also been found to be the subject of undue caution—because the sodium of sodium chloride was thought to cause toxemia. But swelling tissues and soaring blood pressure are now attributed to poor nutrition rather than excess sodium, the need for which is actually increased during pregnancy. Sodium restriction is very important, however, in the treatment of women who enter pregnancy with high blood pressure (hypertension).

prisoners sitting at long tables while dining. Add to the common misconceptions about prison life the classic scene from many old, and some not so old, movies of *The Big House* persuasion: James Cagney, say, sitting in the middle of a long row of men at a long table, banging his tin coffee cup and shouting insurrection.

But modern penologists have long known that such a seating arrangement is just about the worst possible in terms of the kind of tensions symbolized in the scene reconstructed above. So today prisoners are likely to be seated in small groups at small tables, just as in a restaurant. (In Oregon, this has been the practice for years at the state penitentiary.)

Even though not so many can be seated at once in such an arrangement, many prison authorities prefer going to a double shift, if necessary, in order to get away from the benchlike "institutional" feeding that was once common.

professors, time spent waiting for. Scarcely a college campus in the country is free of a myth firmly believed by many students: that there is a fixed number of minutes a class is supposed to wait for a tardy teacher before dismissing itself. Typically, for a full professor one waits fifteen minutes; for an associate professor, twelve minutes; an assistant professor, ten minutes; an instructor, five. Presumably those lowest-ranking workers in the academic vineyard, graduate or teaching assistants, had better be on the dot.

It is not impossible that such a "rule," complete with its implicit rank-conscious snobbism, may have existed on some campus somewhere at some time. If so, however, no one to the knowledge of this writer, who has spent many years on many campuses, has ever discovered it.

Prohibition and women's votes. A complaint often heard in the twenties and thirties—sometimes later, among older generations—was that the so-called Prohibition Amendment (eighteenth to the U.S. Constitution, later repealed by the Twenty-first Amendment in 1933) was voted in by "the women" while the men were fighting World War I.

The Eighteenth Amendment was ratified on January 16, 1919. Women did not achieve nationwide suffrage until more than a year and a half later: the Nineteenth Amendment, ratified on August 20, 1920.

Lest it be argued that it was women's votes in the various states that put the Eighteenth Amendment over, it should be pointed out that women had the vote in only fifteen of the (then) forty-eight states in 1918, the year World War I ended. Three fourths of the states—at that time, this number would have been thirty-six—must approve a constitutional amendment before it takes effect.

proof, shifting the burden of. In logic as in law, the burden of proof lies not with the defense but the offense, though this fact is often overlooked. If you accuse someone of theft or sue for breach of contract, it is obviously up to you to show, beyond a reasonable doubt in the legal phrase, that the object of your accusation or suit has actually committed theft or breached a contract. If you propose that the moon is made of green cheese or that Bacon wrote Shakespeare's plays, you must be prepared to offer convincing proof.

All this seems self-evident enough. But as Professor John R. Cooper of Portland State University reminds us, clairvoyants, spiritualists, astrologers, and other mystics only too frequently propose not that they have evidence of their theories but that anyone who disagrees must provide evidence that the mystic is wrong! Often this takes the form of accusing the skeptic of supposing that the universe is totally explainable in rational or scientific terms, then pointing out how many unsolved mysteries remain. (Not uncommonly, Hamlet's remark to Horatio is adduced: "There are more things in heaven and earth, Horatio, than are dreamt of in your philosophy"—a complete misunderstanding, incidentally, of what Hamlet is saying.)

The skeptic must then defend himself against the charge of arrogant dogmatism, of assuming a certainty about everything that is not justified, when, clearly, it is the mystic who is making the claim that must be defended. It isn't the doubter who should be put on the defense; *he's* not the one who proposes that your grandam's soul inhabits a waterfowl or that your uncle is talking through a levitating megaphone.

It's a very old game. Another term for it is attempting to prove a hypothesis because of lack of evidence against it. But one does not prove something by claiming that it cannot be disproved. One can imagine what would happen to our legal system if this were the case. This is why Congressional or state investigating committees operating outside the laws of evidence can so easily ruin reputations.

A cogent—and pertinent—example is what happened to Professor Melvin Rader of the University of Washington. (He tells the whole story in a fascinating account called *False Witness*, published by the University of Washington Press in 1969.) Through testimony that later was proved to be perjured, Rader was accused by a state legislative committee in 1948 of having attended a school for Communists in New York State in the late 1930s. It then became incumbent upon Rader to prove that he had not attended the school some ten years earlier.

Rader told the committee that he and his wife had been on vacation at a lodge in the State of Washington during the time he was accused of having attended the Communist school. But the guest register at the lodge containing the Raders' names mysteriously disappeared (it was later shown to have been taken by members of the investigating committee). The burden on Rader was thus very nearly intolerable. Only with the help of a Seattle newspaper and its Pulitzer-prizewinning reporter, Ed Guthman, was the evidence of Rader's presence at the Washington lodge finally uncovered.

But it should not have been up to Rader to establish the absence of proof on the part of members of the committee; they were the accusers. Rader was presumed guilty until he could prove his innocence, a gross contradiction of Anglo-American legal principles.

The way charlatans operate in the area of the nonrational illustrates why the principle of presumptive innocence is so firmly a part of our legal system. The number of things an accused *might* have done is limited only by the imagination of the accuser. The number of things *actually* done is limited by experience and opportunities. It is almost impossible to establish an alibi (as the term is used in law: that is, proof that one was at other than the scene of the crime when it was committed) for every hour of one's life, except perhaps in the unlikely circumstance that one has been under constant observation throughout every hour of one's life. Under a system of presumptive guilt, a solitary walk in the woods, a day at the seashore, even a trip to the bathroom are potentially dangerous.

The astrologer says, "You don't believe that I can tell you about your future by observing the conjunctions of the stars and planets. All right; prove that I am wrong. To do that, you must prove that everything in the universe is rational." Actually, the astrologer is under the burden of proving that the universe is *not* rational. Obviously, we have yet to provide a rational explanation for everything that happens; no one denies that. However, the fact that we cannot explain a phenomenon does not mean that the phenomenon has no explanation. We are fairly certain now that lightning is not an irrational manifestation of the power of the gods.

Admittedly, deep within all of us lies the wish that we could explain by avoiding explanation; that we could somehow blame it all on God. Or the gods. Or heredity. Or environment, for that matter. Perhaps we can; who knows? But the ignorance of certainty is a far cry from that ignorance which is a proper human manifestation of *un*certainty. The former works against us; the latter, for us. The former is superstition; the latter, a healthy skepticism.

Prose Edda, the. There are many misunderstandings, even among scholars, concerning this body of Scandinavian literature. In the words of my scholarly correspondent, Gareth Penn:

Edda is the title customarily given both to a collection of anonymous mythological Norse poems and to a poetic handbook written by the Icelandic poet, historian, and politician Snorri Sturluson, about 1220 A.D. However, not only is the title a misnomer, nobody knows what it means, or why it was given to either of the two works. Because the old poetic practices of the skalds, or bards, were falling into disuse in the 13th century (the Church frowned on heathen mythological poetry, and the common folk preferred the simple, light-hearted verses then coming into vogue to the dark, metaphorical court poetry of the ancient Norsemen), Snorri wrote his "poetic," or poet's handbook, setting forth traditional mythological themes, poetic figures of speech (*kenningar,* or involved metaphors), and 120 different meters commonly used in ancient Norse poetry. In a redaction of his poetic written about fifty years after his death at the hands of political assassins, the title *Edda* appears in an inscription added by an unknown editor. In the only other documented occurrences of the word in Icelandic, it means "grandmother," a usage which was apparently obsolete in Snorri's time, and which is difficult to apply to a book on writing poetry. Nonetheless, his book quickly came to be known to Icelanders as the *Edda,* or *Snorra Edda,* "Snorri's Edda." In 1643, a Protestant bishop of Iceland, Brynjolf Sveinsson, published a collection of mythological verses he had discovered written on 45 pages of vellum in prose form. He ascribed these verses to one Saemundr, publishing them under the title *Saemundar Edda,* "Saemund's Edda." Since Brynjolf's time, it has become customary to refer to this collection as "the Edda" or, among the more pedantic, "the Elder Edda," on the assumption that it antedates Snorri's poetic, although no one is sure whether it does or not. It is also known as the "Poetic Edda" because it is written in verse. Nonetheless, Icelanders continue to refer to Snorri's poetic alone when they use the word *Edda.* It is ironic that Snorri's Edda is called the "Prose Edda" by non-Icelanders, since it is poetic, and the work that non-Icelanders call the "Poetic Edda" was written as prose (that is, written down *prorsus,* from one margin to the other, without regard for the verse form).

proverbs, contradictory. To what extent should one govern one's life by folk wisdom and proverbs? A soft answer may turn away wrath, but the squeaky wheel gets the grease, right? Look before you leap; on the other hand, he who hesitates is lost. And though too many cooks spoil the broth, we all know that two heads are certainly better than one, and many hands make light work.

Nothing ventured, nothing gained. Perhaps. But let's remember not to put all our eggs in one basket. (Mark Twain, by way of his fictional character Pudd'nhead Wilson—see BLACK CHILDREN AS RESULT OF TINY PERCENTAGE OF "NEGRO" BLOOD—tells us to go ahead and put all our eggs in one basket; and then watch that basket!) Better safe than sorry.

A miss is as good as a mile. But how about that half a loaf that's better than none? Speaking of one, we all know (see above) that this is what two heads are better than, presumably unless you want a thing done; then you had better do it yourself. And if absence makes the heart grow fonder, how come out of sight, out of mind? Eh?

You want an eye for an eye, a tóoth for a tooth; or do you prefer to turn the other cheek? It's never too late to learn, but you can't teach an old dog new tricks. If you don't seize opportunity by the forelock, it may be that you realize that what you do in haste, you will repent at leisure. And ah, love! If it's indeed blind, how can it find a way?

Bacon thought that the genius, wit, and spirit of a nation are discovered in its proverbs. Shakespeare disagrees: a proverb is something musty. And, says Macaulay, nothing is so senseless as a general maxim. If all generalizations are false, should this one be included?

"psychological moment." "Moment" here did not originally have reference to time. As Fowler reminds us, the original (German) phrase was mistranslated. *Moment* in German means "momentum," not a point in time. Thus the phrase was intended to describe a circumstance in which all psychological factors point toward success. A good salesman, for example, will know when his client has been properly "conditioned," when the psychological momentum is the greatest. If at that point he whips out the contract and the fountain pen, he may be said to be exploiting the "psychological moment" in the customary meaning of the phrase. But the one follows the other: first the "momentum" and then the "moment."

Quaker "church." There is no Quaker church, or Church of the Religious Society of Friends. Quakers were so fed up with what they regarded as church rigamarole that they long ago expunged the word "church" from their vocabulary.

Quads at Cambridge. No; Oxford has Quads, or Quadrangles. Cambridge has Courts. Now you know.

"quick and the dead." Does not contrast those who are agile with those who (obviously) are not. "Quick" here means "alive"—its original meaning, in fact, and the first to be listed by the *Oxford English Dictionary*, with a citation from the ninth century. Thus the contrast is merely between those who have not, and those who have, departed this vale of tears.

"quiz," origin of. A widely believed story has it that one Mr. Daly, the manager of a Dublin theater in the 1780s, coined the word "quiz." Daly and some friends were arguing the gullibility of the public. Daly bet that he could persuade Dubliners to adopt a new word, entirely meaningless, overnight. So he coined "quiz." He and his friends spent the night painting "quiz" on the buildings and pavements of Dublin, presumably without interference from property owners or municipal officials. The next morning everybody in Dublin asked everybody else what "quiz" meant; and so it acquired its present meaning.

It is very unlikely that the tale is true. (It's sometimes

told about Lewis Carroll, real name Charles Lutwidge Dodgson, author of *Alice's Adventures in Wonderland.* But Dodgson [1832–98] was born fifty years after "quiz" made its first appearance in print.) The *Oxford English Dictionary* takes little stock in the story, pointing out that it was first told in 1836 by Benjamin Smart in a book called *Walker Remodelled* (a new version of John Walker's 1791 "critical pronouncing dictionary and expositor of the English language")—but was omitted from the 1840 printing.

The other "early" explanation of the origin of the word, F. T. Porter's *Gleanings and Reminiscences,* did not appear until 1875 and clearly must be thrown out of court, since it gives the date of the Daly story as 1791. "Quiz," although in a different sense from its customary present meaning—it was first used for "an eccentric," as in "He's a quiz"—appeared in print in 1782.

Further, the Daly explanation exhibits that overelaboration that is so common a characteristic of folk etymology. And anyone who knows Latin will at once observe the very close similarity between "quiz" and the Latin interrogative pronoun *quis* ("who?", "what?"). If Mr. Daly was really seeking, as the story has it, an entirely new combination of letters, he couldn't have been trying very hard.

It is also interesting to note that the second—and stressed—syllable of "inquisitive," a word that had been around a long time by the 1780s, contains "quiz," exactly as it is pronounced.

"Quiz" as an informal synonyn for "examination" appears to have been an American innovation. There is also a twentieth-century Australian word, "quizzy," meaning "inquisitive," from which Partridge believes the Australian term is derived.

R

"the rabbit died." This cliché for the confirmation of pregnancy has itself died out; newer and simpler chemical tests are used nowadays. But it never made much sense in the first place, for the rabbit *always* died, whether the finding

was positive or negative: the animal was sacrificed because
the test involved an examination of its ovaries.

Rabelais as creator of Gargantua. The comic and ribald
Rabelais (c. 1495–1553) made Gargantua his own, but he
did not originate either the character or the name. Medieval
legend circulating before Rabelais's work featured a giant
named Gargantua.

rabies. Rabies, or "hydrophobia," is terrifying enough without the myths—some of them potentially dangerous—that
have sprung up concerning it. It is not confined to dogs, as
most people know. Raccoons, badgers, skunks, and bats,
among other warm-blooded creatures, can become rabid—
as can also, of course, cats.

The name by which rabies is also known, hydrophobia,
means "fear or dread of water." But rabid dogs do not
fear or dread water; quite the contrary, they yearn for it
desperately and will drink avidly at the onset of the disease.
Later, when the throat constriction that is one of the characteristics of rabies develops, the dog will still try to drink
even though swallowing may be difficult or impossible.

Nor do rabid dogs necessarily and invariably "foam at
the mouth," as the expression is usually understood, and in
spite of what was a stock comic scene in old movies: the
dog that gets into his master's shaving soap or his mistress's
cream pie and sets off a panic in the populace. The saliva
becomes thick and clings to the mouth and teeth, but its
production is not greatly increased. Sometimes, it is true,
heavy rapid breathing through the mouth will cause froth-
ing of the drooling saliva, which is an indication of progressive laryngeal and pharyngeal paralysis.

It is not necessary to be bitten by a rabid animal to contract rabies. It's the saliva that is dangerous. In a form of
rabies sometimes called "dumb madness," in which the
lower jaw drops open because of paralysis of the masseter
muscles, the animal, in fact, cannot bite. But anyone who
comes into contact with the saliva is in great danger if it
should reach any break or abrasion in the skin. Even airborne transmission and infection through mucous mem-
branes can occur under certain circumstances.

It is not true, as the fearful cry "Mad dog!" implies, that
rabid animals invariably show signs of hostility, snapping
at anything in sight. True, normally friendly animals may

become aggressive. But some animals, in the prodromal, or first, phase, which usually lasts up to thirty-six hours, become, on the contrary, abnormally affectionate. "Mad cat!" comes closer to the truth; cats are more likely to develop the "furious" form of rabies, especially dangerous in cats because of the rapidity with which they can inflict damage if handled.

A little-known fact about rabies, except to veterinarians, is that the incubation period is extremely variable. Clinical signs usually appear fifteen to twenty-five days after exposure. But occasionally the incubation period may be delayed for as long as a year.

As early as 1804 it was known that rabies could be transmitted from one dog to another by way of the saliva. In 1813 it was demonstrated, by injecting dogs with saliva from a human rabies victim, that the rabies agent in persons and dogs is the same. If the great Louis Pasteur (1822–95) had done nothing other than develop his rabies cure, he would be assured of immortality.

It might be said finally, however, that so much is made of the discomfort of the Pasteur rabies treatment (indeed, it appears to be de rigueur in newspaper and broadcast reports to use the term "painful series of inoculations" in describing it) that many people are unnecessarily alarmed at the (admittedly remote) prospect that someday it may have to be done to them. New methods of rabies treatment have considerably lessened the discomfort of the older techniques.

It is commonly believed that untreated rabies is invariably fatal. This is not true, although the facts are grim enough. According to the Center for Disease Control in Atlanta, there are three documented cases in the United States of survival.

radiators, automobile, and distilled water. Distilled water may be fine for those automobile storage batteries that require occasional topping up, although in fact motorists and service stations in many areas use tap water with no discernible harm. But don't use distilled water in your radiator. Or so at least Mercedes-Benz advises; their engineers say that distilled water picks up carbon dioxide and oxygen from the air and can cause corrosion. They add that lime-free water, rainwater, and distilled or desalinated water should not be used under any circumstances; get the water out of the tap.

Obviously, water that is much too hard may cause problems too; Mercedes-Benz suggests having local water analyzed if there is any doubt. But clearly an excess of uninformed caution can be damaging.

A story sometimes taken seriously with respect to automobiles as expensive as the Mercedes-Benz and the Rolls-Royce is that the ideal coolant is champagne. One would suppose that this advice applies to the owner rather than the vehicle, although the thought of checking the radiator to the pleasant aroma of Piper Heidsieck does have some appeal.

"r" and "l"—Japanese/Chinese "confusion" of sounds. Much is made of the difficulty Japanese and Chinese have in distinguishing between the sounds represented in English by the letters "r" and "l." A writer for an automotive magazine once suggested that when the Toyota people marketed a model called the "Corolla," it was obviously designed for the U.S. market, since natives of Japan would find it quite impossible to pronounce "correctly."

But there is nothing surprising in all this. American children often have the same problem. The reason, unlikely as it may seem to those untrained in phonetics, is that there is a close relationship (though rather a complicated one) between these two sounds.

Both involve a similar though not identical position of the tongue. To form the sound represented by "l," one raises the front of the tongue so that it touches the roof of the mouth just behind the teeth. To form the sound of "r," one also raises the tongue; but its tip is turned back, or retroflexed.

So it is not surprising that there is difficulty in distinguishing between these sounds, especially for one who has not yet mastered the rather complicated muscular manipulations involved—or who has been raised in a culture where such manipulations are not necessary.

Each culture has its own uniquely characteristic means of forming the sounds necessary to communicate within that culture. And it might be added that in spite of a tendency to think in terms of "sophisticated" versus "primitive," there is really no such distinction possible when speaking of the phonological aspects of a given language

—if, indeed, there is any such distinction possible when speaking of any aspect of any culture. Forming the sounds of one's language, whatever it may be, is a subtle and sophisticated process, the full understanding of which involves a great deal of study.

rape, prostitution as "cure" for. A common argument for the legalization of prostitution is that where prostitution is permitted, rape is rare. Nothing could be farther from the truth. According to the 1974 FBI Uniform Crime Reports, Nevada, the only state to allow legalized prostitution, also enjoys (if that is the word) a very high forcible-rape ratio: 45.2 per 100,000 population, compared, for example, to Oregon's 32.3, Washington's 29.0, California's 40.6, and Idaho's 16.0. In none of the four states with lower rape figures is prostitution legal.

Rape is a particularly unattractive form of assault and, often enough, battery. If it were, indeed, a "sex crime" arising out of sexual deprivation, then, indeed, legalizing prostitution would help to eliminate it. It doesn't.

"Rape" of the Sabine women. If it happened at all—it's an early tale, very likely a myth, told by later Romans about the followers of Romulus—it was not "rape" as the term is currently understood. In early times, "rape" meant only to capture and carry away, particularly in a hurry (Latin *rapere*). ("Rape" for the crop comes from a quite different source: Latin *rapa*, which also means "turnip.") While it may have had such overtones, the word did not mean, as it now does, sexual assault. The current meaning is an example of what linguists call "specialization."

The phrase "rape and renne [run]," found in Chaucer, merely means to grab and run; in the Canon's Yeoman's Tale it is used in connection with things rather than people. A better term for what happened to the Sabine women would be "abduction."

rector. Not necessarily a term applied only in a religious context. What we would call the President of a university is, in European countries, commonly called the Rector. (The word "rector" derives from the Latin verb *regere*, for "lead" or "direct," the past participle of which is *rectus*.)

religious programming, banning from the air. As of January 10, 1979, the Federal Communications Commission had received nearly *nine million* pieces of mail based on the belief, quite untrue, that the FCC was about to forbid any religious broadcasts and that Madalyn Murray O'Hair and the American Atheist Center were behind a petition designed to end religious broadcasts.

The facts, as stated by Arthur L. Ginsburg, chief of the Complaints and Compliance Division of the FCC, in a letter dated January 10, 1979, are these. Two persons—Jeremy D. Lansman and Lorenzo W. Milam—had asked, in December of 1974, that the FCC "inquire," in Mr. Ginsburg's words, "among other things, into the practices of noncommercial educational broadcast stations, including those licensed to religious educational organizations. Pending the completion of the requested inquiry, Messrs. Lansman and Milam asked that no licenses be granted for any new noncommercial educational station."

This petition (RM-2493) was denied by the commission on August 1, 1975, but that did not stop the spread of unfounded fantasies. Again in Mr. Ginsburg's words, "erroneous rumors began to be circulated about the country to the effect that the petitioners had called for an end to religious broadcasting and that the Commission itself was about to forbid any further religious broadcasts. In recent months, we have received additional mail and telephone calls indicating that many persons believed that Mrs. Madalyn Murray O'Hair was either a party to the original petition or has initiated another proceeding seeking to restrict or abolish religious broadcasting. This rumor is also untrue."

Jon Murray, Director of the American Atheist Center, confirms Mr. Ginsburg's comments. Articles in *TV Guide* and in *Time* magazine, and mention in the *Congressional Record*, have failed to put the rumors to rest. "We wish," says Mr. Ginsburg somewhat plaintively, "that there was some way that we could stop the flow of RM-2493 letters which are based on misinformation."

"resumé." Make up your mind: do you want to spell it in French or in English? If the former, one accent mark won't do; it's "résumé." If the latter, you might as well leave off both accents, in the English fashion.

ribs, men's and women's. A surprising number of persons, including many who do not take the Bible literally, continue to believe that men have fewer ribs than women, presumably because of the creation of Eve from Adam's rib (Genesis 2:21–22). The fact is that men and women have the same number of ribs: an even dozen each.

Maybe Adam grew another one. The Bible doesn't say he did. But it doesn't say he didn't, either.

"Я " in Russian alphabet. The Russian gothic-type "backward R" is not the Russian symbol for the sound of "R" in English, though it is sometimes treated as if it were. The Russian letter corresponding to the English "R" is "P." The Я symbol, the last letter in the Russian alphabet, comes closest to our "Y"; it stands for the sound of the first two letters in the English word "yard."

river canyon, deepest. Claimants are several for the title "Deepest river canyon in the world." The Grand Canyon of the Colorado—which is not in Colorado but in Arizona —is often cited, along with Hell's Canyon of the Snake River on the border between Idaho and Oregon. But the canyon of the Kali Gandaki River in Nepal may be the champion. It is flanked by Annapurna and Dhaulagiri, mountain peaks each over 26,000 feet in height. "Kali" means black, or dark, and the steep walls do give, in Peter Mathiessen's phrase (*The New Yorker*, May 27, 1978, page 49), a "hellish darkness" to the river.

However, one point is often overlooked—a matter of definitions. The Grand Canyon is a great depression in relatively flat country and was carved out by the river. Both Hell's Canyon and the canyon of the Kali Gandaki owe their great depth not to eons of persistent erosion but to the fact that they are surrounded by mountains. It does not seem likely that the mountains are there because the river created them, as it created the Grand Canyon.

rosary as Roman Catholic in origin. There is much debate as to the origin of the rosary, but it did not just arise out of Roman Catholic practice. Hindus had the *japa-mala*, or "muttering chaplet," used to count prayers and promote contemplation. Knots used as a means of aiding memory have arisen in several parts of the world and among several faiths, including not only Hindus, but Buddhists, Muslims, and some Jews.

"Rough" (in golf). Search as one will, there is no acknowledgment that such a phenomenon as "the rough" exists according to the rules of golf. It is purely unwritten convention that differentiates between "fairway" and "rough." (Indeed, there is no "fairway" either; at least, the term is not mentioned in the rules.) A golf course that contained no "rough" at all, every duffer's dream, would be entirely legal.

S

Saint Bernard dogs and their casks of brandy. Firmly fixed in popular belief is the noble Saint Bernard of the Hospice of the St. Bernard Pass in the Swiss Alps, brandy cask slung around its neck as it bravely tracks down and finds the lost and snowbound traveler. But—alas!—it's not so, and never has been. True, the Saint Bernards were originally bred by the monks at the hospice for rescue work; and tales of their shaggy valor, tales that tended to grow with repetition, became widespread. But their principal task was to help the monks themselves find their way in the snow.

And they never, but never, carried that little cask of brandy, or of anything else. According to *Encyclopédie des Idées Reçues* (Vallette & Burnam, 1978), the monks at the hospice have not found in their records, which go back to the seventeenth century, the slightest allusion to the legendary cask.

Ironically, as the *Encyclopédie* points out, the myth has been perpetuated by an illustration on the wrapper of a candy bar showing a Saint Bernard carrying that eternal little barrel. The candy is Swiss chocolate.

Saint Sebastian. This saint, of the third century A.D., is always depicted as a handsome young man, bound to a pillar or a post, and liberally transfixed with arrows. Many who see such depictions—he was a favorite subject of Renaissance painters—assume that Sebastian died in this fashion. Some reference books have contributed to the misconception, too, but the saint's legends do not have it that way.

Sebastian is said to have been a nobleman, a captain of the Praetorian guard, and much favored by the emperor Diocletian. The emperor found out that Sebastian was a Christian and, when he could not persuade his friend to abandon his faith, ordered him shot to death with arrows. Sebastian was left for dead, but he was nursed back to health by a Christian woman named Irene.

When he recovered, Sebastian confounded Diocletian by appearing before him to plead for tolerance of Christians. The emperor, however, would not be swayed; he again ordered Sebastian killed, and the saint was clubbed to death in the amphitheater.

Because Sebastian survived the arrows, his aid was often invoked against the plague. This association, it is said, arose out of an ancient belief that deaths from the plague (as well as other unexplained and nonviolent deaths) were caused by Apollo's arrows. Somewhat oddly—it's as if a Christian martyr were to become the patron saint of lions—Sebastian is the patron saint of archers.

saints, worship of. Roman Catholics do not worship saints; worship belongs exclusively to God. Saints are venerated, not worshiped.

sake (Japanese). This popular beverage, often served heated, is neither wine nor spirits, speaking strictly. It is, rather, a form of what we know as beer, made from fermented rice. It's pretty strong beer, though—about 17 percent alcohol.

"salary" as derived from the Latin for "salt." It is commonly believed that our word "salary" comes from the Latin word *sal* ("salt"), because Roman soldiers were given a regular allowance of salt—their "salary," or, in Latin, *salarium*. And in fact, this is the correct etymology —except that Roman soldiers were not paid in salt during the great days of the Empire. What they got—and what *salarium* stands for—was a money allowance "in lieu of," just as today's soldiers are issued "rations" under certain circumstances (detached service, living off-base, etc.). Today's ration allowances are not in the form of TV dinners, any more than the sophisticated legionnaires who served under Caesar were doled out salt for their services, although this might have been true back in earlier and more primitive Roman times.

The specific word for a soldier's pay (all of it) in the time of the Caesars was *stipendium,* the ancestor of today's "stipend."

salt in prepared foods. There is considerable evidence linking salt intake with high blood pressure. However, those who choose, or are advised, to reduce salt intake may find some surprises; things aren't always what they seem. According to *Consumer Reports* for March 1979, the sodium content of many prepared foods cannot be determined on the basis of taste. (Salt, or sodium chloride, is about 40 percent sodium.)

For example, a one-ounce serving of a popular brand of corn flakes contains nearly twice as much sodium as an ounce of cocktail peanuts. Two slices of a brand of white bread sold nationally contain more sodium than an ounce of potato chips—which is quite a few; commonly, a full bag of potato chips will contain only four or five ounces.

Even those prepared foods that one associates with sugar rather than salt can be high in sodium. Half a cup of one brand of instant chocolate-flavored pudding, for example, exceeds in sodium content three slices of bacon, and by a wide margin. A frozen chicken dinner may contain more than haf of the daily sodium allotment for persons placed on a mild low-sodium diet, a hamburger from one of the large franchised chains about three quarters.

Although there is still some dispute about the exact role salt plays in high blood pressure, several studies have shown that in cultures where salt intake is high, so is the incidence of high blood pressure.

The medical term for high blood pressure is "hypertension." As *Consumer Reports* points out, this term leads many to associate it only with tense, high-strung individuals. But this is a misconception; easygoing, relaxed types are also susceptible.

Those who do associate hypertension with tenseness and "drive," and who may still tend to think, consciously or otherwise, of blacks as happy-go-lucky extroverts should know that hypertension is twice as common among blacks as whites; that in blacks it develops earlier in life and causes higher mortality at younger ages than in whites.

Santa Claus. Add to the various tales purporting to identify Santa Claus one that has him a Turk. That's right—a Turk. According to one rather charming old legend, St. Nicholas was born in Patara, Turkey, and lived most of his life in the vicinity. Travelers today can visit his tomb and a church bearing his name.

It is this St. Nicholas whom the legend credits with having started the stockings-hung-by-the-chimney custom. Said to have been a wealthy young man who liked to give to the poor, St. Nicholas took pity on three impoverished sisters. In one version, he tossed gold through the window of their house two nights in a row. On the third night the window was closed, so he threw the gold down the chimney, where it fell into the sisters' stockings, hung by the fire to dry. Another version that might be defined as set in the pre-chimney era has him dropping gold down the smoke hole, but with the same result: it stuck in the stockings. This variant apparently assumes that stockings were invented before chimneys.

Scopes trial. Few legal proceedings have stirred as much interest as the trial of John Thomas Scopes in Dayton, Tennessee, in 1925, sometimes called the "monkey trial" because of the widespread (but quite mistaken) belief that Darwin said man is descended from monkeys. Scopes was accused of violating Tennessee's "Butler Act," named for John Washington Butler, farmer, part-time schoolteacher, clerk of the Round Lick Association of Primitive Baptists, and legislator who wrote the bill that outlawed teaching evolution in the public schools of the state.

Misinformation about the Scopes trial abounds. In the first place, Scopes is almost always said to have been a biology teacher. He wasn't; his subjects were algebra, chemistry, and physics, and he also did some coaching. Many assume that he won his case. He didn't; he was found guilty and fined $100—but he never paid the fine. The Tennessee Supreme Court set aside the penalty on a technicality without, however, committing itself as to the constitutionality of the Butler Act.

Nor was Scopes an innocent victim of circumstances.

In fact, he had agreed to serve as the focus of a test case. And there is a suggestion that one purpose of the trial was to put Dayton "on the map" so as to encourage an infusion of new capital. By Scopes's own account in *Center of the Storm,* published in 1967, three years before his death, George Rappleyea first suggested Dayton as the place for a test of the law. Rappleyea was manager of a local coal and iron company; the idea of putting Dayton in the limelight seems to have been largely his, perhaps because his company was on the skids. (It later went under; the new capital failed to materialize.) In any case, Rappleyea suggested a test case to F. E. Robinson, a local pharmacist who was chairman of the school board. The two settled on Scopes as a likely candidate; he was known to be opposed to the law and as a young man without family seemed to be a good prospect.

It was all very friendly and small-town, in the beginning. Rappleyea, Robinson, and one or two others were talking at Robinson's drugstore about the possibility of a case. They asked a couple of high school boys, drinking an after-school soda at the fountain, if they would run over to the school and ask Mr. Scopes to drop in. When Scopes arrived he found himself at the center of a discussion of evolution. The test case was proposed, Scopes agreed, and shortly thereafter he and the others were to find themselves at the center of a storm the magnitude of which they could scarcely have anticipated.

There was no dramatic confrontation and arrest. Robinson merely called the *Chattanooga News* and said, "This is Fred Robinson. I'm chairman of the board here. We've just arrested a man for teaching evolution"—all this with Scopes's full participation and agreement.

It is generally thought that the trial took a long time. It did not; it lasted only eleven days (July 10–21), but in those few days the trial attracted worldwide attention. The famed "infidel" lawyer Clarence Darrow led Scopes's defense staff, which also included the noted attorneys Dudley Field Malone and Arthur Garfield Hays. Darrow was chosen by Scopes himself following a visit to New York, where he conferred with the American Civil Liberties Union, whose chairman, Roger Baldwin, had the backing of the ACLU board to raise a special fund to finance Scopes's case. (Darrow had, as a matter of fact, already offered to defend Scopes without fee.)

The attention of journalists, notably H. L. Mencken, was also ensured by the presence, as a witness for the prosecution, of William Jennings Bryan, the orator, religious fundamentalist, and politician (or perhaps "statesman"; he served as Secretary of State during the first eighteen months of the Wilson administration). For a few days the small town of Dayton was indeed Page One material, especially when Darrow subjected Bryan's conservative religious beliefs to a withering cross-examination.

There is a final misconception—and an irony. Scopes never did actually teach the class in which he was accused of teaching evolution. He had assigned, from a textbook that had been in use in Dayton since 1919, a reading of a chapter on the doctrine of evolution and Darwin's theory of natural selection. But Scopes fell ill and did not show up in the classroom to discuss the lesson.

Scopes's failure to appear in the classroom on the appointed day had an effect on the defense: Darrow did not dare to place Scopes himself on the witness stand for fear that, if it became known he had not actually taught the class, the whole case would be thrown out of court.

With Darrow's widely reported assault on Bryan's fundamentalism, the defense felt it had scored all the points it could make in the case, and it pleaded Scopes guilty. This maneuver brought the trial to a close without any opportunity for the great orator to deliver a grand peroration he had composed. Broken, Bryan died five days after the trial ended.

The Butler Act stayed on the books for many years after the Scopes trial; it was not until 1967 that it was finally repealed. Nor was Tennessee the only state to forbid the teaching of evolution. Encouraged, perhaps, by Scopes's failure to win acquittal, both Mississippi and Arkansas, in 1926 and 1927 respectively, passed similar acts. In 1968, the U.S. Supreme Court declared the Arkansas law (and, by inference, Mississippi's) unconstitutional.

sex and athletes. Long enshrined in the mythology of sports is that sexual activity is incompatible with giving one's best when the Big Game comes along. Apparently the myth assumes, perhaps somewhat male-chauvinistically, that sex is so debilitating that athletes should practice continence, at least on the night before.

In past days, a spin-off of this belief on many campuses

even resulted in segregation by sex of the student spectators
at the stadium, sometimes rationalized by the comment that
if one took one's best girl to the game, he would fail to
show the proper school spirit. (The rule was always aimed
at the male spectators, who, if caught accompanied by a
coed, might well be hauled down at halftime and paddled
before the assembled multitude.)

Without mentioning names, surely the fact that some of
professional football's best seem to be as active in the
boudoir as in the ball game should demolish this belief.
Some college coaches still enforce, or try to enforce, a no-
sex-before-the-game rule. However, an attempt to poll
many of them on their attitudes brought only one response,
from Darrell Royal, the renowned University of Texas
athletic director and former head football coach, who
sensibly remarked that not only had he never made a big
point of such matters but did not know how such a rule
could be enforced if it existed. "As a coach," says Mr.
Royal, "I spent most of my time concentrating on those
activities I could control."

It is hard to know where first arose the notion that sex
is debilitating to athletes; at least one recent book (*The
Sports Medicine Book,* by Gabe Mirkin and Marshall Hoffman, 1978) suggests that it may even be traced back to
Old Testament prohibitions on sex before a battle. Certainly medical opinion provides no comfort to those who
enforce a no-sex rule; according to Mirkin and Hoffman,
doctors to Olympic athletes have testified to world records
broken within hours of having sex.

Perhaps the best comment is Casey Stengel's: "It ain't
sex that's troublesome, it's staying up all night looking for
it."

Shakespeare as ignorant and unlettered genius. The notion
that Shakespeare was an ignorant country bumpkin, uneducated and largely unknown in his time and about whose
life little has been discovered, is quite false. Many misap-
prehensions about Shakespeare are the result of unsubstan-
tiated tales told long after his death, among them the story
that his father was a butcher, that he ran away from home
after being caught stealing deer (from a family, it might
be interpolated, that did not own any deer until after the
time of Shakespeare's youth), that his first job in a London

theater was holding horses for the patrons, and so on and so on.

The ironic fact is that the reason so many late legends arose (all of the ones mentioned sprang up at least a century after Shakespeare's day) is that Shakespeare was, indeed, well known during his lifetime; legends tend to cluster around the famous, not the obscure.

As for his education, much—too much—has been made of Ben Jonson's comment that he had "small Latin and less Greek" (often misquoted as "little" Latin). But Jonson says this in a context of praise, not condemnation:

> And though thou hadst small Latin and less Greek,
> From thence to honor thee I would not seek
> For names, but call forth thund'ring Aeschylus,
> Euripides, and Sophocles to us.

And Jonson rounds out his comment by "calling forth" also the names of the greatest Roman playwrights, among them Seneca. It should be noted also that Jonson was the most learned of Elizabethan playwrights and sometimes liked to make something of a point of his learning—possibly because he apparently did not go on to a university and, perhaps, felt thus impelled to prove himself a scholar nonetheless. (Jonson, incidentally, is often said to have been the son of a bricklayer. He was not; his widowed mother married a master bricklayer when Jonson was two years old.) Jonson's knowledge of Latin and Greek was formidable; what looked "small" to him might well have been impressive enough to anyone else.

Shakespeare's father, who when William was fourteen began to undergo a series of financial reverses culminating in bankruptcy, had been an important citizen of Stratford. He held many civic offices, including membership on the town council. It is as certain as anything can be in the absence of written records that the young Shakespeare went to Stratford grammar school. The Elizabethan "grammar school," however, should not be confused with the grammar school of later centuries; it was tough and comprehensive, with much emphasis on Latin particularly. Many cultivated Elizabethans had no formal education beyond grammar school.

There are some gaps in the record, as there are in the records of many a famous man of Shakespeare's time. The great London fire of 1666 destroyed many documents; the records of all writers in Shakespeare's day were affected by this. But we still have more documentary evidence regarding Shakespeare than of any other dramatist of his day, with the possible exception of Ben Jonson (and, some say, George Chapman, much better known then than now).

Jonson and Shakespeare were friends and to some degree competitors—not always the best role to play opposite Jonson, who seems to have been a rather combative sort. He was punished for killing a man in a duel—some say, in self-defense—and he was in and out of trouble much of his life, often because of the sharpness of his satire, not uncommonly directed at persons of influence. That he would write so glowing a tribute as the one from which the foregoing lines are quoted (it was printed in the famous First Folio collection of Shakespeare's plays published in 1623) is a clear indication not only that Jonson admitted and admired Shakespeare's genius but that Shakespeare was scarcely an unknown in his time. Genius, yes; ignorant, unknown, or unlettered, no.

sheik. The popular conception of a sheik is not very close to the truth. Rudolph Valentino and "The Sheik of Araby" hardly summarize the meaning of "sheik" to the Arabs. It may indicate a chief of a tribe, but it is more commonly just a term of respect deriving from its Arabic meaning: "elder," "old man"—to whom the title is often applied.

Though it strains the imagination to its utmost limit to visualize Valentino as a Presbyterian elder, the fact is that "sheik" is also used for elders of the Arabian Presbyterian Church.

"Sheek" has always been the preferred American pronunciation, but some have adopted the fashionable "shayk," apparently on the assumption that it is the Arabic way to say it. It is not, unless one also supplies the guttural sound for the final consonant. The guttural, foreign to English, is roughly the "kh" sound heard in the German "ach."

ship captain, authority to perform marriages. The romantic notion that a shipboard love affair can culminate in a shipboard marriage performed by the captain is just that—a romantic notion. Ship captains have no authority to perform marriages unless they also happen to be ministers of the gospel or justices of the peace. And even then the marriage would have to be repeated ashore, since each jurisdiction has its own requirements (licenses, blood tests, and so on).

Navy regulations, which apply also to the Coast Guard, specifically forbid a commanding officer to perform a marriage ceremony on board his ship—or aircraft. Nor may he even permit such a ceremony to be performed outside U.S. territorial waters unless it is in accordance with local laws *and* those of the state, territory, or district where the parties live, and a U.S. diplomatic or consular official who agrees to issue the certificate and supply such reports as are required by consular regulations is present.

If you want to get married aboard ship, says one captain —in this case of a Dutch liner—you had better bring your own J.P. George J. Bonwich and E. C. Steer, authors of *Ship's Business* (London, 1963, page 69) are even more direct: "Despite the assertions to the contrary of novelists and films, masters of British ships *have no power to perform a marriage ceremony* [their italics]."

Nor is the situation different behind the iron curtain. According to William E. Butler and John B. Quigley, Jr., translators and editors of *The Merchant Shipping Code of the U.S.S.R.* (Johns Hopkins University Press, 1970, page 13), "A master is not . . . empowered by Soviet legislation to celebrate marriages, and if he does so, the 'marriage' has no legal force under Soviet law."

shrews (nonhuman variety). No use baiting a trap for shrews with cheese or grain; they may look like mice, but they belong to a different order, related to moles; they feed on insects, slugs, and, sometimes, each other. They are also notable for their rapid heartbeat; one variety of shrew has a heart that beats 800 times a minute, or a little over thirteen times a second. And they are mean little critters, attacking just about anything they consider edible.

That their bite is poisonous was once thought to be a folktale, but it has been discovered that the saliva of one variety is indeed lethal to mice and can cause considerable pain to humans.

Simon Legree. Almost universally taken to be the archetype of the cruel overseer, Simon Legree was not, in fact, an overseer. He was much more than that; he was a plantation owner. Such dirty work as he does not commit himself he leaves to his own overseers, two blacks named Sambo and Quimbo. Legree, who is nothing if not shrewd, has seen to it that they hate each other and in turn are hated by the field workers, who are also, of course, black.

"sincere"—etymology of. The *Oxford English Dictionary* puts little stock in the old explanation, still often heard, that "sincere" comes from a combination of the Latin words *sine* ("without") and *cera* ("wax"), referring to it as having "no probability."

Actually, "sincere" comes directly from Latin *sincerus,* which originally meant "clean" or "pure." The "without wax" explanation apparently arose, as such explanations so often do, out of an uninformed attempt to create a kind of linguistic fairy tale, like the false explanation that has been proposed for FALSEHOOD (which see): to be without wax is to be true-blue and basic, not all slicked up for appearance's sake.

skid road, skid "row." This term for a seedy street where down-and-outers live does not reflect the fact that they are "on the skids." It comes from the road along which logs were dragged to the sawmill in the Pacific Northwest, usually spelled as one word: skidroad. It might itself be "paved" with logs laid side by side, a type of construction sometimes called "corduroy."

With its sweating horses and no doubt profane drivers, the skidroad was not very genteel, unlikely to be in, or to develop into, the best part of town. This, plus the fact that the term early became extended by loggers to the streets where they gambled, drank, and whored, led to its pejorative implications.

Westerners, particularly old-timers from the Puget Sound area, where the term almost certainly originated, are prone to point out that skid "row," a common variant, is not the right word for it.

"skoal!" or "skaal!" This toast is sometimes said to derive from an old Viking custom: drinking with your friends out of the skulls of your enemies. As usual of such colorful explanations, it's false. "Skoal" is not a variant for "skull"; it comes, prosaically enough, from Old Norse *skál,* meaning "bowl."

"sleep that knits up the ravell'd sleave of care." When Macbeth makes this famous and often-quoted remark (act 2, sc. 2, line 38), he does not have in mind any part of a garment, as countless readers—and more than a few teachers—have incorrectly assumed.

"Sleave" is not "sleeve": indeed, the words are not even directly related, coming as they do from different Old English sources *(slaefan; slefe).* To "sleave" once meant to separate out threads, or filaments, particularly of silk, from the skein. As a noun, the way Shakespeare uses it above, "sleave" may mean either a single filament of silk or a "ravell'd," which is to say "tangled," skein. ("Ravel" once meant to tangle, "unravel" to untangle; but the words have become synonyms.)

Macbeth's metaphor is made both more apt and more vivid when one realizes that the filaments of raw silk are less than one thousandth of an inch thick. A "ravell'd sleave" thus represents a mess that would make untangling a jammed monofilament fishing line seem like child's play.

snakes, poisonous and nonpoisonous. The line between venomous and nonvenomous snakes is no longer considered so clear as it once was. Bites of even the innocent garter snake and the inoffensive hognose have caused severe reactions that cannot be explained on the basis of allergy or infection. So you would be well advised to get quick medical attention if you are bitten by a snake considered nonvenomous, especially if unusual symptoms develop.

snowflakes, no two alike. The persistence of popular notions that cannot possibly have a basis in scientific proof or evidence is well illustrated by the belief that no two snowflakes are ever alike. Many such beliefs exist because it simply isn't worth the trouble, even were it possible, to check them out. There is no way to be sure that no two snowflakes are ever alike unless one examines and compares every snowflake past and present. And even if it could be done, who's to bother?

sound, speed of. Often referred to as if it were a constant, it is not; there is no such figure as "the" speed of sound. Sound travels at widely varying velocities; it all depends on the medium (air, metal, water, e.g.) and the temperature. "Mach 1"—the term derives from Ernst Mach (1838–

1916), an Austrian scientist and philosopher—sounds impressive. But at sea level, under standard atmospheric conditions at a temperature of 32° F. (0° C), sound travels only about 742 miles an hour, a figure even certain land-based vehicles can approach. At high altitudes the speed of sound is much greater. Thus, the higher an airplane flies, the greater the speed it can achieve before reaching (or, as in the *Concorde,* breaking through) the "sound barrier."

sound film, first American. Although *The Jazz Singer* (1927) is justifiably credited with launching the era of "talkies," it had very little talking by its star, Al Jolson, and it was not the first sound picture made in the United States.

It is probably impossible to determine the actual "first" in sound movies, in America or elsewhere; it occurred to many people, almost from the start, that motion pictures might be accompanied by sound. One early method simply extended stage conventions to the movie hall: live voices and sound effects emanated from behind the screen, attempting synchronization with film action. Some screenings of D. W. Griffith's *The Birth of a Nation* were so shown, as late as 1915.

Most efforts, however, were directed toward linking film and phonograph records. More than a decade before the turn of the century Thomas Edison's associate W. K. Laurie Dickson coupled the Gramophone and the Kinetoscope in a device called the Kinetophone (or Kinetophonograph), from which sound was conveyed by a kind of stethoscope. The system was used for years in peep shows, but it created no extraordinary public stir, and the Edison experiments with sound pictures ended in 1914 after a laboratory fire.

Problems with synchronizing film and records encouraged attempts, in America and abroad, to find a way to put the sound directly on the film, and as early as 1904 a former Edison employee, Eugene Lauste, had created a rather sophisticated device for doing just that. Experiments in this direction, however, were frustrated because there was no reliable amplifier to fill an auditorium with sound. Finally, in 1923, Lee De Forest perfected his Phonofilm system, and in the next few years it was demonstrated in theaters all over the United States. The Fox studio bought De Forest's system and, in 1927, incorporated it into its Movietone process.

The sound for *The Jazz Singer* was still supplied by phonograph disks, but when audiences heard Al Jolson exclaim, "Wait a minute! Wait a minute! You ain't heard nothing yet!" they stood and cheered, and the picture became the first box-office smash in sound.

Many arguments rage as to what ought to be regarded as the first American "talkie." Here is a chronology, based on several sources.

August 6, 1926: *Don Juan,* a previously silent film starring John Barrymore and Mary Astor—perhaps the all-time ultimate in typecasting. But it had no dialogue; it was screened to the accompaniment of music recorded, on disks, by the New York Philharmonic. It was a production of Warner Brothers' Vitaphone company.

October 6, 1927: *The Jazz Singer,* sometimes defined as the first talking picture. It was not all talking, however; there was a musical accompaniment, plus a few talking and singing sequences. Another Vitaphone feature.

March 12, 1928: *The Treasurer's Report,* starring Robert Benchley in a monologue that had already made him famous on the stage. It was "all talking," all right, but a short subject. It takes first place if "all talking" is not confined to full-length features.

July 6, 1928: *Lights of New York,* starring Helene Costello and Cullen Landis. Usually regarded as the first all-talking film. Also a Vitaphone production.

September 29, 1928: *The Singing Fool,* another all-talking feature, otherwise memorable because Jolson sang "Sonny Boy."

Another notable first in the all-talking features was *In Old Arizona,* released in January 1929. This was a sound-on-film talkie, done with Fox's Movietone process, and its technical superiority led quickly to the abandonment of all film/disk sound systems. It was also Warner Baxter's first sound film and won him an Academy Award as best actor for his role as the Cisco Kid.

spelling reform. No attempt to overhaul English spelling to remove its obvious inconsistencies has ever succeeded, although passionate campaigns for its reform have been undertaken by such disparate institutions as George Bernard Shaw and Colonel McCormick's *Chicago Tribune.* The reason is that all such attempts are based on a fundamental misconception: that the written word is more important than, and thus takes precedence over, the spoken word.

This is the opposite of the case. Linguists and lexicographers know that speech is the father of writing, not the reverse. Fix the spelling of a word, and sooner or later its sound will depart from that represented by the arbitrary symbols decided on to capture its sound in print—if history is any guide, that is. Then it will be necessary to start all over again.

An analogous dilemma faces those who stress overmuch the value of "phonetics" as an aid to reading. Even in today's environment of tape recorders and similar devices, sounds simply refuse to conform exactly, as printed words do, to an arbitrary standard.

Stamp Act. The hated Stamp Act of 1765, which required the American colonies to affix British stamps costing anywhere from a few pennies to a few pounds to many kinds of papers and objects—mortgages, deeds, playing cards, dice, college diplomas, among others—certainly served as one of the sparks that ignited the revolution to come. Many, however, are unaware of the very short life the Stamp Act enjoyed. So bitter was the opposition to it that Parliament repealed the Act almost at once—in 1766, ten years before the Declaration of Independence.

"Stand up and be counted." This good old American folk proverb, with its foursquare town-hall connotations, flies straight in the face of a better old American tradition: the secret ballot, without which no person can be assured of a franchise free of fear.

steak tartare. Neither the Tartars nor any other Slavic people invented, nor indeed are likely even to know of, the raw chopped and seasoned steak known as "tartare" or "Tartar." It was invented by Jules Verne (1828–1905) to add color to his novel *Michael Strogoff*.

Stokowski, Leopold—and myths about him. Following his death in September of 1977, the concatenation of canards that had wound itself about Stokowski during his lifetime was revived. It was said that his real name was Leo Stokes, "Stokowski" being an affectation to conceal his humble English background; that his musical education was defi-

cient; that his accent was phony; that he did not enjoy
the respect of other musicians; that his transcriptions of
Bach organ music, notably the Toccata and Fugue in D
Minor, were ignorant buffoonery; and that he had no interest in anyone but himself.

None of the above is true. Certainly Stokowski was
"controversial"; his battles with the board of directors of
the Philadelphia Orchestra were legendary, and his marriage to the twenty-one-year-old Gloria Vanderbilt when
he was sixty-three inspired the gossip columnists (who
tended, however, to overlook a fact that flawed the aging
satyr/young virgin theme: Gloria Vanderbilt was actually
Mrs. Gloria Vanderbilt di Cicco at the time).

His name was not Leo Stokes. In full, it was Leopold
Anton Stanislaw Stokowski; he was born in London in
1887, the son of Josef Boleslaw Kopernicus Stokowski, a
Polish cabinetmaker, and an Irish mother. "Stokes" would
have been the affectation—if indeed he ever used it. *Current Biography* says flatly that the story that he was known
as Leo Stokes when he was organist and choirmaster at
St. Bartholomew's Church in New York from 1905 to
1908 is "wholly legendary." *Grove's Dictionary of Music
and Musicians* has him adopting "the name of Stokes" at
some time during "a few years as organist of St. James's,
in Piccadilly." If so, it was while Stokowski was still a
student in his late teens or early twenties—perhaps in
youthful despair at an English congregation's ever assimi-
lating "Stokowski."

Certainly his education was more than adequate. His
parents managed to send him not only to Oxford for his
B. Mus., no small task for a Polish cabinetmaker in turn-
of-the-century London, but also to the Royal College of
Music. It is difficult to determine what kind of accent would
result from a mixture of Polish-Irish parents, a youth spent
in London, and a lifetime in the United States. But
"phony" seems scarcely the word: "interesting," perhaps,
or "unusual."

That he enjoyed the respect of his peers is undoubted.
Not all of them; but no musician was ever respected by all
of his or her peers, artistic jealousies and envies being what
they are. He conducted the Philadelphia Orchestra for
twenty-six years, developing, in the words of *Time* magazine (September 26, 1977, page 54), "a sound equaled by
none and envied by many." No conductor lasts twenty-six

years, especially in an often-adversary position against the directors of his orchestra, without earning the respect of his musicians. He was a highly skilled organist and composer; his Bach transcriptions were disapproved by many purists, but they are in no sense technically deficient.

As for his egotism, or vanity, it was there, all right. Stokowski's abandonment of the baton so he could show off his expressive hands, his obvious awareness of the striking figure he presented, and his willingness to star in such Hollywood productions as *100 Men and a Girl* and *Fantasia* did not endear him to the Old School. But it was not a vanity that excluded help to others of talent, and he used it to call attention as much to others as himself. He insisted on introducing to American audiences the work of such as Mahler, Berg, Stravinsky, Schönberg, Prokofiev, Shostakovich, and other "radicals" and—to Americans—unknowns. When in response to falling receipts in 1932 the directors of the Philadelphia Orchestra forbade further playing of modern compositions or "debatable music," Stokowski said that he would play a modern piece whenever he saw fit to do so and would play it twice for anyone who cared to listen.

And when, in an effort to help young musicians, Stokowski founded the American Symphony Orchestra in 1962, he took no pay and indeed sank $60,000 of his own money into the project.

Stokowski did shake hands with Mickey Mouse—in *Fantasia*. Perhaps this helped to encourage the various attempts, often on the part of purists and snobs, to put him in his place.

There may have been another reason—both unspoken and darker—for some of the attacks on Stokowski. He ignored the prejudice against women and minorities that kept so many symphony orchestras both all-male and all-Caucasian during much of his lifetime. In fact, in 1960 he broke with the management of the Houston Symphony, of which he was then conductor, because the directors of the orchestra refused to permit him, in a projected concert, to use blacks and whites on the same stage.

sun and the seasons. It is naturally assumed by many people in northern latitudes that summer occurs when the earth is nearest the sun, winter when the earth is farthest. Just the opposite is the case; on July 1 the earth is about

94½ million miles from the sun, on December 31 about
91½. This is so because the earth's orbit is an ellipse, not
a circle.

It's the tilt of the earth's axis that brings about the
seasons. As the earth yearly passes around the sun, the
northern latitudes angle away during what we call winter
(in southern latitudes the opposite is the case), and toward
the sun in summer. The earth's winter tilt away from the
sun means that the sun stays closer to the horizon, its rays
thus strike the earth at a more acute angle, and less heat
is distributed per unit of surface area. Also, sunlight must
pass through more of the atmosphere, which absorbs some
of the heat; and to compound it all, the days are shorter.

All this is reversed, obviously, in summer. To those in
northern latitudes the sun is in the best position to send
heat on the last day of spring, usually June 21. One would
expect this to be the hottest time of year, but it is not. The
reason is that it takes time for the earth to warm up—with
the result that the hottest days come long after the nights
have begun to get longer and the sun's rays have long since
begun to strike the earth at a greater angle.

sunrise, sunset. A very common misconception is that after
December 21 (sometimes, December 22) the sun rises a
little earlier and sets a little later each day until late in
June, when the longest day (the day during which the sun
shines the longest) occurs.

Not so. The sun actually rises *later* each day for some
weeks after the winter solstice; it does not start to rise
earlier until January is three fourths gone. It's the progres-
sively later sunsets that account for the increasing amount
of daylight.

swimming pools, "Olympic" size. The phrase "Olympic-size
swimming pool," frequently encountered in real estate advertisements and brochures published by health clubs, often
needs to be taken somewhat less than literally. The Olympic
standard calls for a pool 50 meters in length, or about 162
feet—considerably more than half the length of a football
field.

T

teeth and gums. In spite of popular belief, many more teeth are lost as a result of periodontal (gum and other supporting structures) disease than because of decay. Nor is this true only of human beings; old dogs, cats, lions, and other animals often suffer from deterioration and disease of the supporting bone and periodontal membrane.

Among other myths about periodontal disease, according to the American Academy of Periodontology, are that bleeding always accompanies periodontal disease and that gingivitis, or a superficial inflammation of the gum tissue, is rare (it is common to all ages, including children).

Some periodontists feel that a deficiency in vitamin C, or ascorbic acid, may have something to do with periodontic disease because of the effect vitamin C has on the small blood vessels of the circulatory system.

television. Television is much older than most middle-agers realize. Various TV systems were in operation experimentally as early as the 1920s; by the latter 1930s, regular programs were broadcast from several cities in the United States and England. World War II interrupted any further development.

But TV goes much farther back than the Roaring Twenties; in fact, Mark Twain wrote of a system developed in Europe in the 1890s by Jan Szczepanik, who, to Twain, was "the Austrian Edison." Forgotten today, Szczepanik was internationally known at the turn of the century, not only for his "telelectroscope," or *Fernseher,* but for various important patents involving weaving machinery. Twain's fascination with, and sometimes financially disastrous involvement in, machines and their inventors is well known to Twainians.

So it is not surprising that in 1898 Twain sought out the young (he was twenty-five) Szczepanik in his laboratory;

there is an eyewitness account of Twain's visit by Herman C. Balicer in *Publishers Weekly* for February 20, 1937. As a young man himself, Balicer was a photographic technician for Szczepanik, who, says Balicer, had perfected his TV system several years earlier.

As nearly as can be inferred from drawings and contemporary descriptions, Szczepanik's television was based on a system of mirrors "scanned" by a moving beam that was translated into a varying electric current sent over telegraph wires. It was entirely mechanical/electrical, and that is no doubt why it never reached production. It took the invention of the vacuum tube in 1906 to make long-range transmission of signals feasible, through electronic means.

Still, the telelectroscope attracted enough attention that Szczepanik sold exclusive rights to exploit it to those planning the Paris Exposition of 1900. Whether it was ever actually demonstrated there remains in doubt; accounts of the 1900 Paris Exposition make no mention of it. Szczepanik faded into obscurity, though he continued to be mentioned in the press at least as late as 1909.

Although he did not profit in the usual sense, Twain did make some literary capital out of Szczepanik—and his TV system—in two stories. One is a factual account of Szczepanik's teaching school for one day each year so that he could be legally exempted from military service. It appeared in 1898; Twain called it "The Austrian Edison Keeping School Again."

The other is fiction—a combination of futuristic detective story, satire, and burlesque, not Twain at his best. Purporting to be a news story, its title is "From the London 'Times' of 1904." Twain slyly datelines the "dispatch" April 1 (April Fool's Day), 1904, though the story actually first appeared in 1898. Set, thus, in the future, the story exploits the telelectroscope by making it the means by which a condemned murderer is set free as he is about to be hanged.

In the story, told in the first person, the narrator sees on the telelectroscope the supposed victim, alive and well in Peking. (The "victim" in the story is Szczepanik himself, a rather surprising liberty.) Frantically the narrator manages to stop the execution, just in the nick of time.

The reader never is told the true identity of the corpse, "easily identifiable as Szczepanik's," which was found in the basement of the alleged murderer and on which his conviction (he and Szczepanik are said to have quarreled bitterly, in the story) was based. As is obvious, Twain was not always the world's greatest plotter, at least of detective stories.

Tell, William. Almost certainly the story of William Tell is without any historical foundation—a fact that does not, obviously, detract from its symbolic value or lessen its enduring popularity. It is, in fact, a variation of myths going at least as far back as eleventh-century Norway (Tell is supposed to have shot his famous bolt—he used a crossbow, not a bow—in 1307). Variations of the story can be found in Iceland, Denmark, even in twelfth-century Persia.

As is often the case (Lady Godiva, Betsy Ross), Tell's exploits were recounted long after the presumed dates on which they occurred. Historians cannot find the names Tell or Gessler (the tyrant who forced Tell to shoot the apple off his son's head) in contemporary records. And the canton (Schwyz) where the event is supposed to have taken place has long ceased to regard the episode as verifiable to scholars.

"There is no royal road to learning." According to an early commentator on Euclid, the great geometrician who flourished about 300 B.C., what Euclid actually said to Ptolemy the First was "There is no royal road to geometry."

tepee (or "tipi"); wigwam. Often used interchangeably, but they are not the same. A tepee is a conical tent of the North American Indians, formed of bark, mats, or skins stretched over poles. It was especially characteristic of the Plains Indians.

A wigwam, on the other hand, is a hut or dome-shaped wooden house used especially by the Algonquins of the Eastern woodlands and made of bark mats laid over a frame of poles.

"thunderbolt." No such thing literally; lightning does not hurl solid objects at the earth. But it is easy to see why the expression arose. The intense heat generated by a lightning stroke may fuse various materials together. And damp masonry can be shattered as if hit by a "bolt" because the lightning's heat causes instant boiling of the moisture.

Timbuktu, the magic city. Few names inspire such a romantic longing to escape to far romantic places as Timbuktu. Few places are likely to disappoint the traveler more, says John Darnton, writing in the *New York Times* for January 9, 1978. For in fact, says Darnton, Timbuktu is "a village of mud-brick huts and ankle-deep sand."

Timbuktu, in Mali near the river Niger in northwest Africa, was an important, perhaps even splendid city during the Middle Ages. But by the eighteenth century it had fallen into a poverty and desolation from which, apparently, it is yet to recover.

tinker's dam(n). In times past, itinerant tinkers wandered the countryside repairing holes in pots and pans. In order to keep the hot solder from running all over the place, the tinker would build a small clay surround, or "dam," to hold the molten metal in place until it cooled. Then, having outlived its usefulness, the dam was broken up and discarded. Thus "Not worth a tinker's dam," which isn't really swearing at all—note the "proper" spelling.

Or so the story goes. Unfortunately, it's the kind of story that instantly arouses a scholar's suspicion. For it's more elaborate—a characteristic it shares with all folk etymology—than the circumstances seem to call for.

As evidenced by several citations in the *Oxford English Dictionary,* as early as the fourteenth century tinkers had acquired a reputation for being low, vulgar fellows addicted to cursing and blasphemy. The "tinker's dam" explanation, apparently made up out of whole cloth, did not appear until 1877, in a book by Edward H. Knight called *The Practical Dictionary of Mechanics.* It has become one of the most often cited of linguistic myths.

Titanic: hymn played as it sank. "Nearer, my God, to Thee" was not the hymn played by the ship's band as the *Titanic* went down. According to Walter Lord's *A Night to Remember* (1955), the story that it was arose in the first few days after the sinking, one of a number of such tales.

The band, a brave group if ever there was one, played ragtime until the bridge dipped underwater, at which time the bandmaster led his men in the Episcopal hymn "Autumn." The hymn ended, in Lord's phrase, "in a jumble of falling musicians and instruments."

Apparently none of the band members survived. Harold Bride, surviving wireless operator of the *Titanic*, was quoted as follows in a front-page *New York Times* story dated April 19, 1912:

> The ship was gradually turning on her nose—just like a duck does that goes down for a dive. I had only one thing on my mind—to get away from the suction. The band was still playing. I guess all of the band went down. They were playing "Autumn" then.

tom-tom. Those who associate the beating of the tom-tom with American Indian dances, whether in real life or in the movies, may be surprised to learn that "tom-tom" is not an Indian word at all. At least, not American Indian; the word comes directly from Hindustani and other East Indian dialects (*tam-tam* and other variations). It is onomatopoeic, or echoic: that is, it purports to be the sound of what it names, like "hiss" or "sizzle."

"Trace that call!" For obvious reasons, neither telephone companies nor police departments like to make public the various means involved in tracing phone calls. Nor would it be in the public interest to expose all such means even if they could be ascertained. It can, however, be said that the scene sometimes shown in movies or on TV in which a telephone call is traced within a matter of seconds is unrealistic.

Tracing a phone call to its origin is often complicated—more so than most people realize. The speed with which tracing can be done depends on sophistication of equipment, local regulations, etc. Easiest to trace are repeated calls from the same telephone. In such cases, the recipient may get in touch with the telephone company, which can arrange means enabling the recipient to lock in the call and the company to discover its origin. A hang-up call from a booth, or one that originates from an exchange different from that of the recipient, is much more difficult to trace.

transistor, invention of. Everybody knows at least two things about the transistor. It was the most important electronic invention since Lee De Forest, in 1906, built the first practicable vacuum tube; and it was invented, or discovered, after World War II, by the Bell Telephone Laboratories.

The first part of this statement is true. The second isn't. The transistor was not discovered, or invented, by Bell; it was, rather, *re*discovered. For surprising as it may seem, as early as 1925 Julius Edgar Lilienfeld had filed a Canadian patent application for what is clearly the device we know as the transistor. On January 28, 1930, Lilienfeld was granted a United States patent.

And for twenty years, apparently, nobody noticed. True, Lilienfeld did not apparently fully understand the theory underlying his revolutionary device. But that is unimportant; inventors are not required to understand why their inventions work. The important fact is that they do.

The whole story is told by Theodore L. Thomas in "The Twenty Lost Years of Solid-State Physics" (*Analog: Science Fact and Fiction,* March 1965, pages 8 ff.).

trench mouth (necrotizing ulcerative gingivitis, also called Vincent's infection). Trench mouth—the term comes from its incidence in the trenches of World War I—is not, as so often thought, a highly contagious condition. This is what the American Academy of Periodontology ("Facts About Periodontal Disease," 1970) has to say about it:

> It may be mild or severe, acute or chronic. While it is seen in people of all ages, young people—from 15 to 30 —seem to develop the disease most easily. It has been found that when emotional tension increases, the infection gets worse. The disease is an infection, but apparently not communicable from one individual to another.

true cross, relics of. Tourists are wont to remark, somewhat cynically, that if all the relics of the cross upon which Christ is said to have been crucified were put together, there would be enough material for several crosses. (Mark Twain said the same thing in *Innocents Abroad* more than a hundred years ago.)

But according to the *Maryknoll Catholic Dictionary,* if all the known relics that the Roman Catholic Church believes to exist, or to have existed, were combined, they would make up only a small portion of the original cross.

U

ukulele as Hawaiian. The instrument so indelibly associated
with Hawaii and Arthur Godfrey was not invented by
Hawaiians. The ukulele is a variant of the cavanquinho, a
Portuguese instrument introduced to the Islands in the
1880s by laborers.

In Hawaiian, "ukulele" derives from two words: *uku,*
"small person," "flea," and *lele,* "jumping." The term may
derive, according to the Merriam-Webster Third, from
the nickname given to an Englishman, Edward Purvis, who
helped popularize the ukulele in the Islands.

"Uncle Tom." That the term "Uncle Tom" has come to
stand for the subservient black interested only in pleasing
his white "masters" is somewhat unjust to the "real" Uncle
Tom, a character in Harriet Beecher Stowe's novel *Uncle
Tom's Cabin, or Life Among the Lowly.* True, he's pious
enough, inclined to forgiveness rather than revenge. But it
should also be remembered that when Simon Legree tries
to force Uncle Tom to beat another slave, Tom refuses, and
continues to refuse in the face of continued beatings he
himself undergoes. And his death is the result of a cruel
beating administered by Quimbo and Sambo, Legree's black
overseers, when Tom will not reveal, although he knows,
and they know he knows, where some slaves are hiding.
These are scarcely the actions of an "Uncle Tom" as the
phrase today is so often used.

under the spreading horse chestnut tree. That's not, obviously, what Longfellow wrote. But in the interests of accuracy if not meter, he should have. The most famous tree
in American popular poetry turns out to be not the noble
American chestnut (genus *Castanea*) but the lowly horse
chestnut (genus *Aesculus*).

Solid expert opinion—and concrete evidence, or at least

wooden evidence—exists. According to Dr. Richard Howard, director of the Arnold Arboretum in Massachusetts,
there are no records of the American chestnut growing in
the Harvard Square area of Cambridge. (This was the site
of the blacksmith shop immortalized by Longfellow.)
Horse chestnuts, however, were plentiful there.

Further, in 1876, as reported by Dr. Frank Buda of the
U.S. Department of the Interior, the original "spreading
chestnut tree" was cut down and an armchair made from
its wood. The chair was presented to Longfellow as a birthday present. Not only were the leaves and flowers carved
on it those of the horse chestnut, but an analysis of the
wood proved that the tree was in fact a horse chestnut.

V

veal. The widespread impression that veal must come from
calves fed on a special milk diet is quite false. As a matter
of fact, veal is just about anything the butcher says it is—
and it's all perfectly legal unless the meat is advertised as
sold according to a U.S. Department of Agriculture grade.
Only a small portion of meat sold as veal is actually
graded, and grading is entirely voluntary.

Even graded meat is not all that easy to classify: what's
veal and what isn't is based on such subjective factors as
color, texture, and skeletal characteristics. As a general
rule, according to Herbert C. Abraham of the Meat Quality
Division of the USDA, veal is from animals under three
months of age, calf from three to nine months, and beef
from animals over nine months old. However, milk or milk
substitutes can be fed to older ages and heavier weights,
which can result in those characteristics necessary for clas-
sification as veal.

If all this sounds rather confusing, it is. The truth is that
"veal" comes very close to being meaningless as an accurate and objective term for a specific kind of meat.

vicissitude. "Vicissitude" derives from the Latin for "change, alteration." Thus, it does not necessarily refer only to hardship, though this is how it is commonly used. Perhaps such expressions as "the vicissitudes of fate" have encouraged its pejorative implications.

violet, "shrinking." Whoever coined the phrase "shrinking violet" didn't know very much about violets, says Peter Bernhardt in *Gardening* magazine for June 1978 (pages 17 ff.). In fact, violets are stubborn cusses, common to nearly all major inhabited areas, and have successfully survived even man's attempts to destroy their habitats. Common blue violets can regenerate themselves even after extensive damage because, like many lawn grasses, they propagate from rhizomes, underground stems that are not destroyed if the violet is pulled up.

As Mr. Bernhardt reminds us, Shakespeare knew better than to consider the violet a "frail and modest" flower rather than the aggressive exploiter it actually is. Sonnet XCIX opens as follows:

> The *forward* [italics added] violet thus did I chide:
> Sweet thief, whence didst thou steal thy sweet that smells,
> If not from my love's breath?

vodka as a Russian drink. Pity the poor Poles. Not only are Copernicus and Paderewski forgotten in gales of laughter at the latest Polish joke, but (as Joseph Wechsberg reminds us in *Gourmet* for February 1975, page 28) their best-known native drink, vodka, has been claimed by the Russians. But the Poles were the ones who invented vodka. The Russians merely discovered it.

voltage, high—and its dangers. Signs reading DANGER: HIGH VOLTAGE are, in a sense, misleading—although their warning should by no means be disregarded. For it is not voltage that kills; it's a combination of voltage and "amperage," or current. Voltage, to use an analogy from hydraulics, is pressure: EMF ("electromotive force") to electrical engineers. Amperage, or current, is amount, or "quantity." It takes a combination of both to be dangerous. (Strictly speaking, "ampere" is a measurement of the amount of electric charge flow *per second,* analogous to "gallons per hour." Absolute "quantity" of electricity is expressed in coulombs. An ampere is one coulomb per second.)

The common household current, at 120 volts, can indeed kill under the right circumstances (if one is standing on a wet surface or in water, for example). But automotive mechanics not uncommonly encounter ten thousand volts or more, and while it can certainly be felt, such a current is not likely to kill because its amperage is very small.

Power lines are dangerous because they combine high voltage, or pressure—as much as several hundred thousand volts in long-distance lines—with high current.

Automobile storage batteries can deliver plenty of amperes, as indeed they must to crank a 100-horsepower engine, but since their voltage is low—twelve volts, commonly —they are not dangerous in terms of shock. It should be noted, however, that they can easily involve a considerable fire hazard, as anyone who has inadvertently created a short circuit between their terminals can testify; even a heavy wire will become red-hot in a matter of seconds. (They can also cause a hydrogen-gas explosion if an open flame is near a cell, especially while the battery is being charged; but that's a chemical hazard, not an electrical one.)

Again, by a rough but serviceable analogy with hydraulics, relatively (though not extremely) high voltage is like a thin stream of water under pressure: it may sting, but it won't kill. A lot of water under high pressure, as from a fire hose, is dangerous. That is why a downed power line carrying anything from a few hundred to many thousands of volts is so hazardous: a lot of electricity is under a lot of pressure. Again, however, it's the combination that kills, not just the high voltage.

Von Däniken, Erich. Without getting into the truth or validity of Von Däniken's various theories (he's the *Chariots of the Gods?* author), it can be pointed out that Von Däniken, in spite of various blurbs to the contrary, is not a scientist —at least, not trained as one. He left high school to engage in a variety of jobs: busboy, waiter, cook, working his way up to manager of a resort hotel.

Chariots of the Gods? was his first book; it was originally entitled *Erinnerungen an die Zukunft* ("Memories of the Future") when it was published in Germany. The American translation with the now-famous title was published in 1970 and was an immediate hit.

According to *Current Biography* (1976), the frequent accusations of fraud, forgery, etc., made against Von Däniken are based, according to Von Däniken himself, on a conviction for tax fraud in Switzerland in 1968.

Again, without getting into the furious arguments that have raged around the Von Däniken thesis, or theses, it should in fairness be pointed out that neither lack of formal higher education nor conviction for tax fraud invalidates his conclusions; they must be assessed on their merits.

It is, however, also relevant to point out that no scientist of any reputation has endorsed Von Däniken's speculations.

W

Washington and the cherry tree. No doubt most persons these days take the story of young George Washington and the cherry tree with a fairly large grain of salt. But many may not be aware that "Parson" Weems (full name, Mason Locke Weems, and he was more book peddler than parson) did not include this famous bit of American folklore in the first edition of his *Life and Memorable Actions of George Washington*. Nor the second. Or third. Or fourth. Not until the fifth edition, in 1806, did the cherry-tree story appear. (Washington died in 1799.)

Nor does Weems take credit for the tale. Calling it an anecdote "too valuable to be lost, and too true to be doubted"—a statement which in itself casts a very large cloud over Weems's qualifications as a historian or biographer—Weems attributes it to an "excellent lady," not otherwise identified.

For those interested in what started the whole story, here is the account the "excellent lady" is said to have given "Parson" Weems:

When George was about six years old, he was made the wealthy master of a *hatchet!* of which, like most little boys, he was immoderately fond, and was constantly going about chopping every thing that came in his way. One day, in the garden, where he often amused himself hacking his mother's pea-sticks, he unluckily tried the edge of his hatchet on the body of a beautiful young English cherry-tree, which he barked so terribly, that I don't believe the tree ever got the better of it. The next morning the old gentleman [George's father], finding out what had befallen his tree, which by the by, was a great favorite, came into the house; and with much warmth asked for the mischievous author, declaring at the same time that he would not have taken five guineas for the tree. Nobody could tell him anything about it. Presently George and his hatchet made their appearance. *"George,"* said his father, "do you know who killed that beautiful little cherry tree yonder in the garden?" This was a *tough question;* and George staggered under it for a moment; but quickly recovered himself: and looking at his father, with the sweet face of youth brightened with the inexpressible charm of all-conquering truth, he bravely cried out, "I can't tell a lie, Pa: you know I can't tell a lie. I did cut it with my hatchet."—"Run to my arms, you dearest boy," cried his father in transports, "run to my arms; glad am I, George, that you killed my tree; for you have paid me a thousand fold."

Note that in contrast to popular versions of the story, the tree was not cut down, nor does little George admit to this, nor indeed even to "killing" it. And one might also add that if you are a six-year-old holding a new hatchet in your hand immediately after the discovery of a hacked-up cherry tree, it would be difficult *not* to tell the truth; you've been pretty well caught with the goods.

"water hazard" (golf). Doesn't have to have any water in it, although both the Pacific and Atlantic oceans may quite properly be called water hazards at certain seaside links. A bone-dry ditch, just so it can qualify as an "open water course," is a water hazard. A player whose ball lands in such a hazard can attempt to play out of it without penalty just as he or she can attempt to play out of any other hazard. (Such players cannot, however, "ground" their clubs—that is, touch the playing surface before striking the ball.)

waves, tidal. So-called tidal waves have nothing whatever to do with the tides. Nor do they, in fact, even exist on the open sea—in terms, that is, of 100-foot monsters like the one in *The Poseidon Adventure*. The proper, as well as scientific, term for what most people call a tidal wave is "tsunami," from the Japanese. Tsunamis are quite harmless at sea; many ships have passed harmlessly over a "tidal wave" or, more accurately, have had such a wave zip under them, since the speed of a tsunami may be as high as 450 miles per hour. It is so low in the open sea, however, that it is often unnoticed in the normal ocean swells.

The Japanese name (*tsu,* port, harbor; *nami,* wave) indicates that the great danger from "tidal waves" is not at sea but at the seashore. The *Poseidon* passengers, in real life, would have been quite safe aboard ship, unless in port. What happens is that an earthquake or landslide on the ocean floor disturbs the sea's equilibrium to the point that either a depression or a mound of water is created that spawns the long, low, but fantastically fast waves. As they approach the shore, they slow down and pile up, just like normal surf. Unlike normal surf, however, they may at this point reach heights that indeed approach a hundred feet, and the damage and loss of life can be catastrophic.

Tsunamis have an extraordinary range. In 1883, for example, when volcanic explosions destroyed Krakatoa, an island between Java and Sumatra, seismic waves traveled all around the world. A 1946 earthquake in the Aleutian trench caused a wave that did great damage when it hit the Hawaiian Islands some 2,200 miles away. (Telephone directories in Hawaii routinely include a section on what to do if there is a tsunami warning. The advice can be accurately, if somewhat unscientifically, summarized as "Get the hell out of the way.") The wave that followed the 1964 Good Friday Alaska quake wrought considerable destruction on the Oregon and northern California coasts, including the death of a family camping overnight on an Oregon beach.

A seismic disturbance or a sudden drastic variation in barometric pressure resulting in significant variations in the water level may sometimes cause an oscillating wave, called a "seiche" (pronounced "saysh"), in a lake, a bay, or a gulf. This phenomenon is not unknown on the Great Lakes. On June 26, 1954, a seiche on Lake Michigan created a 10-

foot wave that struck between Waukegan, Illinois, and Whiting, Indiana; it killed eight people.

Welsh rabbit. Yes, that's the correct form, although it is so often rendered as Welsh "rarebit" that most dictionaries accept this variation. "Welsh rabbit" was originally a rather patronizing, not to say snobbish, joke; analogous to "Glasgow capon" for red herring, it implies that the Welsh could afford nothing better—or perhaps wanted nothing better—than melted cheese.

Norman G. Hickman pointed out, in the June 10, 1963, issue of *Nouvelles des Vignobles,* that Welsh rabbit is not a corruption of Welsh rarebit, but rather the reverse. He goes on to remark that the term is comparable to mock turtle, which has no turtle; and Bombay duck, which contains no duck. "Welsh rabbit" is like calling hamburger the "poor man's sirloin." (In Alaska, dried beans are sometimes known as "Alaska strawberries.")

whales "blowing." When a whale blows, as in "Thar she blows!", it is not spouting water from its nostrils, as many assume. Whales no more deliberately take water into their nostrils, or other parts of their breathing apparatus, than human beings do. Whales are, after all, mammals, not fish; they don't want water in their noses.

What happens is that when a whale "sounds," or dives, it naturally enough fills its lungs with air to sustain it underwater. When it comes up, as it finally must, it expels the used air, or "blows." Since this air is almost always warmer than the surface air, the moisture in it condenses into vapor. The exhalation of warm air is through the blowhole, which is closed while the whale is underwater. If the whale should start blowing while still not quite surfaced, as sometimes happens, some water may be mixed with the air. But none of it comes from the whale.

"What big eyes you have!" Surprising as it may seem, the fact is that among most adults there is practically no difference in the size of the eye, which achieves full growth at about the age of nine years. What we perceive as differences is the result of an optical illusion because of such factors as the position of the eye in the skull and the relative prominence of eyebrows or other facial features.

"What's good for General Motors is good for the country."
Although it is widely believed that former GM President
Charles E. Wilson said this, he did not.

During the 1953 hearings before the Senate Committee
on Armed Services of the 83rd Congress (Wilson was being
considered for Secretary of Defense), he was asked about
possible conflict of interest.

This is his answer in full, as reported in the official U.S.
Government report on the hearings. He was asked whether
he could make a decision adverse to the interests of General Motors:

"Yes, sir, I could. I cannot conceive of one because for
years I thought what was good for our country was good
for General Motors, and vice versa. The difference did not
exist."

Oddly, this famous quotation, or misquotation, is not in
Bartlett.

It was no doubt those three words "and vice versa" that
gave rise to the common version of Wilson's remark.

**"When I was fourteen I thought my father was an idiot.
When I reached twenty-one I was amazed at how much he
had learned in seven years."** This statement, or one like it,
has been attributed to Mark Twain, but it obviously has in
it more than a grain of poetic license. Mark Twain's father
died when the young Mark—then known as Samuel Clemens—was only eleven years old.

"Whiff" on teeing ground (golf). Even fairly good golfers
sometimes miss the ball entirely, and it can happen even
when the ball is teed up on the teeing ground. (When it
does happen, it is often on the first tee, with a large crowd
watching.) Such a "whiff," as it's called, is counted as a
stroke, something all but the veriest beginners know. Now
and then a locker-room lawyer will insist that since a stroke
has already been taken and the ball can only be teed up
once, the hapless whiffer must now, for his second attempt, place the ball directly on the ground. This is not,
however, true. According to the rules, you can miss the ball
as many times as you wish, and it may still remain on its
tee—as long as you are on the teeing ground, and the ball
has not moved.

"White Christmas." This popular perennial—sung *ad libitum,* perhaps even *ad nauseam,* during the holidays—was not introduced in the movie called *White Christmas* (released 1954). It was first featured in *Holiday Inn,* winning an Oscar for its composer, Irving Berlin, as the best movie song of 1942. *Holiday Inn* starred Bing Crosby and Fred Astaire; Crosby sang the song.

The 1954 film with the same title as the song was essentially a remake of *Holiday Inn;* it starred Crosby again, but this time he was with Danny Kaye and Rosemary Clooney. Crosby again sings the song, at the beginning and end of the movie. It is easy to see why confusion arises as to its origin.

In an NBC special commemorative program broadcast shortly after Crosby's death in October 1977, Bing is quoted as saying that "White Christmas" was not, as most people would suppose, his biggest-selling record. Another Christmas song, "Silent Night," was.

"Who hath seen the wind?" Sounds properly Biblical, but it isn't. It's often misquoted from a poem by Christina Rossetti (1830–94), the second stanza of which reads as follows:

> Who has seen the wind?
> Neither you nor I;
> But when the trees bow down their heads
> The wind is passing by.

whore, myth of the happy. Firmly enshrined in American mythology is the happy whore—indeed, it's almost a stereotype. Added, often enough, to the stereotype is the prostitute's inherent compassion and nobility, which raise her miles above her "respectable" sisters. From the "soiled dove" of Bret Harte's famous short story "The Outcasts of Poker Flat" to *The World of Susie Wong* and *Never on Sunday,* we are deluged with hookers who, but for the slings and arrows of outrageous fortune, would be—or deserve to be, anyway—the mistress of the manor instead of the man on the street.

Well, it just isn't so. Prostitutes are people, and obviously not all are alike. Some, no doubt, have achieved the respectability—and the status and contentment—that are presumed to go with a secure social position, a nice house in the suburbs, and 2.7 lovely children. Some dance-hall girls married gold-mine millionaires in the Old West (the story of Baby Doe, so fantastic that it simply has to be true, and it is, comes to mind). But in terms of popular belief, practically every miner who struck in rich in Central City married a whore and built her a mansion in Denver, whereupon she revealed her true self as a loyal and faithful helpmate.

But it wasn't, and isn't, that way. Kitty and her "Gunsmoke" colleagues were not the good-hearted, pleasantly cynical but basically healthy people they seemed to be on the TV tube. Not in real life.

More often than not, the later-to-be-glamorized dance-hall girl of the Golden West was sick, sometimes demented, miserable, drug-addicted, exploited by the likes of the likable Kitty. Almost any issue of any newspaper published in the American West during the latter part of the nineteenth century will contain a brief report of the death of a young prostitute, sometimes as a result of an overdose of drugs, very often by suicide or disease.

Nor has the picture changed much. Ask any professional social worker with experience in the red-light district. It is no moral judgment to say that prostitution is not a nice way to earn a living. Nor does it have anything to do with whether or not prostitution should be legalized (although see RAPE, PROSTITUTION AS "CURE" FOR). The survival of the myth of the happy whore, whatever the reasons for it, has little to do with the facts in the case.

Who's Who in America. Many assume that this reference work, published in Chicago since the turn of the century by the A. N. Marquis Company, is connected with *Who's Who,* its British counterpart. It is not.

It *is* true that fake biographies—the Marquis people prefer the somewhat loftier term "dummy sketches"—are included; currently, there are four. But they are not there solely, or even primarily, to prevent copyright violations (see "DORD"—AND OTHER "GHOST WORDS").

DiAnne Halenar, Editorial Director of *Who's Who in America,* explains the dummy sketches as follows:

> We use these sketches (that contain false information but real addresses) to prevent any organization from using our publications as mailing lists. Although the

sketches appearing in our publications are not to be reproduced without our permission, the information itself is available to be used as part of newspaper articles, etc. Since we rely on biographees to provide us with the majority of information contained in our books, we do not want them bothered by solicitations as a result of having their sketches appear in our publications. It is for this reason that we initiated the concept of "dummy sketches."

Obviously, *Who's Who in America* is not about to identify the fictitious biographies in its current editions. It can be revealed, however, that one such in the past was that of "Samuel G. Hansell," said to be an Illinois lawyer. The name and biography were contrived; following *Who's Who* practice, the address was real enough—in this case that of Wheeler Sammons, Jr., then publisher of *Who's Who in America.* (The dummy sketches always give a false name and biography with the address of a real *Who's Who* employee. If the employee then finds himself on a mailing list under the false name, or if the sketch is reprinted verbatim without permission, the company's lawyers know what to do.)

Perhaps because there are many who's whos modeled after the original (well, the original in America, which in turn was admittedly modeled after the British), some of them little more than vanity books into which one buys admission by purchasing a prepublication copy, some believe that *Who's Who in America* operates in this or similar fashion.

The Marquis Company firmly denies this. Perhaps somewhat unfortunately, the company does offer a lower prepublication price to prospective biographees. However, the company will refund any money sent, or cancel an order, if the sketch does not in fact appear. And there are many biographees who never buy a copy, according to Marquis.

Those who rely on *Who's Who in America* for factual data should be aware that it is the biographees themselves who are the primary source of the information. Birth dates particularly must sometimes be taken with a grain of salt; it is said that Henry Adams (1838–1918, according to Merriam-Webster anyway), the great American critic and historian, kept getting younger with every edition. His younger brother finally remarked that he could not very

well be older than his older brother. Those who relied on
Who's Who in America for the late Bing Crosby's birth
date had him dying at seventy-three (1904–1977). Crosby
was born in Tacoma, Washington, in 1901; he was thus
seventy-six when he died.

Obvious falsehoods, like the claim of one prospective
biographee that he had built every new factory in Russia
during World War II, can be and are checked out by the
publisher. Those less obvious—a self-granted honorary degree, for example—are not so easy to spot.

Finally, not all who appear in *Who's Who in America*
are there because they have been invited on account of
what the editors believe to be achievements worthy of note.
Among those automatically listed are all members of Congress, all federal judges, all military officers from major
general or rear admiral and higher, and principal officers
of national and international businesses.

windchill factor. Partly because it is so often adduced by
television and radio weather commentators, "windchill factor" is an oft-heard phrase during the cold months. What
the windchill factor does is to take into account both temperature and wind; for example, at 10° below zero F., a
15-mile-per-hour wind lowers the "chill factor" to a grim
45° below zero.

However, the "factor" applies to exposed flesh, not exposed water pipes or automobile engines, which are quite
indifferent to it. Many people scurry to wrap pipes or
throw blankets over the hood when it is announced that a
10-mile wind and a 35° temperature have resulted in a
chill factor of 22°, well below freezing. But there's no point
in it. True, if the pipes or the automobiles are above 35°,
they will cool down *faster* if exposed to the wind. But they
won't go below the actual temperature (in this example,
35°), no matter how hard the wind blows—and are thus
in no danger of freezing.

Winter Palace, "storming" of the. On November 7, 1917,
occurred a decisive episode in modern history: the taking
of the Winter Palace in Petrograd (until 1914, St. Peters-
burg; since 1924, Leningrad), then the capital of Russia,
once the seat of the Czars and, in 1917, of the government
headed by Prime Minister Alexander Kerensky. Kerensky's
was the third of a series of provisional governments during

these chaotic times. The Kerensky government fell, the Bolsheviks took over, and Soviet Russia was the result.

Perhaps because the event was so pivotal, and without question controversial, an astonishing amount of misinformation surrounds it. The Winter Palace is certain to be pointed out by an Intourist guide, and many have seen the painting by the Soviet artist V. Kuznetsov. It shows the classic, even stereotyped, revolutionary takeover: soldiers, workers, and peasants firing, throwing grenades, advancing on the palace. People lie apparently dead or dying in the square.

Visitors to Leningrad will also be shown the cruiser *Aurora*, permanently anchored in the river Neva, whose guns opened fire as the storming of the Winter Palace began.

But it didn't happen that way—not even remotely. No such storming as the painting shows ever took place. The *Aurora* fired blanks, as those who have read Harrison E. Salisbury's *Russia in Revolution* (1978) are aware.

While the Mensheviks and the Socialist Revolutionists and the Left Socialist Revolutionists and the Bolsheviks and the Menshevik Internationalists, among others, were arguing at the meeting of the All-Russian Soviets at the Smolny Institute, a vast complex miles away where the Bolsheviks were headquartered, Kerensky and other members of the Provisional Government at the Winter Palace nervously awaited what turned out to resemble, in Salisbury's words (page 159), "a theater of the absurd."

The Bolsheviks knew how to exploit confusion and chaos. Their Revolutionary Military Committee had taken over several key points: the post office; the telegraph agency; and the General Staff building, whose capture can serve as something of a symbol of the confusion—its general surrendered because, in Salisbury's words, "he got tired of waiting on the telephone for an answer from the Malachite Chamber," the room in the Winter Palace where Kerensky and his ministers were gathered, like Custer and his men, for a last stand.

But there wasn't any dramatic "last stand." Neither Kerensky nor even the Bolsheviks themselves, apparently, realized how much of Petrograd was in Bolshevik control. Still, the Winter Palace itself had yet to be taken. An ultimatum was delivered—by bicycle; by the time it was presented, it had five minutes to run. Nothing happened.

The Revolutionary Military Committee decided—shades of Paul Revere's ride—to use a red lantern to signal a bombardment. Nobody could find one.

When somebody did, the *Aurora* fired its blank shell, or shells. A few artillery shells, some of these also apparently blanks, came from the Fortress of Peter and Paul, across the Neva River; and there was both small-arms fire and fire from armored cars in the square in front of the Palace. Was this, then, the "storming" celebrated in picture and legend?

Not exactly. In half an hour or so the firing, again in Salisbury's words, simply "petered out." Meanwhile, the American correspondents John Reed and Louise Bryant, who had been waiting for developments—or nondevelopments—at Smolny, decided to hitch a ride to the Winter Palace, and did.

What they found was confusion compounded. Various Bolshevik supporters had infiltrated the palace; when, later, a group of several hundred—perhaps this was the "assault force"?—approached, they simply walked in through various side entrances (the Winter Palace has some 2,000 rooms) and took over. According to Salisbury, total casualties were six men killed.

As for Kerensky himself, one legend, not inconsistent with the tone of other myths surrounding the taking of the Winter Palace, has him fleeing the palace dressed as a nurse. In fact, he simply got into his car with his army chauffeur and, in his own words (*Russia and History's Turning Point*, 1965), "drove off." He was actually saluted by many of the revolutionary sentries as he proceeded on his way out of the city. He went to Paris and finally to the United States, where he wrote and lectured until his death in 1970.

Perhaps one might paraphrase T. S. Eliot. The taking of the Winter Palace started with a bang (of a blank shell) and ended with—well, if not a whimper, exactly, at least in confusion and disorder. However, Americans inclined to scoff overmuch at any Russian tendency to glamorize the conquest of the palace should remind themselves, perhaps, of how far from history departs our own famous painting of Washington crossing the Delaware.

"Winter rules" (golf). There aren't any, really. The United States Golf Association admits reluctantly that many American clubs and courses adopt winter rules, which permit such ordinarily forbidden actions as lifting one's ball and cleaning it while it is in play, improving one's lie, etc. But the USGA does not endorse such conduct and refuses even to enter into any discussion of "winter rules," since they violate golf's most fundamental principle: play it as it lies!

The rationalization for winter rules is that they help protect the course during the season it is most vulnerable to damage. Many greenkeepers argue, however, that in fact they do just the opposite. A player who, under "winter rules," improves the lie of the ball is likely to move it from a bare spot that has already been damaged to a spot that has not been—until he or she takes the divot, that is.

-wise. There is frequent objection to the suffix -wise, as in "He's pretty good, performancewise," or "Salarywise, the job isn't much." It is not a defense of these contrived and awkward examples to point out that most modern English adverbs have arisen out of an analogous process. The suffix -lice, "like," became shortened, over the centuries, to the common adverbial ending -ly. Old English for "friendly," put into contemporary typography, is *freondlice,* or "friendlike." For "fully" it was *fullice,* as in "We support the project full-like"—or, if one dares, ". . . like, fully."

Further, and more directly to the point, the suffix -wise in exactly its current (and felt to be objectionable) sense has given us such entirely acceptable expressions as anywise, crosswise, leastwise, otherwise, sidewise, and slantwise, not to mention likewise, which though it may derive from the phrase "in like wise," or manner, nevertheless is instructive to ponder, wordwise.

"Otherwise, he agrees." "It lay there crosswise." Surely not even the purest purist would object to these sentences. Are they really so different from "Pricewise, it's a problem" or "It's a gamble marketwise"?

"wolf" as synonym for woman-chaser. That aggressive womanizers are often called "wolves" is ironic—and rather unfair to wolves, who as a matter of fact are models of familial propriety. They are monogamous, they mate for life, and they are devoted parents to their young. In short, they never act like—well, like "wolves."

"Workers of the world, unite! You have nothing to lose but your chains!" This oft-quoted revolutionary slogan has a nice ring to it, but it's not really the way the *Communist Manifesto* (Marx and Engels, 1848) puts it. According to the English text of the *Manifesto* generally regarded as standard—a translation by Samuel Moore, revised and edited by Engels himself for the English edition of 1888—here is the actual ending:

> The proletarians have nothing to lose but their chains.
> They have a world to win.
> WORKING MEN OF ALL COUNTRIES, UNITE!

Note that the actual statement starts out in the third person, then switches to the second.

Wright Brothers as lucky bicycle mechanics. Everybody knows the stirring saga of the Wright Brothers: a pair of persistent bicycle mechanics who are said, as F. E. C. Culick puts it ("The Origins of the First Powered, Man-Carrying Airplane," *Scientific American* for July 1979), to have "more or less stumbled on their successful design."

It may be that this notion stems from an American distrust of book-larnin', a tendency to emphasize the practical at the expense of the "theoretical," the pioneer over the professor. Benjamin Franklin is a case in point. Sophisticated enough to be ambassador to France, a scientist who was elected to England's Royal Society while still in his mid-forties, an intellectual holding honorary degrees from St. Andrews and Oxford who founded the American Philosophical Society, he still tends to be remembered for *Poor Richard's Almanac*.

True, the Wright Brothers proceeded by trial and error, as any scientist must; but it was trial preceded by careful analysis of data, much theoretical calculation, and a sophisticated understanding of aerodynamic principles far beyond their time.

Even among aeronautical engineers, says Dr. Culick, who is himself professor of applied physics and jet propulsion at California Institute of Technology, ignorance of the Wright Brothers' accomplishments is widespread. "[But] I have come to recognize," Culick says, "how remarkable their achievements in research, engineering, and testing were."

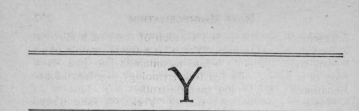

Y

"You have the right to make one phone call." In spite of apparently prevailing opinion among the general public and writers of novels, plays, and TV scripts, the number of phone calls an accused person may make is fixed not by law but by circumstances and customs, which vary widely. The U.S. Constitution provides (Amendment VI, a part of the so-called Bill of Rights) that the accused "shall have the assistance of counsel for his defense."

Incidentally, one so unfortunate as to be arrested, booked, and limited to one call had better not risk a call to a lawyer unless he or she is certain the lawyer is in his or her office. It is better to phone a friend or a relative; the alternate could well be a chat with an answering service, if the lawyer happens to be on vacation or otherwise unavailable.

Yreka ["wye-ree-kuh"], California—origin of its name. We owe to Mark Twain the often repeated tale that—but let Twain tell it in his own words:

> [Bret Harte] had wandered up into the surface diggings of the [mining] camp at Yreka, a place which had acquired its curious name—when in its first days it much needed a name—through an accident. There was a bakeshop with a canvas sign which had not yet been put up but had been painted and stretched to dry in such a way that the word BAKERY, all but the B, showed through and was reversed. A stranger read it wrong end first, YREKA, and supposed that that was the name of the camp. The campers were satisfied with it and adopted it.

Most visitors to Yreka, which is on a main north-south freeway (Interstate 5), some 50 miles north of Mt. Shasta, have heard the tale. But Mark Twain was a better storyteller than etymologist; there's no truth in it. According to

Edragene (Mrs. Robert H.) Gordon of the Yreka Historic
Preservation Corporation, "Yreka" is a transliteration of an
Indian word meaning "white mountain." Too bad, in a
way; as is so often true of folk etymology, the fancied explanation is more colorful than the truth.

However, not all that's said of "Yreka" is false. There
really was once, according to Mrs. Gordon, a bakery there;
some of its old ovens are preserved at the Yrella Gallery in
Yreka (Yrekans do seem to be a Ys group of people). And
so it's true enough that Yreka Bakery was the only such
establishment ever to achieve palindromy without really
trying.

Z

Zion, protocols of. Often as "The Protocols of the Learned
Elders of Zion" are debunked, they regularly pop up again.
Worse, they are still believed by millions. Purporting to be
a secret plot on the part of leaders of world Jewry to
overthrow all governments and establish a Jewish world
empire, the "Protocols" are actually based on a French
pamphlet written by Maurice Joly and published in 1864.
What Joly wrote was a "dialog in hell" between Machia-
velli and Montesquieu; it was intended as a satirical treatment of what Joly believed to be the ambitions for world
domination of Napoleon III. It contains no references
whatever to Jews or Judaism.

The whole sad story of the first forging of the "Protocols," apparently by members of the Czarist Russian
secret police at about the turn of the century, and their subsequent reprintings and exploitations, is too complicated to
tell here. But any standard reference work, Jewish or non-
Jewish, will serve to demolish the myth of the protocols.
They were—and are—taken seriously by some who ought
to know better. One of the darkest marks against the first
Henry Ford is his printing of material drawn from the

"Protocols" in the *Dearborn Independent,* his conservative newspaper.

From 1920 through 1927, the *Dearborn Independent* mounted a series of anti-Semitic attacks unparalleled in American history. W. J. Cameron, who wrote "Mr. Ford's Own Page" for the *Independent,* relied heavily on the "Protocols," contriving contemporary material to enhance the illusion of credibility. In the words of Keith Sward (*The Legend of Henry Ford* [1950], page 150), Cameron "improved on the forgery so skillfully that, in modern dress, it became one of the foremost existing brochures on anti-Semitism."

Finally, in 1927, Ford repudiated his anti-Semitism with an apology to a Jewish lawyer who had sued him for libel (the case was settled out of court) and a general retraction to Jewish people as a whole. In doing so, he claimed that he had no personal knowledge of what had been said in the *Dearborn Independent,* including "Mr. Ford's Own Page." The fact that Henry Ford, for whatever reason or reasons, repudiated the "Protocols" is not always considered by those who wish to use him and the *Dearborn Independent* as "evidence" of the Protocols' "validity."

It was Philip Graves, Istanbul (Constantinople) correspondent for the London *Times,* who in 1921 established that the "Protocols" were, without question, plagiarized from the Joly pamphlet with the addition of the wholly contrived "Jewish" elements. In 1942, a committee of well-known U.S. historians headed by Carlton J. H. Hayes, Allan Nevins, and G. T. Robinson made an exhaustive study, the conclusion of which is that the "Protocols" have no claim to authenticity. Many other experts have come to the same conclusion.

Perhaps the saddest fact of all is that so thoroughly demolished a myth as "The Protocols of the Learned Elders of Zion" continues to flourish.

Word power made·easy with
The Ballantine Reference Library